Series FM1 no.19

Birth statistics

**Review of the Registrar General on births
and patterns of family building
in England and Wales, 1990**

Laid before Parliament pursuant to
Section 19 Registration Service Act 1953

London: HMSO

© *Crown copyright 1992*
First published 1992

ISBN 0 11 691382 7

HMSO

Standing order service

Placing a standing order with HMSO BOOKS enables a customer to receive
other titles in this series automatically as published.
This saves the time, trouble and expense of placing individual orders and avoids the problem of knowing
when to do so.
For details please write to HMSO BOOKS (PC 11C), Publications Centre, PO Box 276, London SW8 5DT
quoting reference X02 02 35.
The standing order service also enables customers to receive automatically as published all material of their
choice which additionally saves extensive catalogue research. The scope and selectivity of the service has
been extended by new techniques, and there are more than 3,500 classifications to choose from. A special
leaflet describing the service in detail may be obtained on request.

Contents

List of tables and appendices

8 Place of confinement (*continued*)

9 Birthplace of parents

10 Cohort Analysis

11 Social class

12 Conceptions

Introduction

This volume *Birth statistics* (Series FM1 no.19) relates to births occurring in England and Wales during 1990. Statistics for earlier years and separate statistics for Scotland, Northern Ireland, and abroad are published as follows:

for England and Wales - in *Birth statistics* from 1974 onwards; (for 1973 and earlier, in the *Registrar General's Statistical Review of England and Wales, Part II*);

for Scotland and Northern Ireland - in the *Annual Reports of the Registrars General for Scotland and Northern Ireland* respectively;

for Europe - in the annual volumes *Recent demographic developments in the member states of the Council of Europe* prepared by the members of the European Population Committee, and *Demographic Statistics* produced by Eurostat;

for United Nations member countries - in the annual *UN Demographic yearbook*.

Notes on the different definitions used by Scotland and Northern Ireland will be published in *Population Trends 67*. (HMSO).

Quarterly estimates of numbers of birth occurrences, seasonally adjusted fertility rates and other fertility statistics for England and Wales are published regularly in *Population Trends* (HMSO). Some recent analytical articles which have been included in *Population Trends* are listed at the end of this introduction.

This volume is divided into twelve sections, each gives statistics on particular characteristics of the birth or of the parents. To economise on printing costs, the time series shown in this volume have been limited to a run of ten years at most. Figures for earlier years are shown in *Birth Statistics* (Series FM1 nos. 1 to 18). This series includes a volume of historical fertility statistics (Series FM1 no.13) containing some time series back to 1838 (the year following the introduction of compulsory registration of births) and some more detailed time series back to 1938 (the year in which the Population (Statistics) Act came into operation).

Changes to existing tables introduced this year

Tables 8.2 and 8.3   Data on maternities by area of occurrence now cover all births in hospital,

in 1989 only births occurring in NHS hospitals were covered.

Birth registration

Birth statistics are compiled annually from the information collected at birth registration for entry into the live birth and stillbirth registers, and from additional confidential particulars collected at the same time under the Population (Statistics) Acts of 1938 and 1960 (see **Appendices A** and **B**).

It should be noted that formal registration began on 1 July 1837 for live births and on 1 July 1927 for stillbirths; it was not until the Population (Statistics) Act, 1938, came into operation on 1 July 1938 that the confidential particulars - excluding the father's date of birth - were ascertained for statistical purposes. (It was also possible to distinguish multiple births on a regular basis as from 1 July 1938.) The Population (Statistics) Act, 1960, with effect from 1 January 1961, added the question on father's date of birth in the case of all births within marriage, and those outside marriage where the father's name is entered in the register. The questions relating to father's and mother's place of birth were introduce on 1 April 1969 by the Registration of Births, Deaths and Marriages Regulations, 1968. Further details on the production of the Registrar General's statistics can be found in *Population and health statistics in England and Wales* (OPCS, 1980), and the companion volume *Vital registration and marriage in England and Wales* (OPCS, 1977).

Accuracy of information

The accuracy of information contained in the draft birth entry form 309 (see **Appendix A**) is the responsibility of the informant(s), usually the mother or the mother and father where the registration is a joint one. Wilfully supplying false information may render the informant(s) liable to prosecution for perjury. It is generally believed that the information supplied by the informant(s) on the draft birth entry is correct. There is no routine statistical verification of the data, although computerised edit checks are applied to detect possible clerical errors which can occur during the transfer of data from the draft entry form onto a computer file.

Explanatory notes

All figures, unless otherwise indicated, refer to those births which occur in a calendar year and are registered by 31 January of the following year. Births registered later than this but occurring in the previous year are included in the following year's figures (for the period 1980-90 there were approximately 1,500-2,000 such cases per year).

Maternity/paternity

A maternity/paternity denotes a pregnancy which resulted in the birth of one or more live or still born children.

Stillbirth

A stillbirth is defined in section 41 of the Births and Deaths Registration Act, 1953 as 'a child which has issued forth from its mother after the twenty-eighth week of pregnancy and which did not at any time after being completely expelled from its mother breathe or show other signs of life'.

Total period fertility rate (*Section 1*)

The total period fertility rate (TPFR) is derived by summing the fertility rates for a given year (live births per woman) by single years of age (or, if not available, by five-year age-groups) up to the age by which the childbearing life span of women is effectively finished, taken to be age 50. Hence, it is a summary measure of the overall level of the year's age-specific fertility rates. It indicates the average number of children which would be born per woman if a group of women were to experience the age-specific fertility rates of the calendar year in question throughout their childbearing lives.

Gross reproduction rate (*Section 1*)

The gross reproduction rate (GRR) is derived by summing female fertility rates (female live births per woman) in the same manner as for the total period fertility rate. It measures the average number of daughters born alive per woman that would result if women survived to the end of their reproductive period, and throughout this period were subject to the age-specific female fertility rates of the calendar year in question.

Net reproduction rate (*Section 1*)

The net reproduction rate (NRR) is similar to the GRR, but allows for the effect of mortality - not all women survive to the end of their reproductive period. It measures the average number of daughters born alive per woman that would result if women were subject, from birth to the end of their reproductive period, to the age-specific female fertility and mortality rates of the calendar year in question.

Births within marriage and sole and joint registration
(*Sections 1 and 3*)

Generally speaking, a birth within marriage is that of a child born to parents who were lawfully married to one another either (a) at the date of the child's birth or (b) when the child was conceived even if they became divorced or the father died before the birth. Only for a birth within marriage will the Registrar enter on the 'draft entry' (Form 309) confidential particulars relating to the date of the parents' marriage, whether the mother has been married more than once and the number of the mother's live and still born children.

If the child is born outside marriage, the father's name and other particulars will be entered on the draft entry by the Registrar only if the information is provided jointly by both the mother and father in person (or if the mother supplied either a statutory declaration by the father acknowledging paternity or an affiliation order).

Information from birth draft entries is used to determine whether the mother and father jointly registering a birth outside marriage were usually resident at the same address at the time of registration; **Table 3.10** shows the statistics obtained. Space 10 on the draft entries is used by the Registrar to record the mother's usual address at the time of the birth. Space 13 is used to record the informant's or informants' address or addresses at the time of registration of the birth. If there is a sole informant whose usual address is the same as that shown in space 10 a line is drawn through space 13. In the case of a birth outside marriage registered by both the father and mother, the father's usual address is always entered in space 13 even if it is the same as the address recorded in space 10. The mother's usual address at registration is recorded in space 13 only if it is different from the father's. The classification of mother's and father's usual addresses shown in **Table 3.10** for jointly registered births outside marriage is therefore defined as follows:

Same address - only one address recorded in space 13;
Different address - two different addresses recorded in space 13.

Seasonality (*Section 2*)

Seasonally adjusted numbers of live births are obtained using the X-11 adjustment package developed by the US Bureau of the Census. Seasonally adjusted TPFRs are based upon these numbers and are estimated using a method due to G. Calot (see Werner, B. A new method to estimating the trend in fertility rates, *Statistical News* 60, HMSO,1983).

Age of parents (*Section 3*)

The mother's or father's date of birth is recorded and translated into the age at the birthday preceding the date of the child's birth. This age is often termed 'age last birthday'. If the mother's date of birth, or the father's date of birth (when applicable) is not given, an age is imputed from the previously processed record with completely stated but otherwise matching particulars. A note of the number of cases dealt with in this way is included with relevant tables.

Previous liveborn children (parity) (*Section 4*)

Information on previous liveborn children is only available

for women having a birth within marriage. Sometimes referred to as 'parity', it relates to the number of previous liveborn children by the present or any former husband, as stated at registration. This use of the term parity should not be confused with those used elsewhere, particularly in the medical literature: for example, the number of preceding births (whether live or still) or total number of liveborn children ever born (whether by the present or a former husband or by some other partner) to a woman. If parity is not given, a value is inputed from the previously processed record with completely stated but otherwise matching particulars. A note of the number of cases dealt in this way is included in the relevant tables.

Duration of marriage (*Section 5*)
Pre-maritally conceived live births are, by convention, taken to be those births where the calculated duration of marriage is less than 8 months - that is 0-7 completed months. As only month and year of marriage are recorded at registration the calculation relates to the interval in completed months between the middle of the month of marriage and the date of the child's birth. Other durations of marriage are computed similarly. If the date of marriage is not given, a value for the duration of marriage is imputed from the previously processed record with completely stated but otherwise matching particulars. For women who have been married more than once, duration of marriage refers to that of the current marriage. Therefore, figures relating to all married women also refer to duration of current marriage.

Multiple births (*Section 6*)
Multiple births arising from a single pregnancy are counted as one maternity/paternity, although each child born is reckoned separately in tables relating to births. In tables which show number of previous liveborn children, multiple births are counted as if they occurred separately, for example, as one first and one second birth.

Area of usual residence (*Section 7*)
Births are assigned to area according to the usual residence of the mother at the time of the child's birth as stated at registration. If the address of usual residence is outside England and Wales the birth is included in any aggregate for England and Wales as a whole, but excluded from the figures for any individual region or area - in 1990 there were 354 such births. Institutional premises are treated as a mother's usual place of residence only if no other address is ascertainable or she normally lives there - for example, a member of the resident staff or a permanent hotel resident.

The areas of usual residence shown in this volume are those as constituted after local government reorganisation in England and Wales on 1 April 1974, and after National Health Service re-structuring on 1 April 1982, as subsequently amended by statutory boundary changes.

Birthweight (*Section 7*)
Birthweight is expressed in grams and is coded on the draft entry form from details given on the birth notification form and made available to registrars. Occurrences where no birthweight is recorded are included in the figures for 'all weights' but are not distributed amongst the individual birthweight categories. In 1990 birthweight was not stated in 3.9 per cent of all livebirth occurrences and 4.67 per cent of all stillbirth occurrences.

Tables 7.1 to 7.4 cover: England and Wales, standard regions, Greater London, metropolitan counties and regional health authorities.

Basic statistics relating to births (and deaths) for all local authority areas, and for regional and district health authorities are published in *Key population and vital statistics: local and health authority areas* (from issue VS no.11/PP1 no.7) (HMSO).

Place of confinement (*Section 8*)
The place of confinement categories in this volume are detailed below:

NHS hospital A. Hospitals and maternity homes under the National Health Service (other than psychiatric hospitals) with beds allocated to GP maternity but not to consultant obstetrics;

NHS hospital B. Hospitals and maternity homes under the National Health Service (other than psychiatric hospitals) with beds allocated to consultant obstetrics, which may or may not also have GP maternity beds.

Other hospitals. Mainly maternity homes not under the National Health Service;

At home. At the usual place of residence of the mother;

Elsewhere. These include all psychiatric institutions, homes for unmarried mothers, remand homes, reception centres and private houses (other than mother's usual residence).

Area of occurrence (*Section 8*)
Births are usually assigned to areas according to the usual residence of the mother at the time of birth as stated at registration (see *Section 7*). However, a birth may take place in an area other than that of the mother's usual residence. **Tables 8.2** and **8.3** show the numbers of maternities, live and still births occurring in hospitals by area of occurrence.

Country of birth of mother (*Section 9*)
Information about the country of birth of parents of children born in England and Wales has been recorded at birth registration since April 1969. Note, however, birthplace

does not always equate with ethnic group. In particular there are an increasing number of women born in Britain from the ethnic minority population in the younger childbearing ages. Any children born to these women will be included in the 'mother born in UK' category although one or both parents would have been from the ethnic minority population. Conversely, the category 'mother born in the New Commonwealth or Pakistan' will include some children born to mothers who, although themselves born in countries of the New Commonwealth and Pakistan, were not of ethnic minority descent. A fuller discussion of this topic is contained in the article 'Components of growth in the ethnic minority populations', published in *Population Trends 52*. (HMSO 1988).

Fertility rates according to mother's country of birth (*Section 9*)

The age-specific fertility rates for women by country of birth are based on population denominators, which were calculated by updating the figures obtained from the 1981 Census. The latter were adjusted to agree with 1981 mid-year female population estimates and then brought up-to-date by taking into account annual numbers of deaths of women by age and country of birth and estimates of net migration, obtained from the International Passenger Survey, for each year since 1981.

Birth cohorts (*Section 10*)

Birth statistics analysed by the year of occurrence and by age of mother have been available since 1938. In *Section 10* these statistics have been rearranged into birth cohorts, i.e. according to the year of birth of the mother. Since analyses of births are only available by calender year of occurrence and age of mother at childbirth, the years of birth shown for the birth cohorts are approximate. For example, women aged 32 giving birth to children in 1990 could have been born in either 1957 or 1958; for convenience such women have been referred to as the 1958 birth cohort. In some earlier volumes (nos. 11 to 16) it was incorrectly stated that such births have been attributed to the earlier cohort. **Tables 10.2, 10.3** and **10.5** now all refer to age in 'completed years'. In the case of Table 10.2 the average number of liveborn children at x completed years for a particular cohort is calculated by summing the age-specific fertility rates for that cohort (shown in **Table 10.1**) up to and including that at age x. For example, **Table 10.2** shows that women born in 1969 averaged 0.22 children after 20 completed years. This was calculated by summing the age-specific fertility rates for the 1969 cohort shown in Table 10.1 up to and including age 20.

i.e. $(3+12+28+46+63+72)/1000 = 0.22$

Social class (as defined by occupation) (*Section 11*)

Live births occurring in a calendar year are sampled for classification by social class. This is derived by coding father's occupation status and allocating to the appropriate social class. The proportion of birth records sampled in each year was 1 in 10.

For each year the occupation of the father shown on the selected birth record was coded using the *Classification of Occupations 1980*. (HMSO, 1980)

Occupation codes were allocated as far as possible to the Registrar General's social classes as used in census reports; this procedure is approximate since the questions asked at the time of a birth registration are less detailed than those in the census schedule.

Broadly speaking the social class categories are:

Non-manual
I	Professional occupation
II	Managerial and technical
IIIN	Skilled occupations (non-manual)

Manual
IIIM	Skilled occupations (manual)
IV	Partly skilled occupations
V	Unskilled occupations

Other — Residual groups including, for example, armed forces, students and those whose occupation was inadequately described.

To improve the quality of the sample estimates and to ensure consistency with sub-totals, the sample figures have been grossed-up to agree with known totals derived from the 100 per cent processing of birth registrations according to mother's age (see **Table 4.1(a)**). **Appendix Tables 3** and **4** give some indication of the 'standard errors' for selected estimated numbers of births and percentages. The 'standard error' is a conventional measure of the sampling variation that occurs by chance when only a part of the total population - in this instance 1 in 10 live births - has been selected. For example, if the estimated number in a particular category was 50.0 thousand then **Appendix Table 3** indicates that the standard error of that estimate would be approximately 0.64 thousand. Statistical theory states that for the type of distribution being considered there is approximately a 95 per cent chance that the 'true' number in the population - that is, the number that would have been obtained had the whole population been covered rather than a 1 in 10 sample - lies within two standard errors of the estimate. The 95 per cent confidence interval, for this example would therefore be

50.0 ± 1.3 thousand
or
48.7 to 51.3 thousand.

Median intervals (*Section 11*)

The median intervals between marriage and first birth

shown in **Table 11.3** are derived from birth registration data and relate to the interval between marriage and the first birth within marriage. As mentioned above (see *Section 4*) information on parity relates to the number of previous liveborn children by the present or any former husband. Therefore, a birth to a remarried woman who had had children in a previous marriage would not be classified as a first birth within marriage. Median intervals between subsequent births are estimated on a 4 per cent sample of new claims for child benefit payments. Here, the parity information relates to all births (i.e. irrespective of whether they occurred inside or outside marriage) and refer to Great Britain, not to England and Wales.

Conceptions (*Section 12*)

Tables 12.1 to **12.9** bring together records of birth registration and of abortions under the 1967 Act; they include all the pregnancies of women usually resident in England and Wales which lead to one of the following outcomes (pregnancies which lead to spontaneous abortions are not included).

(i)   A maternity at which one or more live or still born births occur and are registered in England and Wales.

(ii) A termination of a pregnancy by abortion under the 1967 Act in England and Wales.

Maternities which result in one or more live or still births are counted only once. Such multiple birth maternities are classified as 'live' if at least one live birth is included and as 'still' if all the births are stillbirths.

Estimating date of conception

Dates of conception are not directly available from birth registrations and abortion records; such dates are estimated as follows:

Maternities (one or more live births)
38 weeks before date of birth (the average gestation period, measured between the first day of the last menstrual period and the date of birth is 40 weeks; conception occurs on average 14 days after the first day of the last menstrual period).

Maternities (all stillbirths)
Date of birth minus stated gestation period.

Abortions under the 1967 Act
For conceptions in 1980 and earlier years, date of start of last menstrual period plus 14 days; for conceptions in 1981 and later years date of termination minus stated gestation period plus 14 days (the gestation period is estimated from the first day of the last menstrual period).

Estimating a woman's age at conception

A woman' age at conception is estimated from her date of birth stated on the birth registration or abortion return together with the estimated date of conception. For a small number of cases for which the woman's date of birth was not stated, an age was imputed for the woman by using the date of birth stated on previous comparable record.

Tables 12.5 and **12.7** include conceptions outside marriage which lead to maternities within marriage. In order to maintain consistency with tables elsewhere in the volume, and to avoid erroneous classification of maternities with below average gestation periods, such events have been restricted to those where birth occurred within 8 months (35 weeks) of marriage. The year of conception and age of woman at conception have, however, been estimated at a date 38 weeks before birth as in the case of all other conceptions leading to live births.

True birth order

As noted above (*Section 4*), information on the number of previous liveborn children is only available for births occurring within marriage. However, the proportion of births occurring outside marriage has risen sharply in recent years. Therefore, the information collected on birth order has been supplemented with estimates of overall or 'true' birth order, i.e. regardless of whether the birth occurred inside or outside marriage. **Table 1.7** (mean age at child birth), **Table 10.3** (average number of first births) and **Table 10.5** (distribution of women by number of children) are all based on estimated true birth order.

The volume *Period and cohort birth order statistics* (Series FM1 no. 14) describes how these statistics were estimated.

Base population for fertility rates

Throughout this volume fertility rates have been calculated using appropriate estimates of the population (see **Appendix Tables 1** and **2**). These are currently based on results from the 1981 Census adjusted for estimated under-enumeration. These population bases include residents of England and Wales temporarily outside Great Britain and exclude overseas visitors. Residents of England and Wales temporarily in Scotland are included and residents of Scotland visiting England and Wales are excluded. The estimates are updated each year by allowing for births, deaths and migration. See OPCS Occasional paper 37, *Making a population estimate in England and Wales* for further details.

Births to visitors and births overseas

For birth event numerators for fertility rates to be on exactly the same basis as the population estimate denominators, births to visitors occurring in England and Wales would have to be excluded from the overall counts and births occurring outside the country to England and Wales residents would have to be included. However, the Office of Population Censuses and Surveys collects statistics only of births registered in England and Wales. Therefore, births to residents of England and Wales which are registered elsewhere are excluded from the national statistics but births registered in England and Wales to mothers whose usual residence is elsewhere are included. In 1990 there were 354 live births in England and Wales to visitors whose usual residence was elsewhere.

In 1990, some 15,000 births occurring outside the United Kingdom to British nationals were voluntarily registered with British Consuls, British High Commissioners or HM Armed Forces registration centres. By far the majority of these however, were births to people who had emigrated from the United Kingdom (that is, lived outside the UK for at least one year) and were therefore not residents of England and Wales. Such persons are not included in the estimated base populations. It is estimated that at any given time an average of around 100 thousand women of childbearing age (15-44), usually resident in England and Wales, are temporarily absent overseas. However, the great majority of these women are absent for only a short time and it is unlikely that more than a few hundred per year give birth while overseas. During 1990 the number of births to residents of England and Wales which were registered in Scotland and Northern Ireland were 214 and 29 respectively.

So far as can be established, therefore, it seems that the number of births to residents of England and Wales occurring outside the country is likely to be of about the same magnitude as the number of births occurring in England and Wales to visitors resident elsewhere. The effect on fertility rates of the difference between the definitions used for the birth event numerators and the population denominators can therefore be assumed to be negligible.

Foundlings

By definition few, if any, details are known about abandoned children and therefore they are not included in the statistics given in this volume. However, all children are included in the 'abandoned children register' and in 1990 12 such entries were made.

Symbols and conventions used

:   not appropriate
-       nil
0   less than half the unit under consideration

Where data are not yet available, cells are left blank.

Additional information

The following analytical articles on fertility trends have been included in recent issues of *Population Trends:*

Barry Werner. Fertility trends in the UK and in thirteen other developed countries 1966-1986. *Population Trends 51*. HMSO (1988).

Barry Werner. Birth intervals: results from the OPCS Longitudinal Study. 1972-1984. *Population Trends 51*. HMSO (1988).

Barry Werner. Fertility data from the Population (Statistics) Act in England and Wales: 1938-1988. *Population Trends 52*. HMSO (1988).

Barry Werner. Spacing of births to women born in 1935-1959: evidence from the OPCS Longitudinal Study. *Population Trends 52*. HMSO (1988).

Chris Shaw. The sex ratio at birth in England and Wales. *Population Trends 57*. HMSO (1989).

Chris Shaw. Recent trends in family size and family building. *Population Trends 58*. HMSO (1989)

Chris Shaw. Fertility assumption for 1989-based population projections for England and Wales. *Population Trends 61*. HMSO (1990).

Jacqui Cooper. Births outside marriage: recent trends and associated demographic and social changes. *Population Trends 63*. HMSO (1991).

Jacqui Cooper. The divergence between period and cohort measures of fertility. *Population Trends 63*. HMSO (1991).

Clare Jones. Birth Statistics 1990. *Population Trends 65*. HMSO (1991).

Clare Jones. Fertility of the over thirties. *Population Trends 67*. HMSO (1992).

John Craig. Fertility trends within the United Kingdom. *Population Trends 67*. HMSO (1992).

Other relevant publications

Mortality statistics 1989 - perinatal and infant: social and biological factors (Series DH3 No. 23) contains data on birthweight for regional health authorities analysed separately by age, social class and parity.

Key population and vital statistics 1990: local and health authority areas (Series VS No. 17/PP1 No. 13) contains birth and death rates in local and health authorities of England and Wales for 1990, inluding figures of births occurring inside and outside marriage, the sex of child, deaths, infant deaths and stillbirths.

Vital Statistics 1 (VS1) contains annual data for all local and health authorities in England and Wales, including summary figures of populations, births and deaths; fertility and mortality rates; comparative numbers and rates for the region and for England and Wales.

Vital statistics 2 (VS2) contains annual data for all local and health authorities in England and Wales, including births by age of mother, number of previous children, type of institution in which the birth occurred and birthweight.

Vital statistics 4 (VS4) contains annual summary figures of births and deaths for each ward in England and Wales, including number of live births, still births and deaths by sex.

VS1, VS2 and VS4 are available on paper, microfiche, and tape formats.

Enquiries about the availability of further national birth statistics should be addrssed to the Office of Population Censuses and Surveys (Fertility Statistics Unit), Room 634, St. Catherine's House, 10 Kingsway, London, WC2B 6JP. Telephone 071-242 0262 Ext 2575.

Enquiries about the availability of further birth statistics for particular localities should be addressed to the Office of Population Censuses and Surveys (Vital Statistics Branch), Room 3001, Titchfield, Fareham, Hants, PO15 5RS. Telephone 0329 42511 Ext 3058.

B

Fertility trends in England and Wales: 1980-90

Introduction

This commentary is divided into two parts. The first presents a summary of fertility trends in England and Wales, and sets these in a wider context by comparing them with recent statistics for the United Kingdom, and a selection of Western nations. The second part focuses in more detail on post-war trends in births and conceptions in England and Wales.

Details of methods used to compile the data on births and conceptions are given in the Introduction to this volume, together with explanatory notes on the fertility measures used.

Section I: Overview

Summary birth statistics for England and Wales

There were 706 thousand live births in England and Wales during 1990, 3 per cent more than during 1989, and the highest annual total for 18 years. This represented a return to the upward trend in the number of births each year since 1982, after a slight fall in 1989 (see **Figure 1**). The crude birth rate and general fertility rate also rose in 1990 to 13.9 births per thousand population, and 64.3 births per thousand women aged 15-44 respectively.

The total period fertility rate (TPFR), which is the best period indicator of fertility, showed that there was a genuine rise in the fertility of women. Between 1989 and 1990 the TPFR rose from 1.80 to 1.84, but was still below the value of 1.88 recorded at the most recent peak in 1980.

The trend in mean age of women at childbirth remained upward. At 27.5 years in 1990 the average age was nearly a year greater than in 1980, and the highest since 1961. The mean age of women at first birth also continued to rise, and reached 25.4 years.

Births outside marriage rose by nearly 8 per cent from 1989 to 1990, compared with a rise of less than 1 per cent for births within marriage. In 1990 extra-marital births accounted for 28.3 per cent of all live births, compared with 27.0 per cent in 1989, and 11.8 in 1980.

Table S1 Summary of key birth statistics

Year/Quarter		Number of live births (thousands)	Crude birth rate*	General fertility rate†	Total period fertility rate≠	Mean age at childbirth (years)		Percentage of births outside marriage
						All births	First birth**	
1964 ††		876.0	18.5	92.9	2.93	27.2	24.0	7.2
1977		569.3	11.5	58.1	1.66	26.5	24.4	9.7
1980		656.2	13.2	64.2	1.88	26.7	24.5	11.8
1985		656,4	13.1	61.0	1.78	27.0	24.8	19.2
1988		693.6	13.8	63.0	1.82	27.2	25.1	25.6
1989		687.7	13.6	62.5	1.80	27.3	25.3	27.0
1990		706.1	13.9	64.3	1.84	27.5	25.4	28.3
1989	March	167.0	13.4	62.1	1.79	27.3	25.1	26.9
	June	176.7	14.0	62.8	1.81	27.4	25.3	26.0
	September	175.8	13.8	61.9	1.78	27.4	25.2	27.1
	December	168.2	13.2	63.5	1.82	27.4	25.2	28.0
1990	March	168.3	13.5	62.1	1.80	27.5	25.3	28.0
	June	179.3	14.2	65.5	1.83	27.5	25.4	27.4
	September	184.5	13.8	66.5	1.86	27.5	25.4	28.4
	December	174.5	13.6	63.0	1.88	27.5	25.4	29.5

Note: All quarterly rates are seasonally adjusted.

.. Not available.
* Births per 1,000 population of all ages.
† Births per 1,000 women aged 15-44.
≠ The total period fertility rate is the average number of children which would be born per woman if women experienced the age-specific fertility rates of the period in question throughout their childbearing lifespan.
** Estimated mean age at first birth for all births (whether inside or outside marriage).
†† Figures for 1964 and 1977 are included to allow comparison with the year when post-war fertility in England and Wales was at a maximum and a minimum respectively.

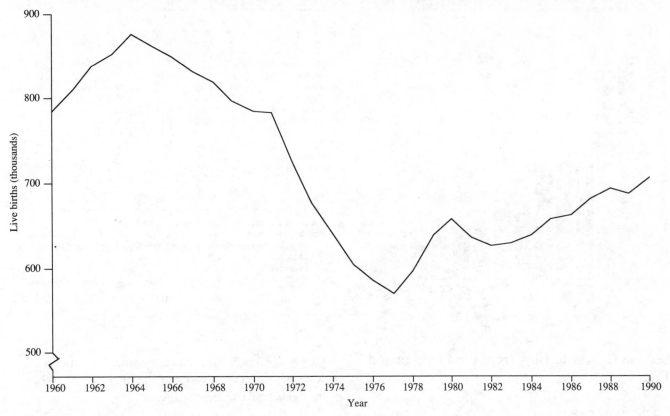

Figure 1 Total live births, 1960-90

Fertility patterns within the United Kingdom

Between 1989 and 1990 the number of births rose in each of the constituent countries of the United Kingdom. Over the past decade, however, trends have varied in different countries; in England the number of births increased by nearly 8 per cent, while in Northern Ireland it fell by over 7 per cent.

Table S2 summarizes the fertility statistics of the four countries in 1990. Northern Ireland, with the highest TPFR (2.26), the lowest proportion of births outside marriage (18.7 per cent), and the highest mean age at child birth (28.0 years), was set apart from the other UK countries. There were also small differences between the fertility profiles of England, Wales and Scotland. The TPFR in Scotland has been lower than England and Wales since 1982, and in 1990 was 1.67. In Wales the proportion of births outside marriage was higher, and the mean age at childbirth lower, than elsewhere.

International fertility trends

Table S3 shows the trend in TPFRs of a number of Western nations. Of these, fertility has remained highest in the Irish Republic, with a TPFR of 2.17 births per woman. Sweden joined the Irish Republic in 1990 in having a level of fertility above that which would lead to the long term 'natural' replacement of the population, as its TPFR rose to 2.13. This represented a marked rise in Swedish fertility over the last 10 years, of 20 per cent, from a relatively low rate in 1980. Recently period fertility levels were lowest in Italy (1.29), Spain (1.30), and West Germany (1.44).

A rise in the proportion of births outside marriage over the last decade has been common to all these countries (see **Figure 2**), though considerable variation in the level persists. Extra-marital births accounted for over a half of all births in Sweden, compared with only 6 per cent in Italy. The United Kingdom and France have experienced similar trends in extra-marital fertility. The proportion of births occurring outside marriage was 28 per cent in 1990 in both countries.

Table S2   Summary of key birth statistics for the United Kingdom and constituent countries 1990

Country	Number of live births (thousands)	Crude birth rate*	General fertility rate†	Total period fertility rate*≠	Mean age at childbirth (years)	Percentage of births outside marriage
United Kingdom	798.6	13.9	64,2	1.84	27.5	27.9
Great Britain	772.1	13.8	63.8	1.83	27.5	28.2
England	666.9	13.6	64.2	1.84	27.5	28.3
Scotland	66.0	12.9	58.8	1.67	27.2	27.1
Wales	38.9	13.5	63.8	1.83	26.9	29.3
Northern Ireland	26.5	16.7	78.0	2.26	28.0	18.7

* See footnotes to table S1.

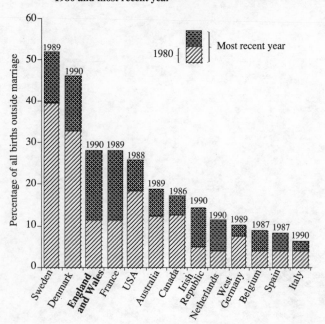

Figure 2 Births outside marriage: an international comparison, 1980 and most recent year

Table S3 International comparison of TPFRs

Country	Year				
	1980	1985	1988	1989	1990
England and Wales	1.88	1.78	1.82	1.80	1.84
Irish Republic	3.23	2.50	2.17	2.11	2.17 (P)
France	1.95	1.82	1.82	1.81	1.80
Belgium	1.69	1.51	1.58 (E)	1.59 (E)	
West Germany	1.45	1.28	1.41	1.44	..
Netherlands	1.60	1.51	1.55	1.55	1.62
Italy	1.69	1.41	1.33	1.32	1.29 (E)
Spain	2.22	1.63	1.38 (E)	1.30 (E)	
Denmark	1.55	1.44	1.56	1.62	1.67 (P)
Swenden	1.68	1.73	1.96	2.02	2.13 (P)
Australia	1.90	1.89	1.84	..	..
Canada	1.74	1.67	1.68	..	..
USA	1.84	1.84	1.93	..	..

Note: For more recent years, some figures are provisional.
Sources: For non-UK figures:Eurostat, Luxembourg; Council of Europe, Strasbourg; national publications of Australia, Canada and USA.
.. Data not available.
(P) Provisional.
(E) Estimate.

Section II: Key fertility trends in England and Wales

Family formation

Total fertility
The total period fertility rate is the most common measure for assessing the level of fertility at a point in time in the population, as it is independent of the number and age structure of women of childbearing age. The TPFR shows the average number of children that would be born per woman if the current age-specific fertility rates persisted throughout her childbearing lifespan.

Figure 3 shows the substantial fluctuations that have occurred in the TPFR of England and Wales over the last 30 years. In 1964 fertility peaked at 2.93 births per woman, and this was followed by a rapid decline to a low of 1.66 in 1977. The TPFR has since remained between 1.7 and 1.9, and the 1990 figure of 1.84 was the highest for 10 years.

Figure 3 Trend in total period fertility rate and average completed family size, 1960-90

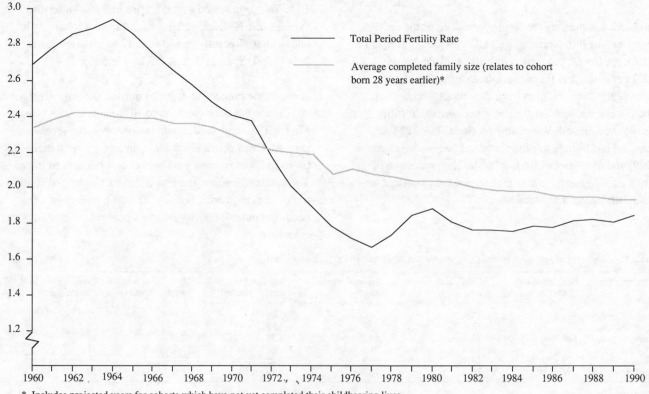

* Includes projected years for cohorts which have not yet completed their childbearing lives.

Figure 4   Trend in monthly total period fertility rate, January 1980 to December 1990

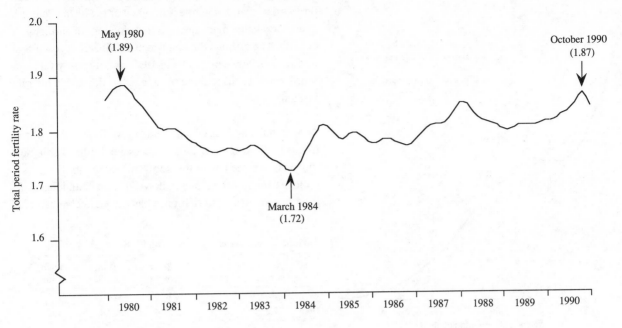

Table S4   Age-specific fertility rates

Year	Live births (thousands)	Births per 1000 women in age-group							TPFR
		All ages	Under 20	20-24	25-29	30-34	35-39	40 and over	
1964	876.0	**92.9**	42.5	181.6	187.3	107.7	49.8	13.7	2.93
1977	569.3	**58.1**	29.4	103.7	117.5	58.6	18.2	4.4	1.66
1980	656.2	**64.2**	30.4	112.7	133.6	70.5	22.3	4.8	1.88
1985	656.4	**61.0**	29.5	94.5	127.6	76.4	24.1	5.0	1.78
1988	693.6	**63.0**	32.4	94.9	123.8	82.7	27.9	5.1	1.82
1989	687.7	**62.5**	31.9	92.9	120.0	83.7	29.4	5.2	1.80
1990	706.1	**64.3**	33.3	91.7	122.4	87.3	31.2	5.3	1.84

Note: The rates for women of all ages, under 20 and 40 and over are based upon the female populations aged 15-44, 15-19 and 40-44 respectively.

During the last decade the seasonally adjusted monthly TPFR was highest in May 1980 (1.89), and lowest in March 1984 (1.72) (see **Figure 4**). The TPFR has been lower than 2.1 - the level that would lead to the long term 'natural' replacement of the population - for the last 18 years. Partly, this is due to the continued widening of the age distribution at which fertility commonly occurs.[1]

The age pattern of fertility and mean age at childbirth
Excepting for the age-group 20-24, whose fertility declined slightly, the increase in fertility between 1989 and 1990 was common to all age-groups. The largest rise, of over 6 per cent, was amongst women aged 35-39, while the rate for women aged 30-34 was the highest since 1968. By comparison, the increase of 2 per cent in fertility of the 25-29 age-group was small.

These latest figures continued the shift to an older age pattern of fertility seen during the 1980s (see **Figure 5**). Although the peak childbearing ages have remained 25-29, the fertility rates of women in their twenties have declined since 1980. In contrast, during the same period, fertility rates amongst ages 30-34 and 35-39 have increased substantially (by 24 and 40 per cent respectively). In 1990, the fertility of women in their early thirties was only slightly less than that of women in their early twenties - 10 years ago it was substantially less.

The fertility of teenagers rose by 4 per cent between 1989 and 1990. This was a continuation of a steady rise in their fertility since 1982 - the rate in 1990 was the highest for 15 years.

Figure 5   Age-specific fertility rates in England and Wales, 1980 and 1990

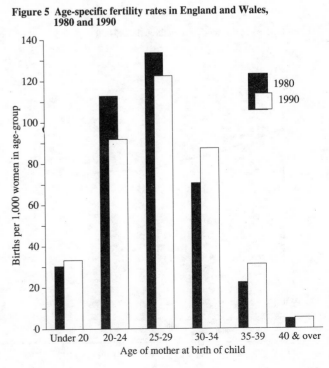

Figure 6 Age-specific fertility rates by marital status, 1990

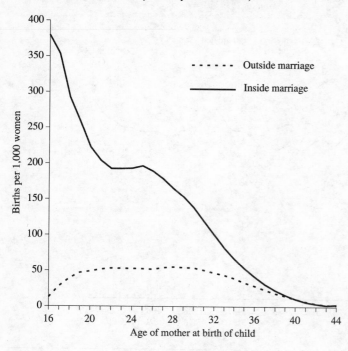

Figure 6 compares marital and extra-marital fertility rates in 1990. Marital fertility rates were particularly high amongst young women and declined with increasing age. In contrast, extra-marital fertility rates, which were generally much lower, peaked amongst women in their late twenties.

Timing and spacing of births
The trends in age-specific fertility rates have contributed to the rising mean age of mothers at childbirth. The mean age for all births in 1990 was 27.5, over a month greater than in 1989, and the highest since 1961. This was also partly due to the small increase in the proportion of women aged 15-44 who are in the older age-groups. **Figure 7** shows that since the mid-1970s the increase in mean age has been common to births both inside and outside marriage.

Table S5 shows estimates of mean age of mother by 'true' birth order, that is regardless of whether the birth occurred inside or outside marriage (see Introduction for further details). The estimated mean age at childbearing rose for all birth orders between 1989 and 1990, and it is only for fourth order births that the mean age has decreased over the last ten years.

Trends in the ages at which women give birth are related to trends in the spacing between successive births. **Table S6** indicates that the recent trend towards more rapid childbearing may be slowing down. The median length of time from marriage to first birth has stayed unchanged at 27

Table S5 Mean age of mothers at childbirth*

Year	All births	First births	Second births	Third births	Fourth births
1980	**26.7**	24.5	27.0	29.2	30.4
1985	**27.0**	24.8	27.4	29.4	30.3
1988	**27.2**	25.1	27.6	29.5	30.2
1989	**27.3**	25.3	27.8	29.6	30.2
1990	**27.5**	25.4	28.0	29.7	30.3

* Includes children born inside and outside marriage (see introduction).

Table S6 Median intervals from first marriage to first birth and between later births

Year	First marriage first birth within marriage	First to second birth*	Second to third birth*
	Median intervals (months)		
1980	29	32	41
1985	28	32	40
1988	27	32	38
1989	27	32	38
1990	27	33	37

* All births (whether inside or outside marriage).
  Based on a 4 per cent sample of child benefit returns for Great Britain.

Figure 7 Mean age of mother at childbirth, 1964-90

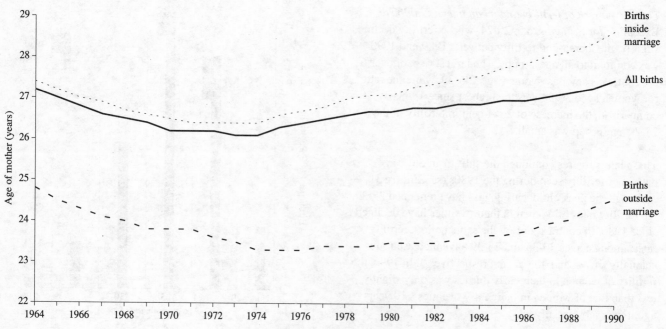

months for the last 5 years, while the average interval between first and second birth of 33 months in 1990 was the highest of the decade. However, the average interval from second to third births continued to fall - to 37 months in 1990.

Average family size
The 'period' measures of fertility discussed are based on one year's data, and are sensitive to short term changes in the timing and patterns of childbearing.[2] A more stable measure is the average completed family size, for successive generations of women. **Figure 3** compares the total period fertility rate for a given year with the average completed family size for the cohort of women born 28 years earlier (28 years being the current mean age of childbearing). The peak in average completed family size in 1964 of 2.4 births per woman was somewhat lower than the TPFR, though since 1972 this cohort measure has been higher than the TPFR. Women currently aged in their mid-twenties are projected to have a completed family size of just under 2 children.

Actual data on final family size is of course limited to women who have reached the end of their childbearing years. The average family size by a given age can be calculated for successive cohorts of women (see **Table S7** and **Figure 8**). A marked decline has occurred in the average family size at younger ages for cohorts born since 1945. Compared with women born 20 years earlier, women born in 1960 had on average half a birth less by the end of their twenties. Amongst recent cohorts there is evidence of delayed childbearing, as the increase in average family size between ages 30 and 35, and between 35 and 40, has risen - though this has not compensated for the shortfall at younger ages, and final average family size to date has declined. In spite of these trends the 1989 General Household Survey

(GHS)[3] indicated that the expected family size of younger women especially had remained little changed from 10 years previously. A family size of two children was still the most common expectation amongst women of all ages.

Childlessness
An important trend amongst successive cohorts of women born since 1945 has been the steady rise in the proportions remaining childless (see **Figure 9**). For the cohort of women born in 1955 just over 20 per cent were still

Table S7   Average achieved family size by age and year of birth of woman 1925-70

Year of birth of woman	Average number of children per woman by age (completed years)					
	20	25	30	35	40	45*
1925	0.14	0.85	1.48	1.88	2.08	2.12
1930	0.19	0.93	1.68	2.15	2.32	2.35
1935	0.20	1.07	1.91	2.29	2.40	2.42
1940	0.28	1.26	2.00	2.27	2.35	2.36
1945	0.35	1.23	1.85	2.10	2.18	2.19
1950	0.36	1.06	1.65	1.94	2.05	
1955	0.31	0.92	1.53	1.87		
1960	0.24	0.81	1.42			
1965	0.20	0.71				
1970	0.22					

	Increase in average family size between given ages					
	By age 20	20 and 25	25 and 30	30 and 35	35 and 40	After age 40
1925	0.14	0.71	0.63	0.40	0.20	0.04
1930	0.19	0.74	0.75	0.47	0.17	0.03
1935	0.20	0.87	0.84	0.38	0.11	0.02
1940	0.28	0.98	0.74	0.27	0.08	0.01
1945	0.35	0.88	0.62	0.25	0.08	0.01
1950	0.36	0.70	0.59	0.29	0.11	
1955	0.31	0.61	0.61	0.34		
1960	0.24	0.57	0.61			
1965	0.20	0.51				
1970	0.22					

* Includes births at ages 45 and over achieved up to the end of 1990.

Figure 8 Average number of children born to women by woman's age and year of birth, 1930-70

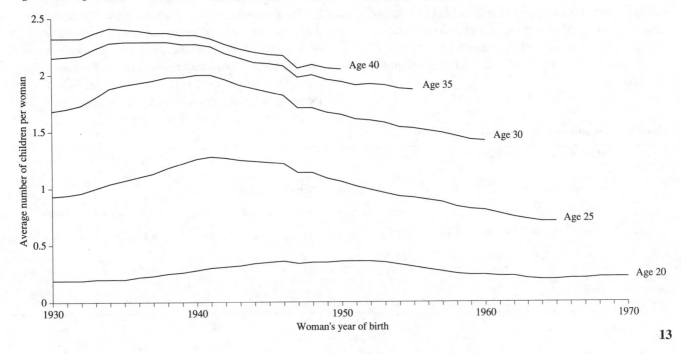

13

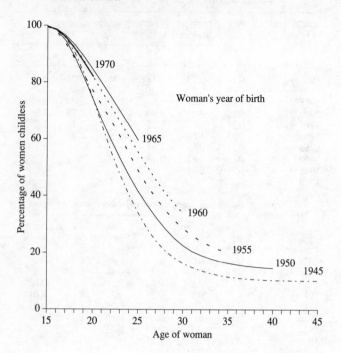

Figure 9 Percentage of women childless at successive ages, 1945-70 cohorts

Woman's year of birth

childless at age 35. In contrast, the corresponding figure for women born 10 years earlier was 12 per cent. Although the current levels of childlessness at younger ages may be partly due to delayed childbearing, it seems unlikely that any childbearing at older ages will be substantial enough to reverse the rising trend in permanent childlessness.

GHS data imply that womens' expectations are not borne out by their actual childbearing patterns. A comparison of the 1979 and 1989 GHS estimates of the number of children expected by women of a given age at the time of interview reveals no increase in expectations of childlessness, and in particular, few young women (aged 25 and under) expected to remain childless.

How far childlessness is involuntary is unknown. However, it does seem highly unlikely that there has been an increase in infecundity, especially given the increasing availability throughout the 1980s of a range of treatments to assist conception (see below). Rather, various social and economic factors may have contributed to a rise in voluntary childlessness.

Multiple births

Although multiple maternities remain rare, their numbers increased steadily during the last decade, from 9.8 per thousand maternities in 1980 to 11.6 per thousand in 1990. This rate rises with age, and in 1990 ranged from 6 per thousand for mothers aged under 20, to 16.9 for mothers aged 35 and over. This oldest age-group also saw the greatest increase in their rate, of 22 per cent, since 1980. The numbers of triplet and higher order maternities rose most. Of the 8,145 multiple maternities in 1990, 211 resulted in triplets or higher order births, an increase of over 8 per cent on the previous year, and more than double the number in 1980.

This recent rise in multiple maternities in thought to be largely due to an increased use of drugs and procedures to assist conception. A study of maternities delivered in 1980 and 1982-1985 showed that 70 per cent of mothers of quadruplets and above, and 36 per cent of mothers of triplets and above, had used drugs for ovulation induction. By comparison, only 6 per cent of mothers of twins and 2 per cent of mothers of singleton births had used these.[4]

Sex ratio at birth

In 1990 there were 104.8 male births for every 100 female births. This was a lower ratio than in 1989 and the same as that in 1988, which was then the lowest ratio recorded since 1933. The fall was totally accounted for by decreases in the sex ratio of births in the quinary age-groups for women aged 25 and over.

The sex ratio has been below 105.5 for the last seven years, and the trend since the 1980s has been generally downward. Thus it would appear that there has been a genuine fall in the sex ratio in the last decade, from a level of around 106 males per 100 females which persisted for almost 40 years previously.

The reasons behind the variations in the sex ratio are largely unknown, although associations with a number of variables, both medical-biological and demographic have been suggested. For example, the statistics indicate that sex ratios are lower for maternities resulting in multiple births, and for births to mothers born outside the United Kingdom. However the rising trends in both of these can not fully account for the overall decline in sex ratio.[5]

Table S8 Maternities with multiple births

| Age of mother | Maternities with multiple births | | | | | | | | | Maternities with multiple births per 1,000 maternities | | |
| | All maternities | | | Twins | | | Triplets or higher | | | | | |
	1980	1989	1990	1980	1989	1990	1980	1989	1990	1980	1989	1990
All ages	**6,404**	**7,774**	**8,145**	**6,308**	**7,579**	**7,934**	**96**	**195**	**211**	**9.8**	**11.4**	**11.6**
Under 20	345	344	333	342	342	328	3	2	5	5.7	6.2	6.0
20-24	1,572	1,641	1,600	1,558	1,623	1,578	14	18	22	7.8	8.9	8.9
25-29	2,315	2,754	2,892	2,281	2,696	2,836	34	58	56	10.4	11.4	11.5
30-34	1,609	2,118	2,287	1,572	2,037	2,200	37	81	87	12.5	14.7	14.8
35 and over	563	917	1,033	555	881	992	8	36	41	13.9	15.7	16.9

Year	Male live births per 100 female live births, by age of mother					
	All ages	Under 20	20-24	25-29	30-34	35 and over
1970	**105.8**	107.1	105.9	105.8	105.9	103.7
1980	**104.9**	105.9	104.2	105.0	105.8	103.8
1985	**105.4**	105.0	106.3	104.8	105.3	105.6
1988	**105.8**	104.7	104.7	104.8	104.6	106.0
1989	**105.1**	105.6	104.9	104.9	105.3	105.5
1990	**104.8**	105.6	105.3	104.7	104.3	104.7

Births outside marriage

One of the most striking trends in recent years has been the rapid rise in both the number and proportion of births that occur outside marriage (see **Figures 10** and **12**).[6] Births outside marriage accounted for over three quarters of the increase of 18.4 thousand in the number of live births from 1989. The number of extra-marital births rose by nearly 8 per cent from 1989 to 200 thousand in 1990, while births within marriage rose by less than 1 per cent. Thus in 1990 the proportion of births outside marriage reached 28.3 per cent, compared with 27.0 per cent in 1989, and 11.3 per cent in 1980 (see **Table S10**).

Figure 10 shows the trends in the proportion of births occurring outside marriage and the extra-marital fertility rate over the last 30 years. While the proportion of births outside marriage has risen steadily from 5.4 per cent in 1960, the extra-marital fertility rate has fluctuated. It rose in the 1960s to 23.0 in 1968, but then fell back to a low of 16.1 in 1977, in line with the general decline in fertility at that time. Since then the rate has increased steeply to 38.9 in 1990.

Figure 10   Extra-marital fertility rate and percentage of births outside marriage, 1960-90

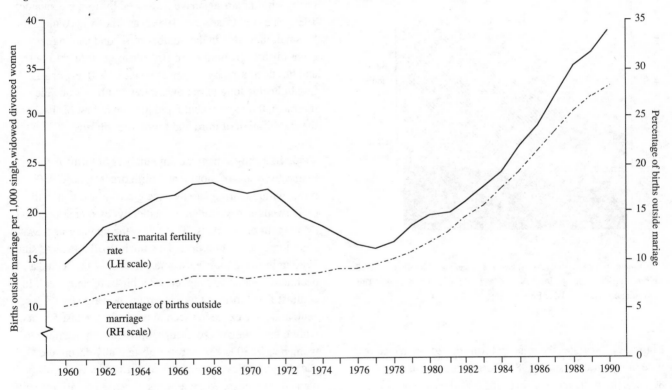

Table S10 Births outside marriage: total number and as a percentage of all births by age of mother, and extra-marital fertility rate

Year	Number of births (thousands)					Percentage of all births in the age-group					Extra-Marital fertility rate*	Mean age at childbirth (in years)
	All ages	Under 20	20-24	25-29	30 and over	All ages	Under 20	20-24	25-29	30 and over		
1964	**63.3**	17.4	20.5	12.1	13.3	7.2	22.6	7.4	4.5	5.3	20.4	24.8
1977	**55.4**	20.1	17.4	9.8	8.2	9.7	36.8	10.0	4.7	6.2	16.1	23.4
1980	**77.4**	25.9	26.6	13.5	11.4	11.3	42.6	13.2	6.0	6.7	19.6	23.5
1985	**126.2**	34.9	47.7	24.2	17.5	19.2	64.8	24.6	10.6	9.3	26.7	23.7
1988	**177.4**	44.6	68.2	38.2	26.4	25.6	76.0	35.2	15.7	13.4	35.1	24.1
1989	185.8	43.5	70.8	41.9	29.6	27.0	78.3	38.2	17.2	14.5	36.4	24.4
1990	200.0	44.6	73.9	47.9	33.6	28.3	80.3	41.1	19.0	15.4	38.9	24.6

* Births per 1,000 unmarried women aged 15-44.

The increase in the number and proportion of all births outside marriage between 1989 and 1990 was common to all age-groups of women. In 1990, extra marital births accounted for over four fifths of teenage births, and over two fifths of births to women aged 20-24. Although the proportion of births that occurred outside marriage was lower among older women, women aged 25-34 have experienced the largest relative rise with numbers more than trebling since 1980. Correspondingly, the mean age of extra-marital childbirth has risen, from 23.5 years in 1980 to 24.6 years in 1990, but was still considerably less than the mean age of 28.7 years of women having births within marriage.

Figure 11 Live births outside marriage as a percentage of total live births, 1980-90

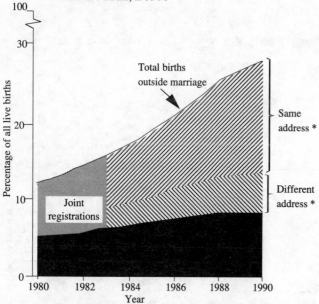

*Estimates of parents' address(es) based on a sample of jointly registered births outside marriage for 1983-85, and all cases for 1986-90. This information is not available for years before 1983.

Figure 11 illustrates the trend in births outside marriage by type of registration since 1980. During this period, over 80 per cent of the increase in births outside marriage arose from the increased number of jointly registered births to unmarried couples. Thus in 1990, 73 per cent of extra-marital births were jointly registered, and in nearly three quarters of these cases the parents stated they were living at the same address, and were therefore presumably cohabiting.

The proportion of births outside marriage which were jointly registered increased with the age of the mother (see Table S11). In 1990, 78 per cent of births outside marriage to women aged over 30 were jointly registered, and of these 82 per cent were registered by co-resident parents. Although the proportions were lower for teenage mothers, some 64 per cent of their births were jointly registered, and 57 per cent were living at the same address as the father.

Table S11 Jointly registered births outside marriage by age of mother

Year	Age of mother					
	All ages	Under 20	20-24	25-29	30-34 .	35 and over
Jointly registered births as a percentage of all births outside marriage						
1980	**57**	46	57	66	71	70
1985	**65**	57	66	70	72	73
1988	**70**	62	70	73	75	77
1989	**71**	63	72	75	77	77
1990	**73**	64	73	77	78	78
Jointly registered births outside marriage where parents were resident at same address as a percentage of all jointly registered births						
1985	**72**	57	74	79	84	82
1986	**71**	56	71	79	81	80
1989	**72**	57	72	79	82	82
1990	**73**	57	73	79	82	82

Births inside marriage: birth order and marriage order
In contrast to the marked rise in births outside marriage, births within marriage have decreased by 13 per cent since 1980. The slight rise since 1989 was wholly accounted for by small increases in the number of second and higher order births - the number of first births continued to fall, and has decreased by 17 per cent since 1980. **Figure 12** highlights the long term upward trend in births outside marriage, the more recent rapid decline in first births, and the stabilisation of third and fourth order births.

Table S13 shows the trends in numbers of births inside marriage by age of mother and birth order. Since 1980 births within marriage to teenage girls and women in their early twenties have fallen dramatically, by 68 per cent and 39 per cent respectively. This fall at the younger ages was common to all birth orders. The much smaller decline since 1980 in births to married women aged 25-29 reflected a decline in second and higher order births of 8 per cent. In contrast first births to this age-group increased by 18 per cent, and have exceeded second births for the last 5 years. Unlike the younger age-groups, births within marriage to women aged 30 and over rose substantially during the decade, and whilst the number of third order births re-mained little changed, first births increased by 40 per cent and second births by 19 per cent. This shift in the age pattern of births within marriage was seen in the continued rise in mean age at childbirth. Mean age at childbirth within marriage rose for all birth orders compared with 1989. Most notably, the mean age for first birth of 27.2 years was 2 years higher than in 1980, and the highest since records began in 1938.

These trends appear to indicate a tendency for delayed childbearing, and also reflect the rise in mean age at marriage[7] and an increase in births to women who have remarried (see **Table S12**). Although the number of births that occurred within a second or later marriage remained virtually unchanged from 1989, they have risen appreciably over the last decade, and in 1990 accounted for over 8 per

Figure 12 Births outside mariage and births inside marriage by birth order, 1960-90

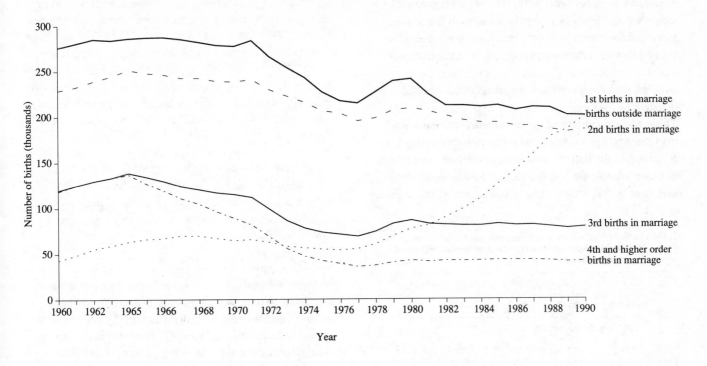

Table S12 Births inside marriage: birth order and mean age of mother

Year	Total births within marriage	Births in second or later marriages	By birth order within marriage (thousands)				Mean age at childbirths (years)		Mean age at marriage (years)	
			First	Second	Third	Fourth or later	All births	First births	All marriages	First marriages
1964	812.6	16.4	286.1	251.3	138.5	136.8	27.4	24.3	25.0	22.8
1977	513.9	28.4	214.6	195.0	68.8	35.5	26.8	25.0	26.6	22.9
1980	578.9	38.5	241.0	209.2	86.3	42.4	27.1	25.2	26.7	23.0
1985	530.2	41.9	212.0	193.1	82.4	42.7	27.8	26.0	27.5	23.8
1988	516.2	42.6	209.3	185.6	79.4	42.0	28.2	26.7	28.3	24.6
1989	501.9	41.4	201.0	182.8	77.5	40.7	28.4	26.9	28.5	24.8
1990	506.1	41.3	200.4	185.3	79.0	41.4	28.7	27.2		

Table S13 Births inside marriage by age of mother and birth order

thousands

Year	Age of mother at birth															
	All births within marriage				First births*				Second births*				Third or later births*			
	Under 20	20-24	25-29	30 and over	Under 20	20-24	25-29	30 and over	Under 20	20-24	25-29	30 and over	Under 20	20-24	25-29	30 and over
1964	59.4	255.6	258.6	239.1	47.4	132.1	73.2	33.4	10.8	84.9	95.8	59.9	1.2	38.6	89.6	145.8
1977	34.4	157.2	198.2	124.1	27.9	83.6	75.4	27.7	6.1	57.8	84.9	46.2	0.4	15.8	37.9	50.2
1980	34.9	174.9	210.0	159.1	28.2	96.4	81.6	34.8	6.3	60.5	84.6	57.8	0.4	18.0	43.8	66.4
1985	20.1	146.3	203.3	160.6	15.8	79.0	79.9	37.3	3.9	50.5	80.0	58.5	0.3	16.7	43.3	64.7
1988	14.1	125.6	205.3	171.3	10.7	68.9	85.8	43.8	3.1	42.4	77.1	62.9	0.3	14.3	42.3	64.5
1989	12.0	114.5	201.0	174.5	9.2	62.1	84.0	45.7	2.6	38.9	76.4	64.9	0.3	13.5	40.6	63.8
1990	11.0	106.2	204.7	184.3	8.3	57.0	86.4	48.6	2.4	36.5	77.7	68.7	0.2	12.7	40.6	66.9

* Birth order is based on all live births within marriage to the mother by her present or any former husband.

cent of all births within marriage. Of these, the majority were third or higher order births. However the greatest increases (of 13 and 14 per cent) occurred in first and second order births, indicating that more women may be starting their childbearing in a second or later marriage.

Distribution of births by father's social class, as defined by occupation
Table S14 indicates trends in the numbers of births inside marriage and jointly registered births outside marriage according to the father's social class as defined by occupation (see Introduction). It should be noted however, that these trends may reflect changes in the proportions of men in each class.

Table S14 Live births within marriage and jointly registered births outside marriage by social class* of father, as defined by occupation *thousands*

Year	All classes (including 'other')	Social class of father (as defined by occupation)			
		I & II	IIIN	IIIM	IV & V
	Live births within marriage				
1980	**578.9**	164.5	61.9	212.2	120.4
1985	**530.2**	158.4	56.2	184.3	105.9
1988	**516.2**	167.7	54.8	175.0	94.1
1989	**501.9**	172.1	49.9	169.7	87.8
1990	**506.1**	177.4	53.2	168.8	85.3
	Jointly registered live births outside marriage				
1980	**44.2**	5.9	2.7	19.6	14.7
1985	**81.8**	10.7	5.0	34.6	27.4
1988	**123.4**	18.8	8.1	51.4	39.7
1989	**132.3**	22.1	7.7	56.3	40.6
1990	**145.2**	23.1	9.5	62.6	44.5

* For definition, see explanatory notes.

Between 1989 and 1990 births within marriage to fathers in Social Classes I and II increased, while births to fathers in Social Classes IIIM, and IV and V decreased. This represented a continuation of trends since 1980. In contrast, births to women married to men in Social Class IIIN experienced an upturn of 7 per cent in 1990, after a ten year period of decline.

Since 1980, jointly registered births outside marriage have increased three to four fold for each social class (as defined by father's occupation). The greatest increase in jointly registered births between 1989 and 1990 occurred amongst Social Class IIIN, though this class accounted for only 7 per cent of all such births.

The distribution of births outside marriage by social class differed appreciably from that for births inside marriage, which may be partly influenced by variations in the age distribution of men in each social class. For example in 1990, Social Classes I and II accounted for 35 per cent of births inside marriage, and only 16 per cent of jointly registered births outside marriage. In contrast Social Classes IV and V accounted for 30 per cent of jointly registered births outside marriage but only 17 per cent of births inside marriage.

Womens' educational attainment and family size
Variations exist by womens' educational level both in the timing of births and in their total family size. Results from the 1989 GHS show that women with no qualifications start their families at younger ages, and have more children by age 25 than do those with qualifications. Among women born in the late 1940s, 69 per cent of those with no qualifications had at least 1 child by age 25, compared with only 27 per cent of women with GCE 'A' Level equivalent or above. Though women with higher qualifications have more births at older ages, particularly in their thirties, it is likely their completed family size will be smaller. For the 1945-49 cohort the number of children born by age 35 ranged from 1.65 amongst those with the highest educational attainment, to 2.24 among women with no educational qualifications.

The stated expected family size also differed by the level of womens' educational attainment. In general, women with no educational qualifications expected to have more children than women with qualifications. Of the 1955-59 cohort with no qualifications, 17 per cent expected to have four or more children, and only 5 per cent expected to remain childless. In contrast, among women with GCE A level or above, only 6 per cent expected four or more children, while 12 per cent expected to remain childless.

Country of birth of mother
Just under 82 thousand births in England and Wales in 1990 were to women born outside the United Kingdom. This was 11.6 per cent of all births, which was virtually unchanged from the previous year, but appreciably less than in 1980. Of these, over 60 per cent were to women born in the New Commonwealth.

Since 1981, TPFRs for women born outside the UK have generally fallen, excepting Caribbean-born women whose level of fertility remained higher than that of UK-born women. Indeed the TPFR of 4.7 for women born in Pakistan and Bangladesh was substantially above that of UK-born women, indicating that larger families are still the norm among these women. In contrast Caribbean-born women had a TPFR of 1.6.

There is wide variation in the proportion of births that occur outside marriage by country of birth of mother. The proportion remained highest amongst Caribbean-born women at 47.8 per cent, but unlike all other groups, the trend was downward. Women born in India and Pakistan and Bangladesh continued however to have extremely low proportions of extra-marital births - 2.4 and 1.0 per cent respectively.

These figures are only a partial indicator of fertility trends among ethnic minority groups. Excluded are births to increasing numbers of women who, although of ethnic minority descent were born in the UK. They also include births to women who were not of ethnic minority descent but were born outside the UK. Analysis of the question on ethnicity on the 1991 Census should provide a better estimate of the fertility of these groups.

Table S15 Live births, TPFRs and births outside marriage by country of birth of mother

Country of birth of mother	All live births											
	Thousands				TPFR				Percentage of births occurring outside marriage			
	1980	1985	1989	1990	1981*	1985	1989	1990	1980	1985	1989	1990
All birthplaces	**656.2**	**656.4**	**687.7**	**706.1**	**1.80**	**1.78**	**1.80**	**1.86**	**11.8**	**19.2**	**27.0**	**28.3**
United Kingdom	569.1	575.2	607.2	624.2	1.7	1.7	1.8	1.8	12.2	20.6	28.9	30.3
Outside United Kingdom	86.8	81.1	80.4	81.9	2.5	2.5	2.3	2.3	9.1	9.7	12.9	13.5
New Commonwealth	55.5	52.7	49.5	49.8	2.9	2.9	2.7	2.6	8.9	8.2	10.0	10.2
India	13.5	11.1	8.8	8.6	3.1	2.9	2.4	2.2	1.2	1.8	2.1	2.4
Pakistan and Bangladesh	16.6	17.9	17.3	18.0	6.5	5.6	4.7	4.7	0.6	0.6	1.0	1.0
East African Commonwealth	6.6	7.1	6.7	6.6	2.1	2.1	1.9	1.8	2.0	3.2	5.6	6.2
Rest of African Commonwealth	3.4	3.6	4.7	5.0	3.4	3.0	4.2	4.1	13.2	19.4	27.0	31.1
Caribbean Commonwealth	7.1	4.9	4.0	3.8	2.0	1.8	1.6	1.6	50.9	48.6	48.1	47.8
Other New Commonwealth	8.3	8.2	7.9	7.9	2.0	2.3	1.8	1.7	5.8	8.7	13.0	12.0
Rest of the World	31.4	28.3	30.9	32.2	2.0	2.0	1.9	2.0	9.4	12.6	17.4	18.4

Table S16 Live births, TPFRs and births outside marriage by region of usual address

Region of usual address	Total live births (thousands)				TPFR				Percentage of births outside marriage			
	1980	1985	1989	1990	1980	1985	1989	1990	1980	1985	1989	1990
England and Wales	661.0	656.4	687.7	706.1	1.88	1.78	1.80	1.84	11.8	19.2	27.0	28.3
England	622.9	619.3	649.4	666.9	1.87	1.78	1.80	1.84	11.9	19.3	27.0	28.3
North	41.5	40.9	39.1	40.7	1.86	1.80	1.71	1.78	12.3	21.1	31.1	32.8
Yorkshire and Humberside	64.9	64.6	66.6	68.9	1.87	1.79	1.79	1.85	12.5	20.7	29.1	30.6
East Midlands	51.7	50.1	53.6	54.8	1.89	1.74	1.77	1.80	11.6	19.6	26.7	28.0
East Anglia	24.9	24.5	26.0	26.6	1.89	1.73	1.73	1.75	9.1	14.5	21.8	22.8
South East	228.1	227.4	243.3	249.6	1.82	1.75	1.83	1.87	11.8	18.0	24.8	25.9
Greater London	94.0	96.5	102.5	105.7	1.77	1.78	1.88	1.92	16.3	22.8	29.8	30.5
South West	52.6	53.5	58.3	59.0	1.80	1.70	1.74	1.76	9.5	15.9	22.9	24.3
West Midlands	71.8	70.4	73.3	75.1	1.96	1.86	1.89	1.94	11.7	19.2	27.8	29.1
North West	87.3	88.1	89.1	92.3	1.92	1.88	1.87	1.93	13.3	23.9	33.1	34.4
Wales	37.6	36.8	38.0	38.9	1.95	1.84	1.79	1.82	10.4	18.9	28.2	29.3

Note: The figures relate to usual area of residence of the mother. Births occurring in England and Wales to mothers usually resident elsewhere are included in the total for England and Wales.

Area of residence

The social and economic circumstances, and ethnic background of women, will influence the regional fertility profiles, as will variations in the distribution of women by age and marital status. **Table S16** shows the trends in total births, TPFRs and the proportion of births outside marriage for each of the standard regions of England and for Wales.[8]

The rise in both the number of births and TPFRs was shared among each of the standard regions of England and Wales. The largest rise occurred in the North where fertility was over 4 per cent higher than last year. However, the TPFR in the North of 1.78 in 1990 was relatively low compared to the West Midlands, North West and Greater London, which each had rates of over 1.9 births per woman. Indeed, Greater London has experienced a marked increase in fertility of 8 per cent from 1980 when it had the lowest rate. In 1990, East Anglia and the South West had the lowest TPFRs (of 1.75 and 1.76 respectively).

Figure 13a shows variation in the standardised fertility ratios (SFRs) of the counties of England and Wales in 1990. These represent the number of births which occurred in each county as a percentage of the number of births that would have occurred had the county experienced the age-specific fertility rates of England and Wales as a whole. (SFRs for local and health authority areas are routinely published in the volume *Key population and vital statistics*,[9] compiled by OPCS.)

The SFR of the West Midlands was over 10 per cent above the national average, and the metropolitan and industrial counties of the North West and South Wales had SFRs over 5 per cent higher than the national average. SFRs were well below average in the south western counties, parts of East Anglia, and the northern most counties; indeed Northumberland had the lowest SFR of 86.

The upward trend in births outside marriage was seen in all regions of England and Wales, and in 1990 extra-marital births accounted for 34.4 per cent of births in the North West and 32.8 per cent in the North, compared with 22.8 per cent in East Anglia and 24.3 in the South West. At county level the variation in the proportions of births outside marriage is even greater. The highest proportions occurred in the metropolitan counties of northern England, for example in Merseyside (39.3 per cent), Tyne and Wear (36.3 per cent) and Greater Manchester (36.2 per cent),

Figure 13 Standardised fertility ratios* and births outside marriage, 1990

a) Standardised fertility ratios*

Less than 95

95-100

100-105

105 or greater

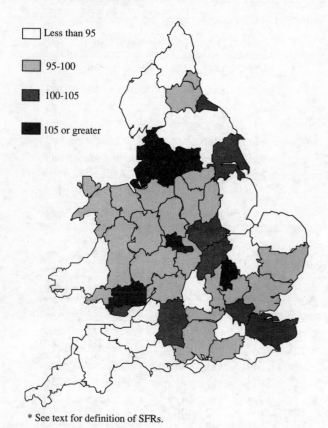

* See text for definition of SFRs.

b) Percentage of births outside marriage

Below 22%

22%-27%

27%-31%

Above 31%

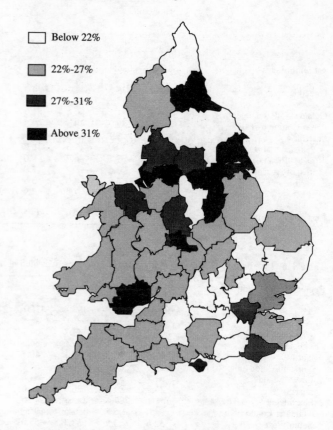

while the lowest portions were recorded in some of the counties of the South East. Surrey was the only county in 1990 where the proportion of births outside marriage was less than one in five.

Patterns of birth occurrence

Seasonal and daily variations in numbers of births
Over the last 30 years there has been a marked shift in the seasonal pattern of births, from a Spring peak to a Summer/early Autumn peak. In 1990, the average monthly number of births (adjusted to allow for the differing number of days in each month) ranged from a peak in September of 4 per cent above average, to a trough in December of 5 per cent below average. In contrast, in 1960, the peak was in March, with 5 per cent above average births, and the trough was in January with 5 per cent below average births.

Figure 14 Monthly variation in numbers of live births (annual average = 100), 1960 and 1990

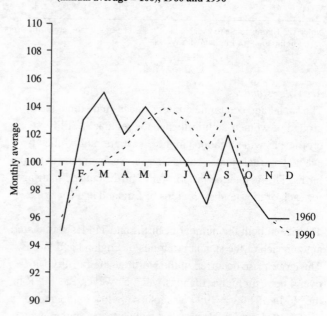

Table S17 Monthly variation in numbers of live births

Year	Daily average* number of births as a proportion of daily average for whole year												
	Jan	Feb	Mar	Apr	May	Jun	Jul	Aug	Sep	Oct	Nov	Dec	Annual average
1960	0.95	1.03	10.5	1.02	1.04	1.02	1.00	0.97	1.02	0.98	0.96	0.96	100.0
1970	0.99	1.03	1.08	1.03	1.03	1.02	1.00	0.98	1.00	0.97	0.94	0.94	100.0
1980	0.97	1.00	1.03	1.02	1.03	1.02	1.03	0.97	1.04	0.99	0.96	0.94	100.0
1985	0.97	0.98	1.00	1.00	1.03	1.03	1.03	1.02	1.05	0.99	0.96	0.95	100.0
1989	0.97	0.99	1.02	1.01	1.03	1.03	1.03	1.01	1.04	0.98	0.95	0.95	100.0
1990	0.96	0.99	1.00	1.01	1.03	1.04	1.03	1.01	1.04	0.98	0.96	0.95	100.0

Births are also unevenly distributed through out the week. Fewer births occur on Friday and at the weekend.

Place of confinement
In 1990, 98 per cent of deliveries took place in National Health Service (NHS) hospitals, 1 per cent in non-NHS hospitals and maternity homes, and 1 per cent in the mother's home. Over the last decade, this distribution has remained almost unchanged. However, when these data were first collected in 1955, over one third of births were delivered at home, while 60 per cent occurred in NHS hospitals, a further 4 per cent in other hospitals, and 2 per cent occurred elsewhere.

Table S18   Place of confinement

Year	Maternities (thousands)	Percentage distribution of maternities by place of confinement			
		NHS hospitals	Other hospitals and maternity homes	At home	Elsewhere*
1980	654.5	97.5	1.1	1.2	0.1
1985	653.1	97.9	1.1	0.9	0.1
1988	689.2	97.8	1.1	0.9	0.1
1989	683.0	97.8	1.1	1.0	0.1
1990	701.0	97.8	1.0	1.0	0.1

* Elsewhere includes psychiatric institutions, homes for unmarried mothers, remand homes, reception centres and private houses (other than the mother's usual residence).

Trends in conceptions: 1979-1989

Outcome of conceptions
The conception statistics reviewed in this section are derived by combining registration records of both live and still births, and of legal terminations under the 1967 Abortion Act. Since many of the births in 1990, and some of the abortions, were conceived in 1989, the latest available conception statistics are for 1989. In that year, an estimated 865 thousand conceptions occurred to women usually resident in England and Wales, over 15 thousand (2 per cent) more than in 1988. Forty-two per cent of these occurred outside marriage, compared with 26 per cent in 1979. Of the 118 thousand conceptions to teenage girls, 89 per cent occurred outside marriage.

For conceptions outside marriage, there was a marked rise in the number and proportion which led to a maternity outside marriage (see **Figure 15** and **Table S19**). Between 1979 and 1989 the proportion rose from 37 to 53 per cent. Correspondingly the proportion that led to a maternity inside marriage fell to only 10 per cent in 1989 compared with 23 per cent in 1979.

Overall, some 20 per cent of conceptions were legally terminated by abortion in 1989, and this proportion has risen gradually since 1979 when it was 16 per cent. During the same period, the proportion of conceptions within marriage that led to an abortion has remained virtually unchanged at 8 per cent, while the corresponding figure for conceptions outside marriage has fallen from 40 to 36 per cent.

Figure 16 shows that the proportion of conceptions which led to a legal abortion was highest among the younger and older age-groups of women. In 1989, however, the proportion of conceptions terminated by legal abortion among older women was less than 10 years earlier, while the converse was true for younger women. These trends may influence the age-specific fertility rates.

Figure 15   Outcome of recorded conceptions, 1979 and 1989

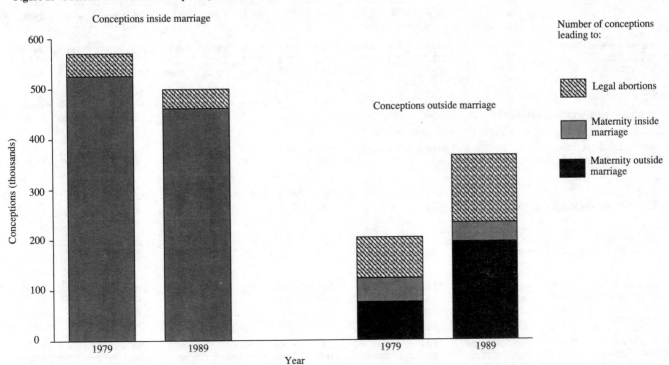

21

Table S19   Outcome of conceptions inside and outside marriage   **Residents of England and Wales**

	Age of woman at conception/year of conception											
	All ages				Under 20				Under 16			
	1979	1984	1988	1989	1979	1984	1988	1989	1979	1984	1988	1989
All conceptions												
Base number (thousands)	**774.1**	**790.1**	**849.5**	**864.7**	**120.9**	**118.2**	**120.7**	**117.5**	**9.1**	**9.6**	**8.8**	**8.4**
Percentage conceived:												
Inside marriage	74	67	59	58	27	17	11	11	0	0	0	0
Outside marriage	26	33	41	42	73	83	89	89	100	100	100	100
Percentage leading to:												
Maternity	84	83	80	80	70	67	64	64	45	44	47	48
Legal abortion*	16	17	20	20	30	33	36	36	55	56	53	52
Conceptions inside marriage												
Base number (thousands)	**570.6**	**526.8**	**498.0**	**499.2**	**32.2**	**20.4**	**13.3**	**12.4**	**0**	**0**	**0**	**0**
Percentage leading to:												
Maternity	92	93	92	92	96	96	95	95	78	89	0	0
Legal abortion	8	7	8	8	4	4	5	5	22	11	0	0
Conceptions outside marriage												
Base number (thousands)	**203.5**	**263.4**	**351.5**	**365.6**	**88.8**	**97.9**	**107.4**	**105.1**	**9.1**	**9.6**	**8.8**	**8.3**
Percentage leading to:												
Maternity outside marriage	37	47	52	53	34	46	52	54	38	41	45	47
Maternity inside marriage	23	16	11	10	26	14	8	7	7	3	2	1
Legal abortion*	40	37	37	36	40	40	40	39	55	56	53	52

* Legal termination under 1967 Abortion Act.

Table S20   Conceptions inside and outside marriage by age of woman and outcome of conception   **Residents of England and Wales**
thousands

Age of woman at conception/ outcome of conception	All conceptions				Conceptions inside marriage				Conceptions outside marriage			
	1979	1984	1988	1989	1979	1984	1988	1989	1979	1984	1988	1989
All ages												
All conceptions	**774.1**	**790.1**	**849.5**	**864.7**	**570.6**	**526.8**	**498.0**	**499.2**	**203.5**	**263.4**	**351.5**	**365.6**
Maternities	**648.5**	**653.8**	**681.8**	**693.5**	**525.8**	**488.5**	**459.6**	**461.1**	**122.7**	**165.3**	**22.3**	**232.4**
Legal abortion*	**125.6**	**136.3**	**167.7**	**171.2**	**44.8**	**38.3**	**38.5**	**38.0**	**80.8**	**98.0**	**129.3**	**133.2**
Under 20												
All conceptions	120.9	118.2	120.7	117.5	32.2	20.4	13.3	12.4	88.8	97.9	107.4	105.1
Percentage leading to legal abortion*	30	33	36	36	4	4	5	5	40	40	40	39
20-24												
All conceptions	241.6	249.1	256.0	251.6	180.4	158.6	127.9	119.6	61.1	90.4	128.1	132.0
Percentage leading to legal abortion*	13	15	21	22	4	4	5	5	39	36	37	37
25-29												
All conceptions	234.8	238.6	267.1	278.0	205.9	196.0	197.8	201.3	28.9	42.6	69.3	76.7
Percentage leading to legal abortion*	9	10	13	13	5	5	5	5	38	33	34	33
30-34												
All conceptions	128.1	126.0	143.1	152.5	112.0	105.7	112.6	118.2	16.1	20.4	30.5	34.3
Percentage leading to legal abortion*	15	13	14	14	11	9	9	9	39	35	32	32
35-39												
All conceptions	38.6	48.5	51.2	53.6	32.0	38.6	38.3	39.6	6.6	9.9	13.0	14.0
Percentage leading to legal abortion*	32	27	24	23	28	22	19	18	49	43	38	38
40 and over												
All conceptions	10.1	9.7	11.3	11.6	8.1	7.5	8.2	8.1	2.0	2.2	3.1	3.5
Percentage leading to legal abortion*	53	47	45	44	51	43	42	40	64	59	54	53

* Legal termination under 1967 Abortion Act.

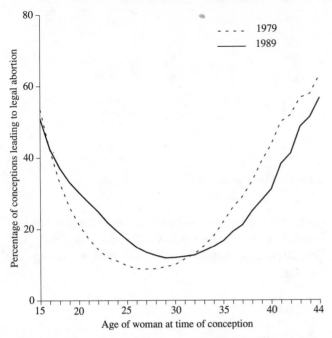

Figure 16 Proportion of all conceptions leading to abortions, by age of woman at time of conception, 1979 and 1989

The proportion of conceptions inside marriage that led to an abortion was very low among women aged under 30, but then increased sharply with age. Abortion was the outcome of 40 per cent of conceptions to women aged 40 and over. By contrast, for conceptions occurring outside marriage, the proportions terminated by abortion were less variable by age, ranging from 30 to 40 per cent for women aged less than 40, and over a half of conceptions to women aged 40 and over.

Conception rates

Conception rates relate the number of conceptions in a given year, to the size, age structure, and/or marital status of the female population of childbearing age. In 1989, there were an estimated 78.6 conceptions per 1,000 women aged 15-44; just under 2 per cent higher than in the previous year.

For each age-group there was a rise in the conception rate from 1989, though trends by age have differed over the last 10 years. Conception rates rose by around 20 per cent for women in their thirties, but fell by over 10 per cent for women aged 20-24 and over 40 years.

Figure 17 shows conception rates by age inside and outside marriage. These are broadly similar to the age profiles for fertility rates (shown in **Figure 6**); any differences arising from the inclusion of abortions, and the fact that a conception can lead to a multiple birth, or stillbirth. Conception rates outside marriage were low among young women, and were highest among women in their twenties. In contrast conception rates among married women were extremely high at younger ages, and declined sharply with increasing age of women. The rates for unmarried and married in their early thirties were similar, and indeed amongst women in their late thirties the conception rate outside marriage slightly exceeded the rate inside marriage.

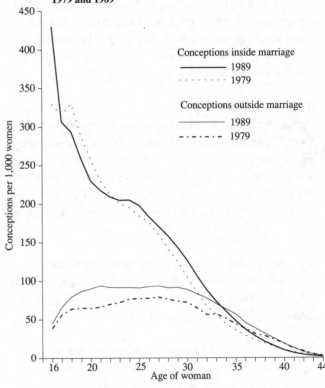

Figure 17 Conception rates by age of woman and marital status, 1979 and 1989

Table S21 Conception rates inside and outside marriage — Residents of England and Wales

Age of woman at conception	All conceptions (per 1,000 women)*				Conceptions outside marriage (per 1,000 unmarried women)*				Conceptions inside marriage (per 1,000 married women)*			
	1979	1984	1988	1989	1979	1984	1988	1989	1979	1984	1988	1989
All ages	**76.8**	**74.2**	**77.2**	**78.6**	**54.0**	**57.5**	**69.6**	**71.7**	**90.5**	**86.7**	**83.6**	**84.6**
Under 20	61.9	59.9	66.6	67.6	48.1	51.2	61.0	62.0	304.4	322.7	267.1	275.4
20-24	139.2	124.2	125.4	125.2	68.6	70.9	88.5	91.7	213.7	217.5	215.7	210.0
25-29	138.7	138.1	135.8	137.4	76.8	80.7	90.4	91.9	156.4	163.4	164.8	169.3
30-34	70.3	75.6	84.0	87.8	60.9	61.2	74.1	77.7	71.9	79.2	87.2	91.2
35-39	26.2	26.7	30.0	31.9	33.6	33.4	37.9	39.9	25.0	25.4	28.0	29.7
40 and over	7.2	6.6	6.4	6.4	10.2	9.2	9.7	10.2	6.8	6.1	5.6	5.5

* Rates for women of all ages, under 20 and 40 and over are based upon the population aged 15-44, 15-19 and 40-44 respectively.

c

Table S22 Numbers and rates of conceptions to teenage girls   **Residents of England and Wales**

Age at conception	All conceptions (base numbers)			Percentage leading to legal abortion*			Conception rates per 1,000 women†		
	1979	1988	1989	1979	1988	1989	1979	1988	1989
Under 14	381	304	250	62.2	54.8	52.4	1.0	1.0	0.9
14	1,904	1,761	1,765	60.1	59.6	55.6	4.7	5.7	6.0
15	6,823	6,716	6,367	53.5	51.4	50.9	16.8	20.4	20.7
16	16,106	15,821	15,176	42.2	43.6	42.4	40.6	45.1	46.0
17	24,868	25,423	24,230	32.9	37.6	37.1	63.3	67.6	68.7
18	32,752	32,208	32,591	26.1	32.7	33.1	84.8	86.9	86.5
19	38,110	38,475	37,120	21.2	30.1	30.2	102.4	100.0	99.8
Total under 20	120,944	120,709	117,499	30.3	35.8	35.6	61.9	66.6	67.6

* Legal terminations under 1967 Abortion Act.
† Rates for women under 14 and under 20 are based on the population of women aged 13 and 15-19 respectively.

The trends over time in conceptions occurring inside and outside marriage by age have also differed. Apart from women aged 40 and over, conceptions rates outside marriage rose dramatically for all age-groups, particularly the youngest. For example the rate for women aged 20-24 increased by 34 per cent from 1979. Over the same period, conceptions inside marriage decreased at these younger ages, as well as for women in their forties. In contrast, women in their thirties experienced a marked rise, and the rate for women aged 30-34 increased by 26 per cent.

Teenage conceptions
Although the number of teenage conceptions fell by just over 3 per cent between 1988 and 1989, the overall teenage conception rate rose slightly, and over the past 10 years has increased by 9 per cent. This was due to a rapid rise in the conception rate of unmarried teenagers, of 30 per cent since 1979, while the rate among married teenagers continued to fall.

The recent slight rise in the teenage conception rate overall, was due to an increase in rates amongst girls aged between 14 and 17. The rates for girls aged under 14, and aged 18 and 19 fell slightly compared with 1988.

Some 36 per cent of conceptions to teenage girls were terminated by abortion in 1989. Over a half of conceptions amongst the youngest ages (14 and under) led to an abortion, although this proportion has fallen significantly since 1979. In contrast, although the corresponding proportions were lower among girls aged 18 and 19 in 1989 (33 and 30 per cent) they have shown a marked rise over the decade.

References

1 Jones C. Fertility of the over thirties *Population Trends 67* HMSO (1992)

2 Cooper JS. Period and cohort measures of fertility *Population Trends 63* HMSO (1991)

3 OPCS *General Household Survey 1989* Series GHS no. 20 HMSO (1991)

4 Macfarlane A, Botting B, and Price F. The study of triplet and higher order births *Population Trends 62* HMSO (1990)

5 Shaw C. The sex ratio at birth in England and Wales *Population Trends 57* HMSO (1989)

6 Cooper JS. Births outside marriage: recent trends and associated demographic and social changes *Population Trends 63* HMSO (1991)

7 OPCS *Marriage and Divorce Statistics 1989* Series FM2 no.17 HMSO (1991)

8 Craig J. Fertility trends within the United Kingdom *Population Trends 67* HMSO (1992)

9 OPCS *Key population and vital statistics: local and health authority areas* Series VS no.17 PP1 no.13 HMSO (1991)

Table 1.1   Live births: occurrence inside/outside marriage and sex, 1980-1990   England and Wales
  a. numbers

Year	Live births								
	All			Within marriage			Outside marriage		
	Total	Males	Females	Total	Males	Females	Total	Males	Females
1980	656,234	335,954	320,280	578,862	296,234	282,628	77,372	39,720	37,652
1981	634,492	325,711	308,781	553,509	284,004	269,505	80,983	41,707	39,276
1982	625,931	321,352	304,579	536,074	275,408	260,666	89,857	45,944	43,913
1983	629,134	323,192	305,942	529,923	272,080	257,843	99,211	51,112	48,099
1984	636,818	326,039	310,779	526,353	269,655	256,698	110,465	56,384	54,081
1985	656,417	336,835	319,582	530,167	271,886	258,281	126,250	64,949	61,301
1986	661,018	338,852	322,166	519,673	266,517	253,156	141,345	72,335	69,010
1987	681,511	349,624	331,887	523,080	268,245	254,835	158,431	81,379	77,052
1988	693,577	354,954	338,623	516,225	264,251	251,974	177,352	90,703	86,649
1989	687,725	352,381	335,344	501,921	257,284	244,637	185,804	95,097	90,707
1990	706,140	361,412	344,728	506,141	259,050	247,091	199,999	102,362	97,637

Table 1.1   Live births: occurrence inside/outside marriage and sex, 1980-1990   England and Wales
  b. rates

Year	Live births							
	Crude birth rate: All births per 1,000 population of all ages	General fertility rate: all births per 1,000 women aged 15-44	Births within marriage per 1,000 married women aged 15-44	Births outside marriage per 1,000 single, widowed and divorced women aged 15-44	Births outside marriage per 1,000 total births	Sex ratio: male births per 1,000 female births		
						All	Within marriage	Outside marriage
1980	13.2	64.2	92.2	19.6	117.9	1,049	1,048	1,055
1981	12.8	61.3	88.8	19.7	127.6	1,055	1,054	1,062
1982	12.6	59.9	86.9	21.0	143.6	1,055	1,057	1,046
1983	12.7	59.7	86.8	22.4	157.7	1,056	1,055	1,063
1984	12.8	59.8	86.7	24.1	173.5	1,049	1,050	1,043
1985	13.1	61.0	87.8	26.7	192.3	1,054	1,053	1,060
1986	13.2	60.6	86.3	28.9	213.8	1,052	1,053	1,048
1987	13.6	62.0	87.1	31.8	232.5	1,053	1,053	1,056
1988	13.8	63.0	86.7	35.1	255.7	1,048	1,049	1,047
1989	13.6	62.5	85.0	36.4	270.2	1,051	1,052	1,048
1990	13.9	64.3	86.7	38.9	283.2	1,048	1,048	1,048

Table 1.2   Stillbirths: occurrence inside/outside marriage and sex, 1980-1990   England and Wales

Year	Stillbirths												
	Numbers									Rates			
	All			Within marriage			Outside marriage			Stillbirths per 1,000 live and still births	Sex ratio: male births per 1,000 female births		
	Total	Males	Females	Total	Males	Females	Total	Males	Females		All	Within marriage	Outside marriage
1980	4,773	2,483	2,290	4,077	2,117	1,960	696	366	330	7.2	1,084	1,080	1,109
1981	4,207	2,186	2,021	3,510	1,817	1,693	697	369	328	6.6	1,082	1,073	1,125
1982	3,939	2,092	1,847	3,282	1,743	1,539	657	349	308	6.3	1,133	1,133	1,133
1983	3,631	1,960	1,671	2,913	1,594	1,319	718	366	352	5.7	1,173	1,208	1,040
1984	3,643	1,967	1,676	2,825	1,533	1,292	818	434	384	5.7	1,174	1,187	1,130
1985	3,645	1,983	1,662	2,773	1,514	1,259	872	469	403	5.5	1,193	1,203	1,164
1986	3,549	1,904	1,645	2,600	1,412	1,188	949	492	457	5.3	1,157	1,189	1,077
1987	3,423	1,869	1,554	2,404	1,297	1,107	1,019	572	447	5.0	1,203	1,172	1,280
1988	3,382	1,811	1,571	2,322	1,265	1,057	1,060	546	514	4.9	1,153	1,197	1,062
1989	3,236	1,762	1,474	2,169	1,173	996	1,067	589	478	4.7	1,195	1,178	1,232
1990	3,256	1,753	1,503	2,176	1,153	1,023	1,080	600	480	4.6	1,166	1,127	1,250

Table 1.3 Natural change in population, 1980-1990 **England and Wales**

Year	Numbers			Rates per 1,000 population of all ages		
	Live births	Deaths	Natural change: live births minus deaths	Live births (crude birth rate)	Deaths (crude death rate)	Natural change
1980	656,234	581,385	74,849	13.2	11.7	1.5
1981	634,492	577,890	56,602	12.8	11.6	1.1
1982	625,931	581,861	44,070	12.6	11.7	0.9
1983	629,134	579,608	49,526	12.7	11.7	1.0
1984	636,818	566,881	69,937	12.8	11.4	1.4
1985	656,417	590,734	65,686	13.1	11.8	1.3
1986	661,018	581,203	79,815	13.2	11.6	1.6
1987	681,511	566,994	114,517	13.6	11.3	2.3
1988	693,577	571,408	122,169	13.8	11.3	2.5
1989	687,725	576,872	110,853	13.6	11.4	2.2
1990	706,140	564,846	141,294	13.9	11.1	2.8

Table 1.4 TPFR, GRR and NRR, 1980-1990 **England and Wales**

Year	Total period fertility rate (TPFR)	Gross reproduction rate (GRR)	Net reproduction rate (NRR)
1980	1.88	0.91	0.90
1981	1.80	0.87	0.85
1982	1.76	0.86	0.84
1983	1.76	0.86	0.84
1984	1.75	0.86	0.84
1985	1.78	0.87	0.86
1986	1.77	0.86	0.85
1987	1.81	0.88	0.87
1988	1.82	0.90	0.88
1989	1.80	0.88	0.87
1990	1.84	0.91	0.89

Table 1.5 Marriages, 1980-1990 **England and Wales**

Year	Number of marriages			Marriage rates				
	All	Bachelors	Spinsters	Crude marriage rate - all persons marrying per 1,000 population of all ages	Males marrying per 1,000 single, widowed and divorced males aged 16 and over	Females marrying per 1,000 single, widowed and divorced females aged 16 and over	Bachelors marrying per 1,000 single males aged 16 and over	Spinsters marrying per 1,000 single females aged 16 and over
1980	370,022	274,140	277,826	14.9	60.4	48.1	56.3	69.6
1981	351,973	259,106	263,368	14.2	55.7	44.7	51.7	64.0
1982	342,166	250,999	255,171	13.8	52.5	42.5	48.7	60.4
1983	344,334	251,845	256,214	13.9	51.2	41.8	47.5	59.1
1984	349,186	255,469	260,359	14.0	50.5	41.6	47.1	58.9
1985	346,389	253,296	258,089	13.9	48.7	40.5	45.6	57.1
1986	347,924	252,953	256,767	13.9	47.7	39.9	44.6	55.7
1987	351,761	258,750	262,958	14.0	47.3	39.8	44.7	56.1
1988	348,492	252,780	256,221	13.8	46.0	38.9	43.1	54.2
1989	346,697	252,230	254,763	13.7	45.0	38.3	42.6	53.5
1990								

Table 1.6 Mean age of women at marriage and at live birth, 1980-1990 **England and Wales**

Year	Mean age at marriage		Mean ages at live birth						
	All brides	Spinsters	**All births**	Births outside marriage	Births within marriage				
					All birth orders	First birth	Second birth	Third birth	Fourth birth
1980	26.7	23.0	**26.7**	23.5	27.1	25.2	27.4	29.5	31.1
1981	26.9	23.1	**26.8**	23.5	27.3	25.4	27.5	29.6	31.1
1982	27.0	23.3	**26.8**	23.5	27.4	25.5	27.5	29.6	31.2
1983	27.1	23.4	**26.9**	23.6	27.5	25.6	27.6	29.7	31.2
1984	27.3	23.6	**26.9**	23.7	27.6	25.8	27.8	29.7	31.2
1985	27.5	23.8	**27.0**	23.7	27.8	26.0	27.9	29.8	31.2
1986	27.8	24.1	**27.0**	23.8	27.9	26.2	28.0	29.8	31.2
1987	27.8	24.3	**27.1**	24.0	28.1	26.5	28.1	29.9	31.3
1988	28.3	24.6	**27.2**	24.1	28.2	26.6	28.3	30.0	31.3
1989	26.1	24.4	**27.5**	24.4	28.4	26.9	28.5	30.1	31.3
1990			**27.5**	24.6	28.7	27.2	28.7	30.3	31.5

Note: Mean ages at live birth for 1981 are based on a 10 per cent sample.

Table 1.7 Mean ages of women at births of different orders*, 1980-1990   England and Wales

Year	Mean age at live birth				
	All births	All births			
		First	Second	Third	Fourth
1980	**26.7**	24.5	27.0	29.2	30.4
1981	26.8	24.6	27.1	29.3	30.5
1982	26.8	24.6	27.1	29.3	30.5
1983	26.9	24.7	27.2	29.4	30.4
1984	26.9	24.7	27.3	29.4	30.4
1985	27.0	24.8	27.4	29.4	30.3
1986	27.0	24.9	27.4	29.5	30.3
1987	27.1	25.0	27.5	29.5	30.3
1988	27.2	25.1	27.6	29.5	30.2
1989	27.3	25.3	27.8	29.6	30.2
1990	27.5	25.4	28.0	29.7	30.3

Note: Mean ages at birth for 1981 are based on a 10 per cent sample.
* Includes children born inside and outside marriage (see Introduction).

Table 1.8 Proportion of total first marriages with a birth within 8 months of marriage, 1979-1989   England and Wales

Year of marriage	Percentage of marriages with a birth within 8 months according to woman's age at marriage				
	Under 45	Under 20	20-24	25-29	30-44
1979	14.1	26.1	9.5	8.5	9.6
1980	14.0	25.5	9.8	9.6	10.7
1981	13.2	25.3	9.7	8.6	8.5
1982	13.5	26.2	9.9	9.3	10.7
1983	13.1	25.5	10.0	9.3	11.3
1984	13.0	26.0	10.4	9.4	10.8
1985	13.4	26.8	10.9	10.4	11.0
1986	13.2	27.2	11.1	10.1	11.8
1987	13.0	26.6	11.1	10.3	12.0
1988	12.5	25.8	11.1	10.0	11.9
1989	12.1	24.9	10.7	10.0	11.9

Notes: 1. The rates are based on the total number of live births occurring to women within a eight-month period - that is, 0-7 completed months - following their first marriage in year x; this period spans the calendar year x and x+1 (see Introduction).
2. Figures for 1980 (partly) and 1981 are based on a 10 per cent sample.

Table 1.9 Components of total period fertility rates, 1980-1990   **England and Wales**

Year	All live births	Live births outside marriage	Live births within marriage All	First	Second	Third	Fourth	Fifth and later	Year	All live births	Live births outside marriage	Live births within marriage All	First	Second	Third	Fourth	Fifth and later
All ages of mother at birth									**25-29**								
1980	**1.88**	0.21	1.66	0.68	0.60	0.25	0.08	0.05	1980	**0.67**	0.04	0.63	0.24	0.25	0.09	0.03	0.01
1981	**1.80**	0.22	1.58	0.63	0.59	0.24	0.08	0.05	1981	**0.65**	0.04	0.60	0.23	0.25	0.09	0.03	0.01
1982	**1.76**	0.24	1.52	0.59	0.57	0.24	0.08	0.04	1982	**0.63**	0.05	0.58	0.22	0.24	0.09	0.03	0.01
1983	**1.76**	0.26	1.49	0.58	0.55	0.23	0.08	0.05	1983	**0.63**	0.05	0.58	0.22	0.23	0.09	0.03	0.01
1984	**1.75**	0.29	1.47	0.57	0.54	0.23	0.08	0.05	1984	**0.63**	0.06	0.57	0.22	0.23	0.09	0.03	0.01
1985	**1.78**	0.33	1.46	0.57	0.53	0.23	0.08	0.05	1985	**0.64**	0.07	0.57	0.22	0.22	0.09	0.03	0.01
1986	**1.77**	0.37	1.41	0.55	0.51	0.22	0.08	0.05	1986	**0.62**	0.07	0.55	0.21	0.21	0.08	0.02	0.01
1987	**1.81**	0.41	1.41	0.55	0.51	0.22	0.07	0.05	1987	**0.62**	0.09	0.54	0.22	0.21	0.08	0.02	0.01
1988	**1.82**	0.46	1.36	0.54	0.49	0.22	0.07	0.04	1988	**0.62**	0.10	0.52	0.22	0.20	0.08	0.02	0.01
1989	**1.80**	0.48	1.31	0.52	0.48	0.22	0.07	0.04	1989	**0.60**	0.10	0.50	0.21	0.19	0.07	0.02	0.01
1990	**1.84**	0.53	1.32	0.51	0.48	0.21	0.07	0.04	1990	**0.61**	0.12	0.50	0.21	0.19	0.07	0.02	0.01
Under 20									**30-34**								
1980	**0.15**	0.07	0.09	0.07	0.02	0.00			1980	**0.35**	0.02	0.33	0.08	0.13	0.08	0.03	0.01
1981	**0.14**	0.07	0.08	0.06	0.02	0.00			1981	**0.35**	0.02	0.33	0.08	0.13	0.08	0.03	0.01
1982	**0.14**	0.07	0.07	0.05	0.01	0.00			1982	**0.35**	0.02	0.33	0.08	0.13	0.08	0.03	0.01
1983	**0.13**	0.07	0.06	0.05	0.01	0.00			1983	**0.36**	0.03	0.33	0.08	0.13	0.08	0.03	0.02
1984	**0.14**	0.08	0.05	0.04	0.01	0.00			1984	**0.37**	0.03	0.34	0.09	0.14	0.08	0.03	0.02
1985	**0.14**	0.09	0.05	0.04	0.01	0.00			1985	**0.38**	0.03	0.35	0.09	0.14	0.08	0.03	0.02
1986	**0.15**	0.10	0.05	0.04	0.01	0.00			1986	**0.39**	0.04	0.35	0.09	0.14	0.08	0.03	0.02
1987	**0.15**	0.11	0.04	0.03	0.01	0.00			1987	**0.41**	0.05	0.36	0.10	0.14	0.08	0.03	0.02
1988	**0.16**	0.12	0.04	0.03	0.01	0.00			1988	**0.41**	0.05	0.36	0.10	0.14	0.08	0.03	0.02
1989	**0.15**	0.12	0.03	0.02	0.01	0.00			1989	**0.41**	0.06	0.36	0.10	0.14	0.07	0.03	0.02
1990	**0.16**	0.13	0.03	0.02	0.01	0.00			1990	**0.43**	0.06	0.37	0.11	0.15	0.08	0.03	0.02
20-24									**35 and over**								
1980	**0.57**	0.07	0.49	0.27	0.17	0.04	0.01	0.00	1980	**0.13**	0.01	0.12	0.02	0.03	0.03	0.02	0.02
1981	**0.53**	0.08	0.45	0.24	0.16	0.04	0.01	0.00	1981	**0.13**	0.01	0.12	0.02	0.03	0.03	0.02	0.02
1982	**0.51**	0.09	0.43	0.22	0.16	0.04	0.01	0.00	1982	**0.13**	0.01	0.12	0.02	0.03	0.03	0.02	0.02
1983	**0.50**	0.09	0.40	0.21	0.14	0.04	0.01	0.00	1983	**0.14**	0.01	0.12	0.02	0.03	0.03	0.02	0.02
1984	**0.48**	0.10	0.38	0.20	0.13	0.04	0.01	0.00	1984	**0.14**	0.02	0.12	0.02	0.04	0.03	0.02	0.02
1985	**0.47**	0.12	0.36	0.19	0.12	0.03	0.01	0.00	1985	**0.15**	0.02	0.13	0.02	0.04	0.03	0.02	0.02
1986	**0.46**	0.13	0.33	0.18	0.11	0.03	0.01	0.00	1986	**0.15**	0.02	0.13	0.02	0.04	0.03	0.02	0.02
1987	**0.47**	0.15	0.33	0.17	0.11	0.03	0.01	0.00	1987	**0.16**	0.02	0.14	0.03	0.04	0.04	0.02	0.02
1988	**0.47**	0.17	0.30	0.17	0.10	0.03	0.01	0.00	1988	**0.17**	0.03	0.14	0.03	0.04	0.03	0.02	0.02
1989	**0.46**	0.18	0.28	0.15	0.10	0.03	0.01	0.00	1989	**0.17**	0.03	0.14	0.03	0.05	0.04	0.02	0.02
1990	**0.46**	0.19	0.27	0.14	0.09	0.03	0.01	0.00	1990	**0.18**	0.03	0.15	0.03	0.05	0.04	0.02	0.02

Notes: 1. Age-standardised rates are calculated by summing rates for each single year of age. The value for all live births is
the total period fertility rate (TPFR) - see Introduction.
2. Figures for 1981 are based on a 10 per cent sample.

Table 2.1 Live births and total period fertility rates:
quarter of occurrence, 1980-1990 — **England and Wales**

Year	Total	Quarter ended				Total	Quarter ended			
		31 March	30 June	30 September	31 December		31 March	30 June	30 September	31 December
	a. Number (thousands)					**b. Total period fertility rate (TPFR)**				
	Live births					Actual TPFR				
1980	**656.2**	162.3	168.1	168.3	157.4	**1.88**	1.86	1.92	1.92	1.79
1981	**634.5**	156.2	160.8	164.3	153.1	**1.80**	1.78	1.83	1.86	1.73
1982	**625.9**	153.4	157.0	162.1	153.4	**1.76**	1.73	1.77	1.82	1.72
1983	**629.1**	152.4	161.3	163.4	151.9	**1.76**	1.71	1.80	1.82	1.69
1984	**636.8**	153.5	157.7	167.1	158.4	**1.75**	1.70	1.74	1.84	1.74
1985	**656.4**	160.4	165.3	172.3	158.5	**1.78**	1.75	1.80	1.87	1.71
1986	**661.0**	160.0	169.0	170.8	161.2	**1.77**	1.72	1.82	1.83	1.72
1987	**681.5**	162.7	174.9	176.6	167.3	**1.81**	1.73	1.86	1.87	1.77
1988	**693.6**	173.4	176.5	179.1	164.6	**1.82**	1.83	1.86	1.88	1.73
1989	**687.7**	167.0	176.7	175.8	168.2	**1.80**	1.75	1.85	1.84	1.76
1990	**706.1**	168.3	179.3	184.0	174.5	**1.84**	1.76	1.87	1.92	1.82
	Seasonally adjusted live births					Seasonally adjusted TPFR				
1980	*Same as above*	163.6	165.0	163.5	162.1	*Same as above*	1.88	1.89	1.87	1.85
1981		159.8	158.3	159.0	157.5		1.82	1.80	1.80	1.78
1982		157.4	154.6	156.6	157.4		1.78	1.74	1.76	1.77
1983		156.9	159.1	157.3	156.2		1.76	1.78	1.75	1.74
1984		156.0	155.8	161.2	162.8		1.73	1.72	1.77	1.78
1985		165.0	162.9	165.9	163.1		1.80	1.77	1.80	1.76
1986		164.7	166.1	164.7	166.1		1.77	1.78	1.76	1.77
1987		167.3	172.0	170.2	172.5		1.78	1.83	1.80	1.82
1988		176.5	173.0	172.8	170.0		1.86	1.82	1.82	1.78
1989		171.6	172.9	170.3	173.6		1.80	1.81	1.78	1.81
1990		172.5	175.9	178.4	179.8		1.80	1.84	1.86	1.88

Table 2.2 Stillbirths: quarter of occurrence, 1980-1990 — **England and Wales**

Year	Total	Quarter ended			
		31 March	30 June	30 September	31 December
1980	**4,773**	1,230	1,263	1,185	1,095
1981	**4,207**	1,042	1,083	1,049	1,033
1982	**3,939**	1,020	955	1,023	941
1983	**3,631**	880	938	900	913
1984	**3,643**	879	932	955	877
1985	**3,645**	891	922	983	849
1986	**3,549**	888	909	909	843
1987	**3,423**	864	842	845	872
1988	**3,382**	861	886	812	823
1989	**3,236**	797	868	769	802
1990	**3,256**	814	820	833	789

Table 2.3 Live births and total period fertility rates: **England and Wales**
month of occurrence, 1980-1990

Year	Total	January	February	March	April	May	June	July	August	September	October	November	December
a) Numbers (thousands)													
Live births													
1980	**656.2**	54.4	51.5	56.4	55.5	57.8	54.7	57.9	54.8	55.6	55.4	50.5	51.6
1981	**634.5**	52.7	48.5	55.0	52.8	54.7	53.4	56.5	54.2	53.6	53.2	49.9	50.0
1982	**625.9**	51.5	47.7	54.3	52.2	53.8	51.0	54.5	53.4	54.2	53.0	49.4	51.0
1983	**629.1**	51.2	47.6	53.6	52.6	54.8	54.0	55.4	53.8	54.3	51.5	49.7	50.7
1984	**636.8**	51.3	48.9	53.3	50.1	54.3	53.4	55.9	55.8	55.4	55.3	52.5	50.6
1985	**656.4**	54.7	49.6	56.0	53.3	57.5	54.5	58.2	57.1	57.0	55.8	51.9	50.7
1986	**661.0**	53.6	49.6	56.7	55.2	58.2	55.7	56.7	57.4	56.7	55.9	51.1	54.2
1987	**681.5**	54.6	50.6	57.6	56.3	59.8	58.9	59.8	58.1	58.7	57.8	53.6	55.9
1988	**693.6**	57.3	55.2	60.8	58.0	60.4	58.1	60.2	59.6	59.3	55.5	53.6	55.5
1989	**687.7**	55.8	52.3	58.9	56.9	60.7	59.1	60.1	58.9	56.8	56.8	55.0	56.4
1990	**706.1**	56.5	52.9	58.9	57.2	61.4	60.7	62.5	61.2	60.3	59.9	57.6	57.1
Seasonally adjusted live births													
1980	*Same as above*	55.2	54.1	54.3	55.3	55.1	54.6	52.2	54.2	54.1	54.4	53.9	53.9
1981		53.5	53.2	53.1	52.7	52.5	53.0	53.4	53.6	52.0	52.6	52.9	52.0
1982		52.4	52.4	52.5	52.2	52.0	50.4	51.7	52.5	52.4	52.6	52.2	52.6
1983		52.3	52.5	52.0	52.8	53.0	53.3	52.8	52.2	52.4	51.3	52.3	52.5
1984		52.4	52.0	51.6	51.0	51.9	52.8	53.4	53.7	54.1	54.6	55.3	52.9
1985		55.4	54.9	54.8	53.9	54.6	54.3	55.2	55.2	55.5	55.2	55.0	52.9
1986		54.1	54.8	55.8	55.3	55.4	55.3	53.8	55.8	55.1	55.2	54.8	56.1
1987		55.5	55.7	56.1	56.8	57.1	58.1	56.4	56.8	57.0	57.6	57.4	57.5
1988		58.8	58.7	59.1	58.2	57.8	57.0	57.4	57.7	57.6	55.9	56.8	57.2
1989		57.3	57.3	57.0	57.6	57.7	57.7	57.7	57.1	55.5	57.1	58.2	58.4
1990		57.6	57.9	57.0	58.2	58.3	59.4	59.7	59.3	59.5	59.8	60.6	59.3
b) Total period fertility rates (TPFR)													
Actual TPFR													
1980	**1.88**	1.87	1.77	1.94	1.91	1.99	1.88	1.99	1.88	1.90	1.89	1.73	1.76
1981	**1.80**	1.80	1.65	1.88	1.80	1.86	1.82	1.92	1.84	1.82	1.81	1.69	1.70
1982	**1.76**	1.75	1.61	1.84	1.77	1.82	1.72	1.84	1.80	1.83	1.79	1.67	1.72
1983	**1.76**	1.72	1.60	1.80	1.76	1.84	1.81	1.85	1.80	1.81	1.72	1.66	1.69
1984	**1.75**	1.71	1.63	1.77	1.66	1.80	1.77	1.85	1.84	1.83	1.82	1.73	1.66
1985	**1.78**	1.80	1.63	1.84	1.74	1.88	1.78	1.90	1.86	1.85	1.81	1.68	1.64
1986	**1.77**	1.74	1.60	1.83	1.78	1.87	1.79	1.82	1.84	1.82	1.79	1.64	1.74
1987	**1.81**	1.74	1.61	1.84	1.79	1.90	1.87	1.90	1.85	1.86	1.83	1.70	1.77
1988	**1.82**	1.82	1.75	1.92	1.83	1.91	1.89	1.90	1.88	1.87	1.75	1.69	1.75
1989	**1.80**	1.76	1.64	1.85	1.79	1.91	1.86	1.89	1.85	1.78	1.78	1.72	1.77
1990	**1.84**	1.77	1.66	1.85	1.79	1.92	1.90	1.96	1.92	1.89	1.87	1.80	1.79
Seasonally adjusted TPFR													
1980	*Same as above*	1.90	1.86	1.87	1.90	1.89	1.87	1.89	1.86	1.85	1.86	1.84	1.84
1981		1.83	1.81	1.81	1.80	1.79	1.80	1.82	1.82	1.77	1.79	1.80	1.76
1982		1.78	1.78	1.78	1.77	1.76	1.70	1.75	1.77	1.77	1.77	1.76	1.77
1983		1.76	1.77	1.75	1.77	1.78	1.78	1.77	1.74	1.75	1.71	1.74	1.75
1984		1.74	1.73	1.71	1.69	1.72	1.75	1.77	1.77	1.78	1.80	1.82	1.74
1985		1.82	1.80	1.79	1.76	1.79	1.77	1.80	1.80	1.80	1.79	1.79	1.71
1986		1.75	1.77	1.80	1.78	1.78	1.78	1.73	1.79	1.77	1.77	1.76	1.79
1987		1.77	1.78	1.79	1.81	1.82	1.85	1.80	1.81	1.81	1.83	1.82	1.82
1988		1.86	1.86	1.87	1.84	1.82	1.80	1.81	1.82	1.82	1.76	1.79	1.80
1989		1.80	1.80	1.79	1.81	1.81	1.81	1.81	1.79	1.74	1.79	1.82	1.83
1990		1.81	1.82	1.78	1.82	1.83	1.86	1.87	1.85	1.86	1.87	1.90	1.86

Table 2.4 Maternities, live and still births: quarter and month of occurrence, occurrence inside/outside marriage and sex, 1990 **England and Wales**

Quarter/month of occurrence	Maternities	Live births			Stillbirths		Live births		Stillbirths	
		Total	Within marriage	Outside marriage	Within marriage	Outside marriage	Male	Female	Male	Female
Annual Total	**701,030**	**706,140**	**506,141**	**199,999**	**2,176**	**1,080**	**361,412**	**344,728**	**1,753**	**1,503**
March quarter	167,142	168,321	121,238	47,083	560	254	86,123	82,198	437	377
June quarter	178,012	179,298	130,179	49,119	552	268	92,022	87,276	436	384
September quarter	182,674	183,990	131,679	52,311	552	281	94,395	89,595	451	382
December quarter	173,202	174,531	123,045	51,486	512	277	88,872	85,659	429	360
January	56,095	56,507	40,381	16,126	192	96	28,902	27,605	146	142
February	52,527	52,908	38,153	14,755	177	84	27,101	25,807	151	110
March	58,520	58,906	42,704	16,202	191	74	30,120	28,786	140	125
April	56,759	57,184	41,578	15,606	178	76	29,422	27,762	129	125
May	60,882	61,365	44,689	16,676	169	102	31,382	29,983	161	110
June	60,371	60,749	43,912	16,837	205	90	31,218	29,531	146	149
July	62,065	62,491	44,906	17,585	183	94	32,036	30,455	148	129
August	60,713	61,195	43,644	17,551	170	95	31,342	29,853	150	115
September	59,896	60,304	43,129	17,175	199	92	31,017	29,287	153	138
October	59,406	59,914	42,720	17,194	154	90	30,560	29,354	134	110
November	57,157	57,558	40,661	16,897	177	84	29,386	28,172	150	111
December	56,639	57,059	39,664	17,395	181	103	28,926	28,133	145	139

Table 2.5 Live birth occurrences in 1990: month of occurrence and of registration **England and Wales**

Quarter/month of occurrence in 1990	Month of registration*												Registration in January 1991	Total
	January	February	March	April	May	June	July	August	September	October	November	December		
Annual total	**26,598**	**52,087**	**59,180**	**55,071**	**61,035**	**60,865**	**62,655**	**62,284**	**56,886**	**64,707**	**58,396**	**46,379**	**39,997**	**706,140**
Quarters ending:														
March	26,598	49,592	59,073	29,700	3,078	115	46	35	18	22	23	14	7	168,321
June	-	20	6	25,356	57,941	60,741	32,363	2,645	85	61	35	21	24	179,298
September	-	30	18	2	6	3	30,245	59,602	56,782	34,716	2,431	96	59	183,990
December	-	2,445	83	13	10	6	1	2	1	29,908	55,907	46,248	39,907	174,531
Months:														
January	26,598	26,372	3,395	64	27	14	10	10	5	5	4	3	-	56,507
February	-	23,213	27,426	2,129	73	17	14	9	7	6	8	4	2	52,908
March	-	7	28,252	27,507	2,978	84	22	16	6	11	11	7	5	58,906
April	-	4	3	25,353	29,224	2,478	67	18	6	12	6	5	8	57,184
May	-	10	2	2	28,717	29,815	2,660	97	17	16	13	7	9	61,365
June	-	6	1	1	-	28,448	29,636	2,530	62	33	16	9	7	60,749
July	-	6	7	-	1	-	30,245	29,695	2,385	102	25	10	15	62,491
August	-	11	3	1	-	-	-	29,907	28,189	2,970	74	23	17	61,195
September	-	13	8	1	5	3	-	-	26,208	31,644	2,332	63	27	60,304
October	-	26	8	3	-	1	-	-	-	29,907	27,612	2,254	103	59,914
November	-	83	10	3	2	3	-	-	-	-	28,294	24,966	4,197	57,558
December	-	2,336	65	7	8	2	1	2	1	1	1	19,028	35,607	57,059

* The figures refer to those births which occurred in 1990 and were registered by 31 January 1991, births registered later than this date will be added to the occurrences for 1991; the above figures similarly include those births which occurred in 1989 but were registered later than 31 January 1990.

Table 3.1 Live births: age of mother and occurrence inside/outside marriage, 1980-1990   **England and Wales**
a. numbers

Year	Age of mother at birth							
	All ages	Under 20	20-24	25-29	30-34	35-39	40-44	45 and over
	All live births							
1980	**656,234**	60,754	201,541	223,438	129,908	33,893	6,075	625
1981	**634,492**	56,570	194,500	215,760	126,590	34,210	6,170	690
1982	**625,931**	55,435	192,322	211,905	120,758	38,992	5,886	633
1983	**629,134**	54,059	191,852	214,078	120,996	41,277	6,210	662
1984	**636,818**	54,508	191,455	218,031	122,774	42,921	6,576	553
1985	**656,417**	56,929	193,958	227,486	126,185	44,393	6,882	584
1986	**661,018**	57,406	192,064	229,035	129,487	45,465	7,033	528
1987	**681,511**	57,545	193,232	238,929	136,558	46,604	8,112	531
1988	**693,577**	58,741	193,726	243,460	140,974	47,649	8,520	507
1989	**687,725**	55,543	185,239	242,822	145,320	49,465	8,845	491
1990	**706,140**	55,541	180,136	252,577	156,264	51,905	9,220	497
	Within marriage							
1980	**578,862**	34,894	174,934	209,976	122,320	30,846	5,314	578
1981	**553,509**	30,140	165,690	201,460	118,720	31,480	5,340	680
1982	**536,074**	26,696	159,911	195,839	112,625	35,310	5,118	575
1983	**529,923**	23,636	155,209	196,162	111,722	37,160	5,422	612
1984	**526,353**	21,373	150,371	197,401	112,660	38,350	5,691	507
1985	**530,167**	20,057	146,262	203,272	114,862	39,293	5,883	538
1986	**519,673**	17,793	137,985	201,323	116,369	39,753	5,959	491
1987	**523,080**	15,588	132,809	206,036	121,252	40,159	6,751	485
1988	**516,225**	14,099	125,575	205,292	123,384	40,400	7,025	450
1989	**501,921**	12,027	114,456	200,961	125,439	41,528	7,079	431
1990	**506,141**	10,958	106,188	204,701	133,384	43,179	7,302	429
	Outside marriage							
1980	**77,372**	25,860	26,607	13,462	7,588	3,047	761	47
1981	**80,983**	26,430	28,810	14,300	7,870	2,730	840	20
1982	**89,857**	28,739	32,411	16,066	8,133	3,682	768	58
1983	**99,211**	30,423	36,643	17,916	9,274	4,117	788	50
1984	**110,465**	33,135	41,084	20,630	10,114	4,571	885	46
1985	**126,250**	36,872	47,696	24,214	11,323	5,100	999	46
1986	**141,345**	39,613	54,079	27,712	13,118	5,712	1,074	37
1987	**158,431**	41,957	60,423	32,893	15,306	6,445	1,361	46
1988	**177,352**	44,642	68,151	38,168	17,590	7,249	1,495	57
1989	**185,804**	43,516	70,783	41,861	19,881	7,937	1,766	60
1990	**199,999**	44,583	73,948	47,876	22,880	8,726	1,918	68

Note: 1981 births for age-groups are based on a 10 per cent sample.

Table 3.1 Live births: age of mother and occurrence inside/outside marriage, 1980-1990   **England and Wales**
       b. rates

Year	Age of mother at birth							
	All ages	Under 20	20-24	25-29	30-34	35-39	40-44	45 and over
	All live births per 1,000 women							
1980	**64.2**	30.4	112.7	133.6	70.5	22.3	4.3	0.5
1981	**61.3**	28.1	105.3	129.1	68.6	21.7	4.4	0.5
1982	**59.9**	27.4	101.6	126.4	69.1	22.8	4.2	0.5
1983	**59.7**	26.9	98.5	126.4	71.5	23.1	4.4	0.5
1984	**59.8**	27.6	95.5	126.2	73.6	23.6	4.5	0.4
1985	**61.0**	29.5	94.5	127.6	76.4	24.1	4.6	0.4
1986	**60.6**	30.1	92.7	124.0	78.1	24.6	4.5	0.4
1987	**62.0**	30.9	93.4	125.1	81.3	26.5	4.8	0.4
1988	**63.0**	32.4	94.9	123.8	82.7	27.9	4.8	0.4
1989	**62.5**	31.9	92.2	120.0	83.7	29.4	4.9	0.3
1990	**64.3**	33.3	91.7	122.4	87.3	31.2	5.0	0.3
	Live births within marriage per 1,000 married women							
1980	**92.2**	340.4	210.8	164.6	78.4	23.6	4.4	0.5
1981	**88.8**	324.8	204.3	161.5	76.9	23.3	4.5	0.6
1982	**86.9**	331.2	204.5	160.0	78.2	24.3	4.3	0.5
1983	**86.8**	329.7	205.8	162.6	81.4	24.7	4.5	0.5
1984	**86.7**	338.7	206.2	164.5	84.4	25.2	4.6	0.4
1985	**87.8**	358.8	209.5	168.9	88.1	25.7	4.7	0.5
1986	**86.3**	360.9	209.8	167.2	90.1	26.2	4.6	0.4
1987	**87.1**	302.1	213.2	170.6	93.9	28.2	4.8	0.4
1988	**86.7**	283.7	211.7	171.1	95.5	29.6	4.8	0.4
1989	**85.0**	266.7	201.0	169.0	96.8	31.2	4.8	0.4
1990	**86.7**	277.0	197.3	175.3	101.8	33.2	4.9	0.4
	Live births outside marriage per 1,000 single, widowed and divorced women							
1980	**19.6**	13.7	27.8	33.9	26.8	14.5	3.8	0.2
1981	**19.7**	13.7	27.8	33.7	26.0	11.9	4.1	0.1
1982	**21.0**	14.8	29.2	35.4	26.4	14.4	3.6	0.3
1983	**22.4**	15.7	30.7	36.8	29.0	14.7	3.5	0.2
1984	**24.1**	17.3	32.2	39.1	30.4	15.4	3.8	0.2
1985	**26.7**	19.7	35.2	41.8	32.6	16.2	4.0	0.2
1986	**28.9**	21.3	38.2	43.1	35.8	17.2	4.0	0.2
1987	**31.8**	23.1	41.8	46.8	39.5	19.3	4.5	0.2
1988	**35.1**	25.3	47.1	49.7	42.7	21.2	4.6	0.2
1989	**36.4**	25.7	49.1	50.2	45.0	22.6	5.2	0.2
1990	**38.9**	27.4	51.9	53.5	47.7	24.1	5.4	0.2

Notes: 1. 1981 births for age-groups are based on a 10 per cent sample.
     2. The rates for women of all ages, under 20 and 45 and over are based upon the population of women aged 15-44, 15-19 and 45-49 respectively.

Table 3.2 Maternities, live and still births: age of mother, occurrence inside/outside marriage and sex, 1990

Age of mother at birth	Maternities			Births			
	Total	Within marriage	Outside marriage	Live		Still	
				Total	Female only	Total	Female only
All ages	**701,030**	**501,942**	**199,088**	**706,140**	**344,728**	**3,256**	**1,503**
11	-	-	-	-	-	-	-
12	-	-	-	-	-	-	-
13	16	1	15	16	7	-	-
14	188	3	185	188	89	-	-
15	1,103	8	1,095	1,102	538	5	-
16	4,165	228	3,937	4,166	1,962	17	5
17	10,337	1,057	9,280	10,335	5,008	62	28
18	16,539	3,067	13,472	16,536	8,056	98	45
19	23,187	6,583	16,604	23,198	11,357	150	74
Under 20	**55,535**	**10,947**	**44,588**	**55,541**	**27,017**	**332**	**152**
20	26,510	10,549	15,961	26,580	12,911	116	51
21	31,725	15,696	16,029	31,811	15,484	155	77
22	35,677	20,737	14,940	35,861	17,419	152	70
23	40,458	26,574	13,884	40,692	19,857	163	67
24	44,947	32,108	12,839	45,192	22,078	219	99
20-24	**179,317**	**105,664**	**73,653**	**180,136**	**87,749**	**805**	**364**
25	49,835	37,978	11,857	50,115	24,497	209	101
26	51,567	41,032	10,535	51,929	25,431	228	102
27	52,173	42,700	9,473	52,540	25,704	219	103
28	50,292	41,926	8,366	50,741	24,745	188	83
29	46,803	39,456	7,347	47,252	22,997	198	95
25-29	**250,670**	**203,092**	**47,578**	**252,577**	**123,374**	**1,042**	**484**
30	42,059	35,801	6,258	42,521	20,862	164	79
31	36,400	31,179	5,221	36,739	17,886	148	74
32	30,718	26,366	4,352	31,075	15,174	141	64
33	25,070	21,365	3,705	25,374	12,465	131	66
34	20,306	17,195	3,111	20,555	10,091	85	46
30-34	**154,553**	**131,906**	**22,647**	**156,264**	**76,478**	**669**	**329**
35	16,006	13,516	2,490	16,206	7,960	97	38
36	12,916	10,806	2,110	13,101	6,386	67	30
37	9,782	8,097	1,685	9,897	4,804	62	27
38	7,175	5,877	1,298	7,262	3,515	48	25
39	5,380	4,331	1,049	5,439	2,665	40	15
35-39	**51,259**	**42,627**	**8,632**	**51,905**	**25,330**	**314**	**135**
40	3,778	3,006	772	3,809	1,918	24	7
41	2,408	1,892	516	2,417	1,182	24	11
42	1,586	1,251	335	1,580	770	17	4
43	967	757	210	965	457	10	5
44	454	366	88	449	213	8	4
40-44	**9,193**	**7,272**	**1,921**	**9,220**	**4,540**	**83**	**31**
45	217	179	38	215	115	3	3
46	103	87	16	103	45	1	-
47	57	49	8	53	27	4	2
48	41	37	4	41	19	-	-
49	27	26	1	26	12	1	1
45-49	**445**	**378**	**67**	**438**	**218**	**9**	**6**
50	17	17	-	17	9	-	-
51	12	12	-	14	3	-	-
52	10	9	1	9	4	1	1
53	6	6	-	6	1	1	1
54	8	7	1	8	4	-	-
55	5	5	-	5	1	-	-
50-55	**58**	**56**	**2**	**59**	**22**	**2**	**2**

The following cases in which the mother's age was not stated have been included in the above table (for method of distribution see Introduction).

	1,190	805	385	1,153	577	51	19

Within marriage				Outside marriage				Age of mother at birth
Live		Still		Live		Still		
Total	Female only	Total	Female only	Total	Female only	Total	Female only	
506,141	**247,091**	**2,176**	**1,023**	**199,999**	**97,637**	**1,080**	**480**	**All ages**
-	-	-	-	-	-	-	-	11
-	-	-	-	-	-	-	-	12
1	-	-	-	15	7	-	-	13
3	-	-	-	185	89	-	-	14
8	5	-	-	1,094	533	5	-	15
228	102	1	-	3,938	1,860	16	5	16
1,061	513	4	3	9,274	4,495	58	25	17
3,073	1,550	17	11	13,463	6,506	81	34	18
6,584	3,148	43	22	16,614	8,209	107	52	19
10,958	**5,318**	**65**	**36**	**44,583**	**21,699**	**267**	**116**	**Under 20**
10,587	5,161	43	22	15,993	7,750	73	29	20
15,729	7,697	74	41	16,082	7,787	81	36	21
20,839	10,089	94	44	15,022	7,330	58	26	22
26,727	13,016	104	40	13,965	6,841	59	27	23
32,306	15,785	132	66	12,886	6,293	87	33	24
106,188	**51,748**	**447**	**213**	**73,948**	**36,001**	**358**	**151**	**20-24**
38,199	18,699	157	73	11,916	5,798	52	28	25
41,338	20,249	154	66	10,591	5,182	74	36	26
43,021	20,993	160	77	9,519	4,711	59	26	27
42,311	20,601	153	69	8,430	4,144	35	14	28
39,832	19,417	165	83	7,420	3,580	33	12	29
204,701	**99,959**	**789**	**368**	**47,876**	**23,415**	**253**	**116**	**25-29**
36,205	17,762	133	63	6,316	3,100	31	16	30
31,490	15,308	118	58	5,249	2,578	30	16	31
26,667	13,027	116	53	4,408	2,147	25	11	32
21,624	10,575	110	51	3,750	1,890	21	15	33
17,398	8,553	73	41	3,157	1,538	12	5	34
133,384	**65,225**	**550**	**266**	**22,880**	**11,253**	**119**	**63**	**30-34**
13,699	6,661	81	33	2,507	1,299	16	5	35
10,961	5,385	58	27	2,140	1,001	9	3	36
8,194	3,977	52	21	1,703	827	10	6	37
5,948	2,896	35	20	1,314	619	13	5	38
4,377	2,150	27	11	1,062	515	13	4	39
43,179	**21,069**	**253**	**112**	**8,726**	**4,261**	**61**	**23**	**35-39**
3,039	1,515	16	3	770	403	8	4	40
1,901	923	18	8	516	259	6	3	41
1,245	598	14	3	335	172	3	1	42
755	359	7	3	210	98	3	2	43
362	172	7	4	87	41	1	-	44
7,302	**3,567**	**62**	**21**	**1,918**	**973**	**21**	**10**	**40-44**
178	98	2	2	37	17	1	1	45
87	36	1	-	16	9	-	-	46
45	23	4	2	8	4	-	-	47
37	17	-	-	4	2	-	-	48
25	11	1	1	1	1	-	-	49
372	**185**	**8**	**5**	**66**	**33**	**1**	**1**	**45-49**
17	9	-	-	-	-	-	-	50
14	3	-	-	-	-	-	-	51
8	3	1	1	1	1	-	-	52
6	1	1	1	-	-	-	-	53
7	3	-	-	1	1	-	-	54
5	1	-	-	-	-	-	-	55
57	**20**	**2**	**2**	**2**	**2**	**-**	**-**	**50-55**
787	390	29	9	366	187	22	10	

Table 3.3 Live births within marriage: age of father, 1980-1990   **England and Wales**

Year	Age of father at birth											
	All ages	Under 20	20-24	25-29	30-34	35-39	40-44	45-49	50-54	55-59	60-64	65 and over
	Numbers											
1980	**578,862**	9,889	108,836	202,446	166,174	60,084	20,984	6,967	2,368	756	259	99
1981	**553,509**	7,970	102,130	191,030	160,250	60,290	21,030	7,020	2,660	760	280	120
1982	**536,074**	7,126	96,046	185,471	150,346	66,064	20,212	7,147	2,489	809	271	93
1983	**529,923**	6,192	90,466	184,214	148,058	68,833	20,635	7,581	2,689	872	256	99
1984	**526,353**	5,371	86,263	183,174	147,749	70,512	21,593	7,705	2,657	929	304	96
1985	**530,167**	4,941	83,152	184,986	149,651	72,904	22,470	7,947	2,658	1,019	327	112
1986	**519,673**	4,466	76,895	180,926	149,531	72,745	23,146	7,646	2,817	1,057	332	112
1987	**519,474**	3,740	72,058	181,617	152,823	72,002	24,984	7,634	2,951	1,141	385	139
1988	**516,225**	3,274	67,771	179,254	154,973	72,533	26,144	7,554	3,030	1,148	395	149
1989	**501,921**	2,780	59,895	172,273	155,118	72,707	26,735	7,731	3,015	1,111	404	152
1990	**506,141**	2,549	55,251	171,895	161,251	74,916	27,586	7,942	3,015	1,138	420	178
	Rates: Live births within marriage per 1,000 married men in the age-group											
1980	**47.0**	462.1	224.8	186.3	112.6	46.6	17.2	5.9	2.0	0.6	0.3	0.0
1981	**45.2**	408.7	219.3	180.8	110.4	45.5	17.6	6.0	2.3	0.6	0.3	0.1
1982	**44.2**	439.9	223.9	180.8	111.7	46.6	17.1	6.2	2.1	0.7	0.3	0.0
1983	**44.0**	430.0	227.7	183.8	115.4	47.3	17.2	6.5	2.3	0.8	0.2	0.0
1984	**43.8**	429.7	228.0	185.3	118.5	48.1	17.6	6.6	2.4	0.8	0.3	0.0
1985	**44.3**	445.1	235.5	189.8	122.9	49.7	18.0	6.8	2.4	0.9	0.3	0.1
1986	**43.7**	451.1	238.7	189.3	124.7	50.2	17.9	6.7	2.5	1.0	0.3	0.1
1987	**43.8**	347.3	231.8	193.9	128.0	53.0	17.9	6.7	2.7	1.0	0.4	0.1
1988	**43.7**	330.7	224.8	196.5	130.7	55.8	18.2	6.5	2.7	1.1	0.4	0.1
1989	**42.6**	315.9	208.3	193.2	131.3	57.4	18.5	6.5	2.7	1.0	0.4	0.1
1990	**43.1**	335.4	205.6	197.1	137.0	60.5	19.2	6.6	2.7	1.1	0.4	0.1

Note: 1981 births for five-year age-groups are based on a 10 per cent sample.

Table 3.4 Paternities, live and still births: age of father, occurrence inside/outside marriage and sex, 1990

England and Wales

Age of father at birth	Paternities within marriage	Births within marriage				Births outside marriage registered* on joint information of parents			
		Live		Still		Live		Still	
		Total	Male only	Total	Male only	Total	Male only	Total	Male only
All ages	**501,942**	**506,141**	**259,050**	**2,176**	**1,153**	**145,168**	**74,387**	**691**	**400**
11	0	0	0	0	0	1	1	0	0
12	0	0	0	0	0	2	1	0	0
13	3	3	1	0	0	0	0	0	0
14	·1	1	1	0	0	19	15	0	0
15	1	1	0	0	0	78	38	1	1
16	10	10	6	0	0	437	230	2	2
17	112	112	64	2	1	1,352	689	6	4
18	582	584	302	2	2	3,337	1,713	21	15
19	1,835	1,838	950	8	5	6,128	3,250	25	18
Under 20	**2,544**	**2,549**	**1,324**	**12**	**8**	**11,354**	**5,937**	**55**	**40**
20	3,621	3,629	1,942	32	14	7,800	4,023	38	23
21	6,520	6,544	3,311	31	16	9,366	4,821	41	17
22	10,273	10,321	5,279	51	29	10,104	5,128	50	24
23	14,618	14,699	7,497	59	33	10,398	5,347	55	34
24	19,968	20,058	10,341	94	57	10,253	5,248	46	32
20-24	**55,000**	**55,251**	**28,370**	**267**	**149**	**47,921**	**24,567**	**230**	**130**
25	25,920	26,105	13,441	103	55	9,866	5,046	52	27
26	31,463	31,660	16,179	126	64	9,490	4,863	32	15
27	35,567	35,812	18,241	142	71	8,517	4,363	31	15
28	38,407	38,701	19,792	151	89	7,853	4,089	41	24
29	39,291	39,617	20,320	146	74	6,859	3,436	38	25
25-29	**170,648**	**171,895**	**87,973**	**668**	**353**	**42,585**	**21,797**	**194**	**106**
30	38,229	38,572	19,727	143	70	6,106	3,063	19	9
31	35,908	36,252	18,575	146	75	5,264	2,679	23	14
32	32,874	33,145	16,934	128	74	4,487	2,310	19	12
33	28,455	28,690	14,622	132	66	3,909	2,019	15	7
34	24,314	24,592	12,525	112	62	3,383	1,705	17	11
30-34	**159,780**	**161,251**	**82,383**	**661**	**347**	**23,149**	**11,776**	**93**	**53**
35	20,487	20,704	10,649	92	41	2,838	1,410	9	7
36	17,550	17,780	9,114	70	36	2,585	1,307	14	7
37	14,668	14,839	7,606	61	38	2,177	1,124	14	9
38	11,784	11,928	6,054	49	24	1,905	978	12	11
39	9,592	9,665	4,978	41	23	1,625	859	9	5
35-39	**74,081**	**74,916**	**38,401**	**313**	**162**	**11,130**	**5,678**	**58**	**39**
40	7,871	7,966	4,035	34	10	1,463	768	6	4
41	6,573	6,663	3,384	39	23	1,338	671	8	5
42	5,326	5,359	2,726	32	21	1,162	564	12	2
43	4,480	4,523	2,367	29	12	1,054	571	7	3
44	3,044	3,075	1,582	15	13	752	417	8	5
40-44	**27,294**	**27,586**	**14,094**	**149**	**79**	**5,769**	**2,991**	**41**	**19**
45	2,484	2,506	1,330	14	7	558	269	1	1
46	1,964	1,986	1,023	14	8	497	245	5	4
47	1,437	1,450	717	12	7	430	221	4	1
48	1,103	1,104	604	11	6	310	158	1	1
49	883	896	470	8	3	274	140	2	1
45-49	**7,871**	**7,942**	**4,144**	**59**	**31**	**2,069**	**1,033**	**13**	**8**
50-54	2,987	3,015	1,496	25	14	807	403	3	3
55-59	1,136	1,138	571	12	8	250	125	2	1
60-64	424	420	209	8	2	96	59	1	1
65-69	135	135	62	1	0	29	17	1	0
70-74	26	26	13	1	0	7	3	0	0
75 and over	**16**	**17**	**10**	**0**	**0**	**2**	**1**	**0**	**0**

The following births in which the age of the father was not stated have been included in the above table (for method of distribution see Introduction)

	598	**585**	**319**	**17**	**11**	**740**	**372**	**12**	**8**

* 54,831 live births and 389 stillbirths which occurred outside marriage and were registered without any information on the child's father are excluded from this table.

Table 3.5   Paternities within marriage: live and still birth rates, age of father and sex, 1990   **England and Wales**

| Age of father | Estimated number of married men (thousands) | Paternities within marriage per 1,000 married men | Births within marriage per 1,000 married men | | | |
| | | | Live | | Still | |
			Total	Male only	Total	Male only
All ages	**11,732.2**	**42.8**	**43.1**	**22.1**	**0.19**	**0.10**
Under 20	7.6	334.7	335.4	174.2	1.58	1.05
20-24	269.3	204.2	205.2	105.3	0.99	0.55
25-29	871.9	195.7	197.1	100.9	0.77	0.40
30-34	1,177.1	135.7	137.0	70.0	0.56	0.29
35-39	1,238.8	59.8	60.5	31.0	0.25	0.13
40-44	1,439.9	19.0	19.2	9.2	0.10	0.05
45-49	1,207.7	6.5	6.6	3.4	0.05	0.03
50-54	1,119.9	2.7	2.7	1.3	0.02	0.01
55-59	1,054.5	1.1	1.1	0.5	0.01	0.01
60-64	1,008.4	0.4	0.4	0.2	0.01	0.00
65 and over	2,337.0	0.1	0.1	0.0	0.00	0.00

Table 3.6   Live births within marriage: age of mother and father, 1990   **England and Wales**

| Age of father at birth | Age of mother at birth | | | | | | | | |
	All ages	Under 20	20-24	25-29	30-34	35-39	40-44	45-49	50 and over
All Ages	**506,141**	**10,958**	**106,188**	**204,701**	**133,384**	**43,179**	**7,302**	**372**	**57**
Under 20	**2,549**	1,407	992	122	22	6	-	-	-
20-24	**55,251**	6,408	37,076	10,003	1,461	268	34	1	-
25-29	**171,895**	2,374	50,402	101,206	15,778	1,908	217	8	2
30-34	**161,251**	558	13,303	71,348	68,042	7,360	617	23	-
35-39	**74,916**	127	2,960	15,584	35,154	19,598	1,470	21	2
40-44	**27,586**	49	954	4,471	9,227	9,845	2,982	57	1
45-49	**7,942**	22	286	1,311	2,446	2,580	1,162	133	2
50-54	**3,015**	9	141	401	817	1,054	485	85	23
55-59	**1,138**	4	47	167	281	367	222	29	21
60-64	**420**	-	16	60	99	146	83	12	4
65 and over	**178**	-	11	28	57	47	30	3	2

Table 3.7   Stillbirths within marriage: age of mother and father, 1990   **England and Wales**

| Age of father at birth | Age of mother at birth | | | | | | | | |
	All ages	Under 20	20-24	25-29	30-34	35-39	40-44	45-49	50 and over
All Ages	**2,176**	**65**	**447**	**789**	**550**	**253**	**62**	**8**	**2**
Under 20	**12**	8	4	-	-	-	-	-	-
20-24	**267**	42	164	49	7	3	2	-	-
25-29	**668**	8	201	369	78	9	3	-	-
30-34	**661**	3	60	279	274	40	5	-	-
35-39	**313**	2	11	60	130	106	4	-	-
40-44	**149**	-	5	19	39	60	24	2	-
45-49	**59**	1	-	6	16	17	15	4	-
50-54	**25**	1	2	1	3	11	5	2	-
55-59	**12**	-	-	3	1	4	3	-	1
60-64	**8**	-	-	3	1	2	1	-	1
65 and over	**2**	-	-	-	1	1	-	-	-

Table 3.8 Live births outside marriage: England and Wales
           age of mother and father and type of registration, 1990

Age of father at birth	Age of mother at birth							
	All ages	Under 20	20-24	25-29	30-34	35-39	40-44	45 and over
	(i) Total live births outside marriage							
	199,999	44,583	73,948	47,876	22,880	8,726	1,918	68
	(ii) Solely registered							
	54,831	16,191	20,135	11,140	5,006	1,933	413	13
	(iii) Jointly registered							
All ages	**145,168**	**28,392**	**53,813**	**36,736**	**17,874**	**6,793**	**1,505**	**55**
Under 20	**11,354**	8,447	2,378	411	95	16	7	-
20-24	**47,921**	14,798	25,136	6,213	1,418	311	44	1
25-29	**42,585**	3,879	18,168	15,311	4,083	978	163	3
30-34	**23,149**	883	5,419	9,050	5,968	1,577	247	5
35-39	**11,130**	223	1,647	3,398	3,645	1,882	328	7
40-44	**5,769**	95	725	1,490	1,747	1,301	393	18
45-49	**2,069**	42	225	561	591	451	191	8
50-54	**807**	17	79	199	232	183	90	7
55-59	**250**	3	25	73	62	63	22	2
60 and over	**134**	5	11	30	33	31	20	4

D

Table 3.9 Live births outside marriage: age of mother and sole/joint **England and Wales**
registration, 1980-1990

Year		a. Number (thousands)						b. Percentage sole/joint in each age-group					
		All ages	Under 20	20-24	25-29	30-34	35 and over	All ages	Under 20	20-24	25-29	30-34	35 and over
1980	Total	77.4	25.9	26.6	13.5	7.6	3.9						
	Sole	33.2	14.0	11.3	4.5	2.2	1.1	42.9	54.3	42.6	33.5	28.7	29.6
	Joint	44.2	11.8	15.3	8.9	5.4	2.7	57.1	45.7	57.4	66.5	71.3	70.4
1981	Total	81.0	26.4	28.8	14.3	7.9	3.6						
	Sole	33.8	13.7	12.0	4.8	2.3	1.1	41.8	51.7	41.6	33.4	29.7	29.9
	Joint	47.1	12.8	16.8	9.5	5.5	2.5	58.2	48.3	58.4	66.6	70.3	70.1
1982	Total	89.9	28.7	32.4	16.1	8.1	4.5						
	Sole	36.5	14.5	13.0	5.4	2.3	1.3	40.6	50.3	40.1	33.5	28.3	29.5
	Joint	53.4	14.3	19.4	10.7	5.8	3.2	59.4	49.7	59.9	66.5	71.7	70.5
1983	Total	99.2	30.4	36.6	17.9	9.3	5.0						
	Sole	38.4	14.4	14.1	5.8	2.7	1.5	38.7	47.2	38.5	32.5	28.6	30.3
	Joint	60.8	16.1	22.6	12.1	6.6	3.5	61.3	52.8	61.5	67.5	71.4	69.7
1984	Total	110.5	33.1	41.1	20.6	10.1	5.5						
	Sole	40.6	14.9	14.9	6.4	2.8	1.6	36.7	45.1	36.2	30.9	27.9	28.8
	Joint	69.9	18.2	26.2	14.2	7.3	3.9	63.3	54.9	63.8	69.1	72.1	71.2
1985	Total	126.2	36.9	47.7	24.2	11.3	6.1						
	Sole	44.5	15.9	16.4	7.4	3.1	1.6	35.2	43.0	34.5	30.4	27.8	26.7
	Joint	81.8	21.0	31.3	16.9	8.2	4.5	64.8	57.0	65.5	69.6	72.2	73.3
1986	Total	141.3	39.6	54.1	27.7	13.1	6.8						
	Sole	47.8	16.4	17.9	8.2	3.5	1.8	33.8	41.3	33.1	29.8	26.5	26.3
	Joint	93.5	23.2	36.2	19.5	9.6	5.0	66.2	58.7	66.9	70.2	73.5	73.7
1987	Total	158.4	42.0	60.4	32.9	15.3	7.9						
	Sole	50.5	16.8	18.9	8.9	3.9	2.0	31.9	40.0	31.4	27.1	25.3	24.9
	Joint	108.0	25.2	41.5	24.0	11.4	5.9	68.1	60.0	68.6	72.9	74.7	75.1
1988	Total	177.4	44.6	68.2	38.2	17.6	8.8						
	Sole	53.9	17.1	20.3	10.2	4.3	2.0	30.4	38.3	29.9	26.7	24.6	22.6
	Joint	123.4	27.5	47.8	28.0	13.3	6.8	69.6	61.7	70.1	73.3	75.4	77.4
1989	Total	185.8	43.5	70.8	41.9	19.9	9.8						
	Sole	53.5	16.1	20.2	10.4	4.6	2.2	28.8	37.1	28.5	24.8	23.1	22.7
	Joint	132.3	27.4	50.6	31.5	15.3	7.5	71.2	62.9	71.5	75.2	76.9	77.3
1990	Total	200.0	44.6	73.9	47.9	22.9	10.7						
	Sole	54.8	16.2	20.1	11.1	5.0	2.4	27.4	36.3	27.2	23.3	21.9	22.0
	Joint	145.2	28.4	53.8	36.7	17.9	8.4	72.6	63.7	72.8	76.7	78.1	78.0

Note: Figures for jointly registered live births outside marriage include a small number of cases registered by the mother alone for which the father's name
was included in the birth register.

Table 3.10 Jointly registered births outside marriage: age of mother and same/different addresses of parents usual residence, 1983-1990

England and Wales

Year	Addresses of mother and father	Age of mother											
		All ages	Under 20	20-24	25-29	30-34	35 and over	All ages	Under 20	20-24	25-29	30-34	35 and over
		a. Numbers of jointly registered births outside marriage						b. Percentage same/different addresses in each age-group					
1983	Total	10,157	2,679	3,755	1,999	1,124	571						
	Same	7,427	1,513	2,860	1,661	924	457	73.1	56.5	76.2	83.1	82.2	80.0
	Different	2,730	1,166	895	338	200	114	26.9	43.5	23.8	16.9	17.8	20.0
1984*	Total	12,216	2,771	4,803	2,587	1,302	732						
	Same	8,843	1,550	3,505	2,098	1,066	609	72.4	55.9	73.0	81.1	81.9	83.2
	Different	3,373	1,221	1,298	489	236	123	27.6	44.1	27.0	18.9	18.1	16.8
1985*	Total	14,234	3,646	5,380	3,019	1,379	787						
	Same	10,274	2,084	3,971	2,394	1,162	649	72.2	57.2	73.8	79.3	84.3	82.5
	Different	3,960	1,562	1,409	625	217	138	27.8	42.8	26.2	20.7	15.7	17.5
1986	Total	93,523	23,234	36,157	19,466	9,639	5,027						
	Same	65,844	12,908	25,760	15,300	7,849	4,027	70.4	55.6	71.2	78.6	81.4	80.1
	Different	27,679	10,326	10,397	4,166	1,790	1,000	29.6	44.4	28.8	21.4	18.6	19.9
1987	Total	107,957	25,170	41,479	23,984	11,431	5,893						
	Same	75,572	13,808	29,114	18,671	9,210	4,769	70.0	54.9	70.2	77.8	80.6	80.9
	Different	32,385	11,362	12,365	5,313	2,221	1,124	30.0	45.1	29.8	22.2	19.4	19.1
1988	Total	123,408	27,544	47,801	27,983	13,270	6,810						
	Same	87,601	15,304	33,994	22,070	10,765	5,468	71.0	55.6	71.1	78.9	81.1	80.3
	Different	35,807	12,240	13,807	5,913	2,505	1,342	29.0	44.4	28.9	21.1	18.9	19.7
1989	Total	132,267	27,374	50,604	31,462	15,281	7,546						
	Same	95,858	15,686	36,582	24,859	12,543	6,188	72.5	57.3	72.3	79.0	82.1	82.0
	Different	36,409	11,688	14,022	6,603	2,738	1,358	27.5	42.7	27.7	21.0	17.9	18.0
1990	Total	145,168	28,392	53,813	36,736	17,874	8,353						
	Same	106,001	16,311	39,062	29,181	14,585	6,862	73.0	57.4	72.6	79.4	81.6	82.2
	Different	39,167	12,081	14,751	7,555	3,289	1,491	27.0	42.6	27.4	20.6	18.4	17.8

* Births registered in July and November each year.

Table 4.1 Live births within marriage: previous liveborn children and age of mother (five-year age-groups), 1980-1990 **England and Wales**
/a. all married women

Year	Number of previous liveborn children						Year	Number of previous liveborn children					
	Total	0	1	2	3	4 or more		Total	0	1	2	3	4 or more
	All ages of mother at birth							**25-29**					
1980	**578,862**	240,975	209,164	86,336	27,537	14,850	1980	**209,976**	81,554	84,580	31,461	8,988	3,393
1981	**553,520**	224,290	205,690	82,400	26,160	14,980	1981	**201,460**	77,200	82,750	29,480	8,660	3,380
1982	**536,074**	211,862	200,681	81,431	27,123	14,977	1982	**195,839**	73,585	80,633	29,194	8,882	3,545
1983	**529,923**	211,753	195,630	80,728	26,646	15,166	1983	**196,162**	75,876	78,657	29,291	8,788	3,550
1984	**526,353**	210,421	193,093	80,643	26,860	15,336	1984	**197,401**	77,208	78,280	29,323	8,895	3,695
1985	**530,167**	212,017	193,058	82,403	26,865	15,824	1985	**203,272**	79,906	80,043	30,546	8,977	3,800
1986	**519,673**	206,942	189,186	80,842	26,920	15,783	1986	**201,323**	79,255	78,858	30,243	9,123	3,844
1987	**523,080**	209,971	189,370	81,180	26,593	15,966	1987	**206,036**	83,941	78,907	30,467	9,041	3,680
1988	**516,225**	209,291	185,553	79,411	26,379	15,591	1988	**205,292**	85,848	77,129	29,666	9,040	3,609
1989	**501,921**	200,970	182,765	77,518	25,807	14,861	1989	**200,961**	83,987	76,381	28,571	8,750	3,281
1990	**506,141**	200,394	185,334	79,040	25,984	15,389	1990	**204,701**	86,432	77,678	28,684	8,431	3,476
	Under 20							**30-34**					
1980	**34,894**	28,189	6,307	386	12	-	1980	**122,320**	28,907	48,205	30,052	10,063	5,093
1981	**30,140**	23,650	6,090	390	10	-	1981	**118,720**	27,800	47,680	28,720	9,430	5,090
1982	**26,696**	21,071	5,231	377	17	-	1982	**112,625**	26,272	45,255	26,592	9,454	5,052
1983	**23,636**	18,723	4,577	319	16	1	1983	**111,722**	27,264	44,807	25,364	8,983	5,304
1984	**21,373**	16,865	4,204	290	14	-	1984	**112,660**	28,261	44,946	25,196	8,907	5,350
1985	**20,057**	15,811	3,941	287	17	1	1985	**114,862**	29,477	45,225	25,690	8,894	5,576
1986	**17,793**	13,837	3,641	285	29	1	1986	**116,369**	30,754	45,543	25,565	8,907	5,600
1987	**15,588**	11,882	3,439	241	23	3	1987	**121,252**	33,284	47,081	26,036	8,999	5,852
1988	**14,099**	10,695	3,124	256	19	5	1988	**123,384**	34,377	48,394	26,018	8,898	5,697
1989	**12,027**	9,180	2,586	254	7	-	1989	**125,439**	35,873	49,488	25,760	8,883	5,435
1990	**10,958**	8,334	2,409	205	9	1	1990	**133,384**	38,277	52,462	27,616	9,422	5,607
	20-24							**35 and over**					
1980	**174,934**	96,393	60,501	14,830	2,772	438	1980	**36,738**	5,932	9,571	9,607	5,702	5,926
1981	**165,690**	89,460	59,040	14,070	2,640	480	1981	**37,500**	6,180	10,130	9,740	5,410	6,030
1982	**159,911**	84,438	58,064	14,248	2,707	454	1982	**41,003**	6,496	11,498	11,020	6,063	5,926
1983	**155,209**	82,829	55,380	13,915	2,668	417	1983	**43,194**	7,061	12,209	11,839	6,191	5,894
1984	**150,371**	80,585	52,782	13,867	2,694	443	1984	**44,548**	7,502	12,881	11,967	6,350	5,848
1985	**146,262**	78,992	50,526	13,587	2,706	451	1985	**45,714**	7,831	13,323	12,293	6,271	5,996
1986	**137,985**	74,695	47,519	12,708	2,591	472	1986	**46,203**	8,401	13,625	12,041	6,270	5,866
1987	**132,809**	71,957	45,829	12,202	2,396	425	1987	**47,395**	8,907	14,114	12,234	6,134	6,006
1988	**125,575**	68,919	42,372	11,549	2,345	390	1988	**47,875**	9,452	14,534	11,922	6,077	5,890
1989	**114,456**	62,068	38,867	10,823	2,271	427	1989	**49,038**	9,871	15,443	12,110	5,896	5,718
1990	**106,188**	56,995	36,532	10,144	2,118	399	1990	**50,910**	10,356	16,253	12,391	6,004	5,906

Note: 1981 figures are based on a 10 per cent sample.

Table 4.1 Live births within marriage: previous liveborn children and age of mother (five-year age-groups), 1980-1990
b. women married once only

Year	Number of previous liveborn children						Year	Number of previous liveborn children					
	Total	0	1	2	3	4 or more		Total	0	1	2	3	4 or more
	All ages of mother at birth							**25-29**					
1980	**540,375**	231,270	197,102	76,755	23,080	12,168	1980	**196,740**	77,373	80,075	28,523	7,815	2,954
1981	**514,760**	214,840	192,730	73,080	21,850	12,250	1981	**188,020**	73,460	77,720	26,360	7,530	2,950
1982	**497,183**	202,166	188,118	71,976	22,556	12,367	1982	**182,493**	69,355	76,031	26,314	7,714	3,079
1983	**490,198**	201,487	182,694	71,126	22,266	12,625	1983	**182,691**	71,485	74,042	26,377	7,681	3,106
1984	**485,364**	199,827	179,788	70,871	22,157	12,721	1984	**183,809**	77,770	73,628	26,467	7,706	3,238
1985	**488,303**	200,955	179,509	72,457	22,270	13,112	1985	**189,675**	75,516	75,272	27,703	7,873	3,311
1986	**477,934**	195,906	175,382	71,149	22,353	13,144	1986	**188,114**	75,083	74,236	27,455	7,968	3,372
1987	**480,139**	198,325	175,446	71,208	21,879	13,280	1987	**192,723**	79,649	74,414	27,614	7,866	3,180
1988	**473,572**	197,779	171,662	69,462	21,742	12,927	1988	**192,334**	81,530	72,892	26,852	7,898	3,162
1989	**460,501**	189,944	169,067	67,935	21,336	12,219	1989	**188,622**	80,080	72,201	25,883	7,641	2,817
1990	**464,830**	189,322	171,848	69,562	21,368	12,730	1990	**192,837**	82,564	73,765	26,179	7,349	2,980
	Under 20							**30-34**					
1980	**34,831**	28,146	6,289	384	12	-	1980	**107,747**	25,562	43,675	26,135	8,293	4,082
1981	**30,050**	23,580	6,070	390	-	-	1981	**104,650**	24,370	43,050	25,220	7,930	4,090
1982	**26,668**	21,052	5,224	376	16	-	1982	**98,288**	23,031	40,465	22,954	7,677	4,161
1983	**23,586**	18,687	4,565	318	15	1	1983	**97,166**	23,671	39,903	21,847	7,353	4,392
1984	**21,344**	16,850	4,193	288	13	-	1984	**97,665**	24,528	39,852	21,577	7,232	4,476
1985	**20,021**	15,786	3,933	285	16	1	1985	**99,477**	25,421	40,135	22,028	7,255	4,638
1986	**17,744**	13,813	3,625	281	25	-	1986	**100,959**	26,663	40,204	22,076	7,308	4,708
1987	**15,542**	11,864	3,425	234	18	1	1987	**105,012**	28,820	41,653	22,334	7,281	4,924
1988	**14,069**	10,682	3,112	252	18	5	1988	**107,135**	30,144	42,761	22,201	7,282	4,747
1989	**12,001**	9,168	2,574	252	7	-	1989	**109,731**	31,681	44,107	22,174	7,253	4,516
1990	**10,935**	8,323	2,400	202	9	1	1990	**117,147**	33,930	46,962	23,927	7,689	4,639
	20-24							**35 and over**					
1980	**171,274**	95,154	59,049	14,091	2,591	389	1980	**29,783**	5,035	8,014	7,622	4,369	4,743
1981	**162,090**	88,260	57,540	13,430	2,460	400	1981	**29,960**	5,170	8,340	7,680	3,930	4,820
1982	**156,887**	83,411	56,902	13,603	2,547	424	1982	**32,847**	5,317	9,496	8,729	4,602	4,703
1983	**152,352**	81,910	54,211	13,317	2,526	388	1983	**34,403**	5,734	9,973	9,267	4,691	4,738
1984	**147,579**	79,716	51,662	13,277	2,515	409	1984	**34,967**	5,963	10,453	9,262	4,691	4,598
1985	**143,522**	78,091	49,492	12,998	2,521	420	1985	**35,608**	6,141	10,677	9,443	4,605	4,742
1986	**135,359**	73,777	46,500	12,190	2,463	429	1986	**35,758**	6,570	10,817	9,147	4,589	4,635
1987	**130,118**	71,038	44,795	11,655	2,247	383	1987	**36,744**	6,954	11,160	9,371	4,461	4,792
1988	**123,084**	68,024	41,472	11,038	2,188	362	1988	**36,950**	7,399	11,425	9,119	4,356	4,651
1989	**112,282**	61,354	38,060	10,363	2,120	385	1989	**37,865**	7,661	12,125	9,263	4,315	4,501
1990	**104,294**	56,358	35,810	9,762	1,990	374	1990	**39,617**	8,147	12,911	9,492	4,331	4,736

Note: 1981 figures are based on a 10 per cent sample.

Table 4.1 Live births within marriage: previous liveborn children and age of mother (five-year age-groups), 1980-1990
c. remarried women

England and Wales

Year	Total	0	1	2	3	4 or more	Year	Total	0	1	2	3	4 or more
	All ages of mother at birth							**25-29**					
1980	**38,487**	9,705	12,062	9,581	4,457	2,682	1980	**13,236**	4,181	4,505	2,938	1,173	439
1981	**38,750**	9,450	12,960	9,320	4,300	2,720	1981	**13,440**	3,740	5,020	3,120	1,130	430
1982	**38,891**	9,696	12,563	9,455	4,567	2,610	1982	**13,346**	4,230	4,602	2,880	1,168	466
1983	**39,725**	10,266	12,936	9,602	4,380	2,541	1983	**13,471**	4,391	4,615	2,914	1,107	444
1984	**40,989**	10,594	13,305	9,772	4,703	2,615	1984	**13,592**	4,438	4,652	2,856	1,189	457
1985	**41,864**	11,062	13,549	9,946	4,595	2,712	1985	**13,597**	4,390	4,771	2,843	1,104	489
1986	**41,739**	11,036	13,804	9,693	4,567	2,639	1986	**13,209**	4,172	4,622	2,788	1,155	472
1987	**42,941**	11,646	13,923	9,972	4,714	2,686	1987	**13,313**	4,292	4,493	2,853	1,175	500
1988	**42,653**	11,512	13,891	9,949	4,637	2,664	1988	**12,958**	4,318	4,237	2,814	1,142	447
1989	**41,420**	11,026	13,698	9,583	4,471	2,642	1989	**12,339**	3,898	4,180	2,688	1,109	464
1990	**41,311**	11,072	13,486	9,478	4,616	2,659	1990	**11,864**	3,868	3,913	2,505	1,082	496
	Under 20							**30-34**					
1980	**63**	43	18	2	-	-	1980	**14,573**	3,345	4,530	3,917	1,770	1,011
1981	**90**	60	20	-	10	-	1981	**14,070**	3,440	4,630	3,500	1,500	1,010
1982	**28**	19	7	1	1	-	1982	**14,337**	3,241	4,790	3,638	1,777	891
1983	**50**	36	12	1	1	-	1983	**14,556**	3,593	4,904	3,517	1,630	912
1984	**29**	15	11	2	1	-	1984	**14,995**	3,733	5,094	3,619	1,675	874
1985	**36**	25	8	2	1	-	1985	**15,385**	4,056	5,090	3,662	1,639	938
1986	**49**	24	16	4	4	1	1986	**15,410**	4,091	5,339	3,489	1,599	892
1987	**46**	18	14	7	5	2	1987	**16,240**	4,464	5,428	3,702	1,718	928
1988	**30**	13	12	4	1	-	1988	**16,249**	4,233	5,633	3,817	1,616	950
1989	**26**	12	12	2	-	-	1989	**15,708**	4,192	5,381	3,586	1,630	919
1990	**23**	11	9	3	-	-	1990	**16,237**	4,347	5,500	3,689	1,733	968
	20-24							**35 and over**					
1980	**3,660**	1,239	1,452	739	181	49	1980	**6,955**	897	1,557	1,985	1,333	1,183
1981	**3,600**	1,200	1,490	640	180	80	1981	**7,550**	1,010	1,800	2,050	1,480	1,210
1982	**3,024**	1,027	1,162	645	160	30	1982	**8,156**	1,179	2,002	2,291	1,461	1,223
1983	**2,857**	919	1,169	598	142	29	1983	**8,791**	1,327	2,236	2,572	1,500	1,156
1984	**2,792**	869	1,120	590	179	34	1984	**9,581**	1,539	2,428	2,705	1,659	1,250
1985	**2,740**	901	1,034	589	185	31	1985	**10,106**	1,690	2,646	2,850	1,666	1,254
1986	**2,626**	918	1,019	518	128	43	1986	**10,445**	1,831	2,808	2,894	1,681	1,231
1987	**2,691**	919	1,034	547	149	42	1987	**10,651**	1,953	2,954	2,863	1,667	1,214
1988	**2,491**	895	900	511	157	28	1988	**10,925**	2,053	3,109	2,803	1,721	1,239
1989	**2,174**	714	807	460	151	42	1989	**11,173**	2,210	3,318	2,847	1,581	1,217
1990	**1,894**	637	722	382	128	25	1990	**11,293**	2,209	3,342	2,899	1,673	1,170

Note: 1981 figures are based on a 10 per cent sample.

Table 4.2 Live births within marriage: previous liveborn children and age of mother (single years of age), 1990
a. all married women

England and Wales

Age of mother at birth	Number of previous liveborn children												
	Total	0	1	2	3	4	5	6	7	8	9	10-14	15 and over
All ages	506,141	200,394	185,334	79,040	25,984	8,638	3,518	1,724	767	370	207	161	4
Under 16	12	10	-	1	1	-	-	-	-	-	-	-	-
16	228	219	8	1	-	-	-	-	-	-	-	-	-
17	1,061	937	116	6	1	-	1	-	-	-	-	-	-
18	3,073	2,498	541	34	-	-	-	-	-	-	-	-	-
19	6,584	4,670	1,744	163	7	-	-	-	-	-	-	-	-
Under 20	10,958	8,334	2,409	205	9	-	1	-	-	-	-	-	-
20	10,587	6,627	3,383	513	60	2	2	-	-	-	-	-	-
21	15,729	8,884	5,504	1,171	155	12	3	-	-	-	-	-	-
22	20,839	11,281	7,184	1,976	357	38	2	1	-	-	-	-	-
23	26,727	13,919	9,246	2,835	611	95	18	1	2	-	-	-	-
24	32,306	16,284	11,215	3,649	935	197	22	3	1	-	-	-	-
20-24	106,188	56,995	36,532	10,144	2,118	344	47	5	3	-	-	-	-
25	38,199	18,404	13,730	4,456	1,256	292	54	6	1	-	-	-	-
26	41,338	18,877	15,295	5,184	1,470	407	77	23	5	-	-	-	-
27	43,021	18,131	16,460	5,958	1,764	526	132	40	8	2	-	-	-
28	42,311	16,639	16,482	6,365	1,931	626	185	64	16	3	-	-	-
29	39,832	14,381	15,711	6,721	2,010	660	230	83	30	4	2	-	-
25-29	204,701	86,432	77,678	28,684	8,431	2,511	678	216	60	9	2	-	-
30	36,205	11,999	14,402	6,604	2,132	651	283	95	24	11	3	1	-
31	31,490	9,342	12,624	6,240	2,120	729	277	103	36	15	3	1	-
32	26,667	7,313	10,589	5,662	1,920	645	318	136	58	20	3	3	-
33	21,624	5,443	8,436	4,902	1,750	581	265	146	60	25	10	6	-
34	17,398	4,180	6,411	4,208	1,500	592	258	144	57	30	12	6	-
30-34	133,384	38,277	52,462	27,616	9,422	3,198	1,401	624	235	101	31	17	-
35	13,699	3,144	4,853	3,345	1,345	507	243	128	63	38	22	11	-
36	10,961	2,373	3,725	2,655	1,234	476	230	122	72	36	20	18	-
37	8,194	1,665	2,581	2,077	953	424	206	155	63	38	18	14	-
38	5,948	1,124	1,900	1,470	737	329	155	111	65	20	25	12	-
39	4,377	784	1,324	1,069	590	235	179	102	39	20	13	22	-
35-39	43,179	9,090	14,383	10,616	4,859	1,971	1,013	618	302	152	98	77	-
40	3,039	559	805	735	415	204	131	85	47	24	18	16	1
41	1,901	322	497	450	282	138	79	45	35	26	15	11	1
42	1,245	186	304	290	198	110	56	37	26	18	11	8	1
43	755	105	160	174	122	80	39	29	19	12	6	9	-
44	362	47	60	74	68	36	27	19	11	8	7	4	1
40-44	7,302	1,219	1,826	1,723	1,085	568	332	215	138	88	57	48	3
45	178	28	33	32	25	14	15	11	7	7	1	5	-
46	87	10	5	11	15	11	10	8	5	2	8	2	-
47	45	4	5	4	7	2	6	6	5	3	1	2	-
48	37	-	-	2	4	6	3	4	3	4	6	5	-
49 and over	82	5	1	3	9	13	12	17	9	4	3	5	1
45 and over	429	47	44	52	60	46	46	46	29	20	19	19	1

Notes: 1. 787 cases in which age of mother at birth, and 182 cases in which the number of previous liveborn children was not stated, have been included with the stated cases (for method of distribution see 'Introduction').
2. The distribution of live births within marriage in the '10-14' and '15 and over' categories is given below:

Number of previous liveborn children

10	11	12	13	14	15	16	17	18	19	20
85	40	20	14	2	2	2	-	-	-	-

Table 4.2 Live births within marriage: previous liveborn children and age of mother (single years of age), 1990
b. women married once only

Age of mother at birth	Number of previous liveborn children												
	Total	0	1	2	3	4	5	6	7	8	9	10-14	15 and over
All ages	464,830	189,322	171,848	69,562	21,368	6,920	2,964	1,508	666	325	188	155	4
Under 16	12	10	-	1	1	-	-	-	-	-	-	-	-
16	227	218	8	1	-	-	-	-	-	-	-	-	-
17	1,058	936	115	5	1	-	1	-	-	-	-	-	-
18	3,066	2,494	538	34	-	-	-	-	-	-	-	-	-
19	6,572	4,665	1,739	161	7	-	-	-	-	-	-	-	-
Under 20	10,935	8,323	2,400	202	9	-	1	-	-	-	-	-	-
20	10,536	6,606	3,359	508	59	2	2	-	-	-	-	-	-
21	15,599	8,841	5,444	1,151	149	11	3	-	-	-	-	-	-
22	20,575	11,195	7,079	1,917	343	38	2	1	-	-	-	-	-
23	26,171	13,736	9,043	2,709	574	90	16	1	2	-	-	-	-
24	31,413	15,980	10,885	3,477	865	180	22	3	1	-	-	-	-
20-24	104,294	56,358	35,810	9,762	1,990	321	45	5	3	-	-	-	-
25	36,839	17,930	13,290	4,183	1,135	244	50	6	1	-	-	-	-
26	39,437	18,225	14,654	4,805	1,300	356	73	20	4	-	-	-	-
27	40,542	17,310	15,644	5,446	1,531	457	113	31	8	2	-	-	-
28	39,462	15,747	15,537	5,742	1,675	526	163	56	13	3	-	-	-
29	36,557	13,352	14,640	6,003	1,708	548	202	73	25	4	2	-	-
25-29	192,837	82,564	73,765	26,179	7,349	2,131	601	186	51	9	2	-	-
30	32,788	10,995	13,229	5,858	1,803	541	249	78	22	9	3	1	-
31	28,047	8,401	11,454	5,470	1,751	588	239	93	33	14	3	1	-
32	23,307	6,421	9,428	4,903	1,577	506	283	116	48	19	3	3	-
33	18,510	4,644	7,394	4,191	1,398	456	214	125	53	20	9	6	-
34	14,495	3,469	5,457	3,505	1,160	462	218	130	50	26	12	6	-
30-34	117,147	33,930	46,962	23,927	7,689	2,553	1,203	542	206	88	30	17	-
35	11,126	2,535	3,998	2,726	1,031	404	198	116	51	36	20	11	-
36	8,713	1,872	3,021	2,090	926	376	200	109	61	26	16	16	-
37	6,417	1,304	2,063	1,605	685	325	167	144	58	35	17	14	-
38	4,524	864	1,458	1,115	537	230	118	96	56	19	21	10	-
39	3,286	604	1,028	772	409	159	145	86	34	15	13	21	-
35-39	34,066	7,179	11,568	8,308	3,588	1,494	828	551	260	131	87	72	-
40	2,217	428	599	498	279	147	99	76	39	20	16	16	-
41	1,341	241	360	304	176	85	58	37	33	24	12	10	1
42	883	143	211	195	134	76	42	29	20	14	10	8	1
43	517	81	108	110	72	57	27	20	17	11	5	9	-
44	255	39	36	47	43	23	19	18	10	8	7	4	1
40-44	5,213	932	1,314	1,154	704	388	245	180	119	77	50	47	3
45	128	21	24	14	17	8	13	11	7	7	1	5	-
46	64	7	2	10	6	7	9	7	4	2	8	2	-
47	36	4	2	3	3	1	6	6	5	3	1	2	-
48	32	-	-	1	4	4	2	4	2	4	6	5	-
49 and over	78	4	1	2	9	13	11	16	9	4	3	5	1
45 and over	338	36	29	30	39	33	41	44	27	20	19	19	1

Notes: 1. 736 cases in which age of mother at birth, and 181 cases in which the number of previous liveborn children was not stated, have been included with the stated cases (for method of distribution see Introduction).
2. The distribution of live births within marriage in the '10-14' and '15 and over' categories is given below:

Number of previous liveborn children

10	11	12	13	14	15	16	17	18	19	20
80	39	20	14	2	2	2	-	-	-	-

Table 4.2 Live births within marriage: previous liveborn children and age of mother (single years of age), 1990
c. remarried women

England and Wales

Age of mother at birth	Number of previous liveborn children												
	Total	0	1	2	3	4	5	6	7	8	9	10-14	15 and over
All ages	41,311	11,072	13,486	9,478	4,616	1,718	554	216	101	45	19	6	-
Under 16	-	-	-	-	-	-	-	-	-	-	-	-	-
16	1	1	-	-	-	-	-	-	-	-	-	-	-
17	3	1	1	1	-	-	-	-	-	-	-	-	-
18	7	4	3	-	-	-	-	-	-	-	-	-	-
19	12	5	5	2	-	-	-	-	-	-	-	-	-
Under 20	23	11	9	3	-	-	-	-	-	-	-	-	-
20	51	21	24	5	1	-	-	-	-	-	-	-	-
21	130	43	60	20	6	1	-	-	-	-	-	-	-
22	264	86	105	59	14	-	-	-	-	-	-	-	-
23	556	183	203	126	37	5	2	-	-	-	-	-	-
24	893	304	330	172	70	17	-	-	-	-	-	-	-
20-24	1,894	637	722	382	128	23	2	-	-	-	-	-	-
25	1,360	474	440	273	121	48	4	-	-	-	-	-	-
26	1,901	652	641	379	170	51	4	3	1	-	-	-	-
27	2,479	821	816	512	233	69	19	9	-	-	-	-	-
28	2,849	892	945	623	256	100	22	8	3	-	-	-	-
29	3,275	1,029	1,071	718	302	112	28	10	5	-	-	-	-
25-29	11,864	3,868	3,913	2,505	1,082	380	77	30	9	-	-	-	-
30	3,417	1,004	1,173	746	329	110	34	17	2	2	-	-	-
31	3,443	941	1,170	770	369	141	38	10	3	1	-	-	-
32	3,360	892	1,161	759	343	139	35	20	10	1	-	-	-
33	3,114	799	1,042	711	352	125	51	21	7	5	1	-	-
34	2,903	711	954	703	340	130	40	14	7	4	-	-	-
30-34	16,237	4,347	5,500	3,689	1,733	645	198	82	29	13	1	-	-
35	2,573	609	855	619	314	103	45	12	12	2	2	-	-
36	2,248	501	704	565	308	100	30	13	11	10	4	2	-
37	1,777	361	518	472	268	99	39	11	5	3	1	-	-
38	1,424	260	442	355	200	99	37	15	9	1	4	2	-
39	1,091	180	296	297	181	76	34	16	5	5	-	1	-
35-39	9,113	1,911	2,815	2,308	1,271	477	185	67	42	21	11	5	-
40	822	131	206	237	136	57	32	9	8	4	2	-	-
41	560	81	137	146	106	53	21	8	2	2	3	1	-
42	362	43	93	95	64	34	14	8	6	4	1	-	-
43	238	24	52	64	50	23	12	9	2	1	1	-	-
44	107	8	24	27	25	13	8	1	1	-	-	-	-
40-44	2,089	287	512	569	381	180	87	35	19	11	7	1	-
45	50	7	9	18	8	6	2	-	-	-	-	-	-
46	23	3	3	1	9	4	1	1	1	-	-	-	-
47	9	-	3	1	4	1	-	-	-	-	-	-	-
48	5	-	-	1	-	2	1	-	1	-	-	-	-
49 and over	4	1	-	1	-	-	1	1	-	-	-	-	-
45 and over	91	11	15	22	21	13	5	2	2	-	-	-	-

Notes: 1. 51 cases in which age of mother at birth, and 1 case in which the number of previous liveborn children was not stated, have been included with the stated cases (for method of distribution see Introduction).
2. The distribution of live births within marriage in the '10-14' and '15 and over' categories is given below:

Number of previous liveborn children

10	11	12	13	14	15	16	17	18	19	20
5	1	-	-	-	-	-	-	-	-	-

Table 4.3   Live and still births within marriage: previous liveborn children, age of mother and sex, 1990   **England and Wales**

Age of mother at birth	Sex	Number of previous liveborn children												
		Total	0	1	2	3	4	5	6	7	8	9	10-14	15 and over
		Numbers												
All ages	M	260,203	103,199	94,859	40,602	13,623	4,433	1,824	885	393	198	107	79	1
	F	248,114	98,158	91,070	38,792	12,505	4,270	1,718	852	386	174	101	85	3
Under 20	M	5,669	4,285	1,270	108	5	-	1	-	-	-	-	-	-
	F	5,354	4,101	1,152	97	4	-	-	-	-	-	-	-	-
20-24	M	54,674	29,464	18,706	5,186	1,104	187	24	3	-	-	-	-	-
	F	51,961	27,793	17,960	4,995	1,023	161	24	2	3	-	-	-	-
25-29	M	105,163	44,595	39,627	14,756	4,397	1,295	355	108	25	4	1	-	-
	F	100,327	42,232	38,257	14,060	4,071	1,227	328	109	36	5	1	1	-
30-34	M	68,443	19,532	26,880	14,217	4,949	1,614	727	323	126	52	15	8	-
	F	65,491	18,936	25,747	13,510	4,516	1,606	682	307	113	49	16	9	-
35-39	M	22,251	4,680	7,411	5,445	2,571	1,008	523	298	155	80	47	33	-
	F	21,181	4,467	7,037	5,232	2,324	979	496	324	151	73	52	46	-
40-44	M	3,776	618	947	863	564	309	169	124	74	50	30	27	1
	F	3,588	607	890	871	539	268	166	93	65	39	27	21	2
45 & over	M	227	25	18	27	33	20	25	29	13	12	14	11	-
	F	212	22	27	27	28	29	22	17	18	8	5	8	1
Not stated	M	417	155	128	93	19	10	5	2	4	-	1	-	-
	F	399	146	117	71	38	10	5	6	1	3	2	-	-
Ratio: male births inside marriage per 1,000 female births inside marriage														
All ages		1,049	1,051	1,042	1,047	1,089	1,038	1,062	1,039	1,018	1,138	1,059	929	-
Under 20		1,059	1,045	1,102	1,113	1,250	-	-	-	-	-	-	-	-
20-24		1,052	1,060	1,042	1,038	1,079	1,161	1,000	1,500	-	-	-	-	-
25-29		1,048	1,056	1,036	1,050	1,080	1,055	1,082	991	694	800	-	-	-
30-34		1,045	1,031	1,044	1,052	1,096	1,005	1,066	1,052	1,115	1,061	938	889	-
35-39		1,051	1,048	1,053	1,041	1,106	1,030	1,054	920	1,026	1,096	904	717	-
40-44		1,052	1,018	1,064	991	1,046	1,153	1,018	1,333	1,138	1,282	1,111	1,286	-
45 and over		1,071	1,136	667	1,000	1,179	690	1,136	1,706	722	1,500	2,800	1,375	-

Notes: 1. 816 cases in which the age of mother at birth, and 188 cases in which the number of previous liveborn children was not stated have been included with the stated cases (for method of distribution see Introduction).
2. The distribution of births within the '10-14' and '15 and over' categories is given below.

Number of previous liveborn children								
10	11	12	13	14	15	16	17	18
87	41	20	14	2	2	2	-	-

Table 5.1 First live births within marriage: duration of marriage and age of mother, 1980-1990
a. all married women

England and Wales

Year	All durations	Completed months		Completed years												
		0-7	8-11	0	1	2	3	4	5	6	7	8	9	10-14	15-19	20 and over
Age of mother at birth: All ages																
1980	**240,975**	39,329	18,704	58,033	49,048	36,727	28,401	21,867	15,921	10,940	7,611	4,567	2,912	4,403	486	59
1981	**224,290**	35,830	17,210	53,040	47,300	36,220	25,250	18,830	14,490	9,920	6,950	4,410	2,750	4,520	550	70
1982	**211,862**	33,595	16,157	49,752	44,587	34,822	24,341	17,593	12,728	9,066	6,489	4,290	2,910	4,749	480	55
1983	**211,753**	32,824	16,431	49,255	44,272	34,657	25,877	17,628	12,383	8,689	6,289	4,149	2,896	5,059	544	55
1984	**210,421**	32,573	16,785	49,358	44,596	33,207	25,084	18,549	12,447	8,373	5,863	4,165	3,027	5,105	600	47
1985	**212,017**	33,675	17,592	51,267	46,184	33,118	23,575	17,985	12,765	8,408	5,910	3,888	2,890	5,356	612	59
1986	**206,943**	32,935	17,567	50,502	45,742	32,610	22,798	16,205	12,326	8,465	5,590	3,696	2,650	5,519	782	58
1987	**209,971**	32,125	17,706	49,831	46,949	33,949	23,921	16,584	11,502	8,484	6,020	3,787	2,587	5,459	822	76
1988	**209,291**	31,367	18,637	50,004	47,604	33,689	23,738	16,525	11,269	7,872	5,787	3,932	2,626	5,207	950	88
1989	**200,970**	29,341	17,849	47,190	46,149	32,780	22,733	15,840	10,914	7,434	5,383	3,868	2,594	5,127	876	82
1990	**200,394**	27,130	18,024	45,154	46,764	32,856	23,345	15,762	11,117	7,533	5,158	3,633	2,705	5,410	871	86
Under 20																
1980	**28,189**	17,277	4,147	21,424	5,784	869	106	6	-	-	-	-	-	-	-	-
1981	**23,650**	14,400	3,500	17,900	5,000	700	50	-	-	-	-	-	-	-	-	-
1982	**21,071**	12,931	3,097	16,028	4,205	732	100	6	-	-	-	-	-	-	-	-
1983	**18,723**	11,557	2,825	14,382	3,696	546	93	6	-	-	-	-	-	-	-	-
1984	**16,865**	10,232	2,735	12,967	3,337	477	76	8	-	-	-	-	-	-	-	-
1985	**15,811**	9,497	2,599	12,096	3,185	457	70	3	-	-	-	-	-	-	-	-
1986	**13,837**	8,383	2,283	10,666	2,767	351	48	5	-	-	-	-	-	-	-	-
1987	**11,882**	7,294	1,951	9,245	2,238	333	61	5	-	-	-	-	-	-	-	-
1988	**10,695**	6,211	1,878	8,089	2,215	344	38	9	-	-	-	-	-	-	-	-
1989	**9,180**	5,204	1,616	6,820	1,953	350	53	4	-	-	-	-	-	-	-	-
1990	**8,334**	4,429	1,534	5,963	1,970	333	64	4	-	-	-	-	-	-	-	-
20-24																
1980	**96,393**	15,378	9,198	24,576	27,779	20,651	12,984	6,903	2,673	666	120	37	4	-	-	-
1981	**89,460**	14,940	8,240	23,180	26,940	19,720	10,880	5,630	2,360	640	90	20	10	-	-	-
1982	**84,438**	14,063	8,010	22,073	25,288	19,007	10,358	5,153	1,940	489	113	12	5	-	-	-
1983	**82,829**	13,962	8,229	22,191	24,672	18,304	10,755	4,659	1,710	443	77	17	1	-	-	-
1984	**80,585**	14,396	8,264	22,660	24,399	16,999	9,891	4,570	1,595	389	68	11	3	-	-	-
1985	**78,992**	15,162	8,681	23,843	24,341	16,020	8,659	4,259	1,450	353	55	10	2	-	-	-
1986	**74,695**	14,877	8,570	23,447	23,315	14,918	7,822	3,524	1,264	326	67	10	2	-	-	-
1987	**71,957**	14,427	8,297	22,724	22,977	14,211	7,476	3,252	1,017	231	56	11	2	-	-	-
1988	**68,919**	13,955	8,643	22,598	22,269	13,344	6,744	2,814	872	204	61	12	1	-	-	-
1989	**62,068**	12,558	7,909	20,467	20,357	12,010	5,873	2,367	754	192	32	11	5	-	-	-
1990	**56,995**	11,029	7,457	18,486	18,952	11,068	5,541	2,115	618	160	33	15	7	-	-	-
25-29																
1980	**81,554**	4,411	3,509	7,920	10,790	11,581	12,201	12,166	10,603	7,806	4,903	2,282	944	358	-	-
1981	**77,200**	4,200	3,610	7,810	10,770	11,680	11,410	10,620	9,770	7,100	4,550	2,170	860	450	-	-
1982	**73,585**	4,349	3,350	7,699	10,488	11,434	11,045	10,071	8,500	6,452	4,203	2,192	1,003	498	-	-
1983	**75,876**	4,794	3,604	8,398	11,151	12,037	11,865	10,335	8,333	6,080	3,956	2,159	1,007	555	-	-
1984	**77,208**	5,153	3,838	8,991	11,936	11,900	12,018	11,122	8,315	5,687	3,641	2,037	1,055	506	-	-
1985	**79,906**	6,060	4,218	10,278	13,062	12,647	11,735	10,920	8,629	5,614	3,603	1,900	973	545	-	-
1986	**79,255**	6,359	4,571	10,930	13,938	12,953	11,558	9,769	8,278	5,623	3,239	1,670	802	495	-	-
1987	**83,941**	6,760	4,919	11,679	15,343	14,507	12,585	10,254	7,761	5,569	3,398	1,604	773	468	-	-
1988	**85,848**	7,288	5,468	12,756	16,457	14,895	12,950	10,388	7,533	5,038	3,120	1,644	697	370	-	-
1989	**83,978**	7,361	5,539	12,900	16,675	15,028	12,644	9,838	7,150	4,506	2,785	1,519	627	306	-	-
1990	**86,432**	7,422	5,929	13,351	17,839	15,659	13,166	9,937	7,078	4,486	2,554	1,371	678	313	-	-
30 and over																
1980	**34,839**	2,263	1,850	4,113	4,695	3,626	3,110	2,792	2,645	2,468	2,588	2,248	1,964	4,045	486	59
1981	**33,980**	2,310	1,860	4,170	4,590	4,120	2,900	2,580	2,360	2,180	2,300	2,220	1,880	4,060	550	70
1982	**32,768**	2,252	1,700	3,952	4,606	3,649	2,838	2,363	2,288	2,125	2,173	2,086	1,902	4,251	480	55
1983	**34,325**	2,511	1,773	4,284	4,753	3,770	3,164	2,628	2,340	2,166	2,256	1,973	1,888	4,504	544	55
1984	**35,763**	2,792	1,948	4,740	4,924	3,831	3,099	2,849	2,537	2,297	2,154	2,117	1,969	4,599	600	47
1985	**37,308**	2,956	2,094	5,050	5,596	3,994	3,111	2,803	2,686	2,441	2,252	1,978	1,915	4,811	612	59
1986	**39,156**	3,316	2,143	5,459	5,722	4,388	3,370	2,907	2,784	2,516	2,284	2,016	1,846	5,024	782	58
1987	**42,191**	3,652	2,543	6,195	6,391	4,898	3,799	3,073	2,723	2,684	2,565	2,172	1,812	4,983	820	76
1988	**43,829**	3,913	2,648	6,561	6,663	5,106	4,006	3,314	2,864	2,630	2,606	2,276	1,928	4,837	950	88
1989	**45,744**	4,218	2,785	7,003	7,164	5,392	4,163	3,631	3,010	2,736	2,566	2,338	1,962	4,821	876	82
1990	**48,633**	4,250	3,104	7,354	8,003	5,796	4,574	3,706	3,421	2,887	2,571	2,247	2,020	5,097	871	86

Note: 1981 live births are based on a 10 per cent sample.

Table 5.1 First live births within marriage: duration of marriage and age of mother, 1980-1990
b. women married once only

England and Wales

Year	All durations	Completed months		Completed years												
		0-7	8-11	0	1	2	3	4	5	6	7	8	9	10-14	15-19	20 and over
Age of mother at birth: All ages																
1980	**231,270**	36,892	17,419	54,311	46,300	35,282	27,634	21,432	15,664	10,799	7,532	4,514	2,882	4,376	478	66
1981	**214,840**	33,440	15,910	49,350	45,000	34,860	24,470	18,240	14,180	9,770	6,810	4,360	2,700	4,500	540	70
1982	**202,166**	31,233	14,934	46,167	41,859	33,294	23,562	17,163	12,462	8,910	6,384	4,238	2,878	4,716	478	55
1983	**201,487**	30,305	15,168	45,473	41,388	33,126	25,016	17,156	12,093	8,521	6,164	4,094	2,853	5,007	541	55
1984	**199,827**	29,953	15,363	45,316	41,792	31,656	24,241	18,038	12,140	8,170	5,736	4,092	2,964	5,038	597	47
1985	**200,955**	30,794	16,183	46,977	43,092	31,675	22,737	17,448	12,429	8,214	5,782	3,820	2,839	5,276	607	59
1986	**195,907**	30,012	16,174	46,186	42,858	31,094	21,927	15,656	11,999	8,259	5,449	3,625	2,592	5,424	780	58
1987	**198,325**	29,066	16,190	45,256	43,820	32,340	23,057	16,072	11,191	8,261	5,842	3,695	2,535	5,368	812	76
1988	**197,779**	28,204	17,154	45,358	44,602	32,140	22,902	15,979	10,947	7,662	5,620	3,831	2,569	5,136	945	88
1989	**189,944**	26,409	16,422	42,831	43,274	31,261	21,920	15,298	10,615	7,221	5,241	3,777	2,525	5,033	866	82
1990	**189,322**	24,304	16,547	40,851	43,751	31,374	22,498	15,280	10,778	7,320	5,024	3,547	2,655	5,296	862	86
Under 20																
1980	**28,146**	17,248	4,141	21,389	5,778	867	106	6	-	-	-	-	-	-	-	-
1981	**23,580**	14,350	3,480	17,830	5,000	710	50	-	-	-	-	-	-	-	-	-
1982	**21,052**	12,916	3,096	16,012	4,204	730	100	6	-	-	-	-	-	-	-	-
1983	**18,687**	11,532	2,820	14,352	3,692	545	92	6	-	-	-	-	-	-	-	-
1984	**16,850**	10,221	2,733	12,954	3,335	477	76	8	-	-	-	-	-	-	-	-
1985	**15,786**	9,484	2,595	12,079	3,180	455	69	3	-	-	-	-	-	-	-	-
1986	**13,813**	8,370	2,278	10,648	2,761	351	48	5	-	-	-	-	-	-	-	-
1987	**11,864**	7,283	1,950	9,233	2,232	333	61	5	-	-	-	-	-	-	-	-
1988	**10,682**	6,202	1,876	8,078	2,214	343	38	9	-	-	-	-	-	-	-	-
1989	**9,168**	5,198	1,614	6,812	1,950	349	53	4	-	-	-	-	-	-	-	-
1990	**8,323**	4,422	1,531	5,953	1,970	332	64	4	-	-	-	-	-	-	-	-
20-24																
1980	**95,154**	14,823	9,014	23,837	27,433	20,547	12,949	6,892	2,669	666	120	37	4	-	-	-
1981	**88,260**	14,330	8,020	22,350	26,780	19,560	10,840	5,620	2,350	640	90	20	10	-	-	-
1982	**83,411**	13,606	7,832	21,438	25,007	18,933	10,330	5,148	1,936	489	113	12	5	-	-	-
1983	**81,910**	13,560	8,073	21,633	24,419	18,225	10,736	4,650	1,709	443	77	17	1	-	-	-
1984	**79,716**	13,979	8,112	22,091	24,181	16,934	9,878	4,568	1,593	389	68	11	3	-	-	-
1985	**78,091**	14,710	8,540	23,250	24,102	15,977	8,645	4,249	1,448	353	55	10	2	-	-	-
1986	**73,777**	14,399	8,411	22,810	23,096	14,878	7,805	3,521	1,263	325	67	10	2	-	-	-
1987	**71,038**	13,980	8,127	22,107	22,752	14,156	7,464	3,246	1,015	230	56	11	1	-	-	-
1988	**68,024**	13,519	8,504	22,023	22,017	13,291	6,733	2,811	872	203	61	12	1	-	-	-
1989	**61,354**	12,217	7,777	19,994	20,172	11,968	5,864	2,363	753	192	32	11	5	-	-	-
1990	**56,358**	10,751	7,327	18,078	18,774	11,031	5,531	2,112	617	160	33	15	7	-	-	-
25-29																
1980	**77,373**	3,362	2,895	6,257	9,495	10,928	11,898	12,004	10,546	7,781	4,892	2,273	942	357	-	-
1981	**73,470**	3,280	3,020	6,290	9,590	11,220	11,110	10,420	9,720	7,090	4,540	2,160	860	470	-	-
1982	**69,355**	3,282	2,784	6,066	9,179	10,734	10,712	9,925	8,432	6,426	4,196	2,189	1,001	495	-	-
1983	**71,485**	3,673	2,997	6,670	9,754	11,359	11,515	10,198	8,273	6,057	3,941	2,157	1,006	555	-	-
1984	**72,770**	3,985	3,172	7,157	10,609	11,217	11,699	10,955	8,248	5,662	3,632	2,034	1,053	504	-	-
1985	**75,516**	4,811	3,583	8,394	11,713	12,041	11,434	10,762	8,570	5,595	3,592	1,899	973	543	-	-
1986	**75,083**	5,172	3,928	9,100	12,700	12,368	11,283	9,616	8,224	5,599	3,232	1,667	801	493	-	-
1987	**79,649**	5,530	4,272	9,802	14,004	13,889	12,324	10,145	7,713	5,547	3,388	1,600	772	465	-	-
1988	**81,530**	6,000	4,821	10,821	15,141	14,278	12,722	10,253	7,476	5,020	3,112	1,643	694	370	-	-
1989	**80,080**	6,193	4,919	11,112	15,550	14,474	12,406	9,720	7,114	4,481	2,779	1,514	625	305	-	-
1990	**82,564**	6,237	5,324	11,561	16,674	15,143	12,932	9,836	7,039	4,474	2,552	1,368	676	309	-	-
30 and over																
1980	**30,597**	1,459	1,369	2,828	3,594	2,940	2,681	2,530	2,449	2,352	2,520	2,204	1,936	4,019	478	66
1981	**29,540**	1,490	1,390	2,880	3,630	3,380	2,470	2,210	2,100	2,040	2,180	2,180	1,830	4,030	540	70
1982	**28,348**	1,429	1,222	2,651	3,469	2,897	2,420	2,084	2,094	1,995	2,075	2,037	1,872	4,221	478	55
1983	**29,405**	1,540	1,278	2,818	3,523	2,997	2,673	2,302	2,111	2,021	2,146	1,920	1,846	4,452	541	55
1984	**30,491**	1,768	1,346	3,114	3,667	3,028	2,588	2,507	2,299	2,119	2,036	2,047	1,908	4,534	597	47
1985	**31,562**	1,789	1,465	3,254	4,097	3,202	2,589	2,434	2,411	2,266	2,135	1,911	1,864	4,733	607	59
1986	**33,234**	2,071	1,557	3,628	4,301	3,497	2,791	2,514	2,512	2,335	2,150	1,948	1,789	4,931	780	58
1987	**35,774**	2,281	1,845	4,126	4,832	3,962	3,208	2,676	2,462	2,484	2,397	2,084	1,762	4,895	810	76
1988	**37,543**	2,483	1,953	4,436	5,230	4,228	3,409	2,906	2,599	2,439	2,447	2,176	1,874	4,766	945	88
1989	**39,342**	2,801	2,112	4,913	5,602	4,470	3,597	3,211	2,748	2,548	2,430	2,252	1,895	4,728	866	82
1990	**42,077**	2,894	2,365	5,259	6,333	4,868	3,971	3,328	3,122	2,686	2,439	2,164	1,972	4,987	862	86

Note: 1981 live births are based on a 10 per cent sample.

Table 5.1 First live births within marriage: duration of marriage and age of mother, 1980-1990 c. remarried women

England and Wales

Year	All durations	Completed months		Completed years													
		0-7	8-11	0	1	2	3	4	5	6	7	8	9	10-14	15-19	20 and over
Age of mother at birth: All ages																	
1980	**9,705**	2,437	1,285	3,722	2,748	1,445	767	435	257	141	79	53	30	27	1	-
1981	**9,450**	2,360	1,270	3,630	2,380	1,370	753	421	355	144	90	51	30	29	2	-
1982	**9,696**	2,362	1,223	3,585	2,728	1,528	779	430	266	156	105	52	32	33	2	-
1983	**10,266**	2,519	1,263	3,782	2,884	1,531	861	472	290	168	125	55	43	52	3	-
1984	**10,594**	2,620	1,422	4,042	2,804	1,551	843	511	307	203	127	73	63	67	3	-
1985	**11,062**	2,881	1,409	4,290	3,092	1,443	838	537	336	194	128	68	51	80	5	-
1986	**11,036**	2,923	1,393	4,316	2,884	1,516	871	549	327	206	141	71	58	95	2	-
1987	**11,646**	3,060	1,516	4,576	3,129	1,609	864	512	311	223	178	92	51	91	10	-
1988	**11,512**	3,163	1,483	4,646	3,002	1,549	836	546	322	210	167	101	57	71	5	-
1989	**11,026**	2,932	1,427	4,359	2,875	1,519	813	542	299	213	142	91	69	94	10	-
1990	**11,072**	2,826	1,477	4,303	3,013	1,482	847	482	339	213	134	86	50	114	9	-
Under 20																	
1980	**43**	29	6	35	6	2	-	-	-	-	-	-	-	-	-	-
1981	**60**	40	10	50	10	-	-	-	-	-	-	-	-	-	-	-
1982	**19**	15	1	16	1	2	-	-	-	-	-	-	-	-	-	-
1983	**36**	25	5	30	4	1	1	-	-	-	-	-	-	-	-	-
1984	**15**	11	2	13	2	-	-	-	-	-	-	-	-	-	-	-
1985	**25**	13	4	17	5	2	1	-	-	-	-	-	-	-	-	-
1986	**24**	13	5	18	6	-	-	-	-	-	-	-	-	-	-	-
1987	**18**	11	1	12	6	-	-	-	-	-	-	-	-	-	-	-
1988	**13**	9	2	11	1	1	-	-	-	-	-	-	-	-	-	-
1989	**12**	6	2	8	3	1	-	-	-	-	-	-	-	-	-	-
1990	**11**	7	3	10	-	1	-	-	-	-	-	-	-	-	-	-
20-24																	
1980	**1,239**	555	184	739	346	104	35	11	4	-	-	-	-	-	-	-
1981	**1,200**	580	210	790	210	150	34	8	4	-	-	-	-	-	-	-
1982	**1,027**	457	178	635	281	74	28	5	4	-	-	-	-	-	-	-
1983	**919**	402	156	558	253	79	19	9	1	-	-	-	-	-	-	-
1984	**869**	417	152	569	218	65	13	2	2	-	-	-	-	-	-	-
1985	**901**	452	141	593	239	43	14	10	2	-	-	-	-	-	-	-
1986	**918**	478	159	637	219	40	17	3	1	1	-	-	-	-	-	-
1987	**919**	448	170	618	225	55	12	6	2	1	-	-	-	-	-	-
1988	**895**	436	139	575	252	53	11	3	-	1	-	-	-	-	-	-
1989	**714**	341	132	473	185	42	9	4	1	-	-	-	-	-	-	-
1990	**637**	278	130	408	178	37	10	3	1	-	-	-	-	-	-	-
25-29																	
1980	**4,181**	1,049	614	1,663	1,295	653	303	162	57	25	11	9	2	1	-	-
1981	**3,740**	920	590	1,510	1,200	601	283	137	55	23	8	5	2	2	-	-
1982	**4,230**	1,067	566	1,633	1,309	700	333	146	68	26	7	3	2	3	-	-
1983	**4,391**	1,121	607	1,728	1,397	678	350	137	60	23	15	2	1	-	-	-
1984	**4,438**	1,168	666	1,834	1,327	683	319	167	67	25	9	3	2	2	-	-
1985	**4,390**	1,249	635	1,884	1,349	606	301	158	59	19	11	1	-	2	-	-
1986	**4,172**	1,187	643	1,830	1,238	585	275	153	54	24	7	3	1	2	-	-
1987	**4,292**	1,230	647	1,877	1,339	618	261	109	48	22	10	4	1	3	-	-
1988	**4,318**	1,288	647	1,935	1,316	617	228	135	57	18	8	1	3	-	-	-
1989	**3,898**	1,168	620	1,788	1,125	554	238	118	36	25	6	5	2	1	-	-
1990	**3,868**	1,185	605	1,790	1,165	516	234	101	39	12	2	3	2	4	-	-
30 and over																	
1980	**4,242**	804	481	1,285	1,101	686	429	262	196	116	68	44	28	26	1	-
1981	**4,450**	810	470	1,280	970	739	436	277	200	126	85	47	30	29	2	-
1982	**4,420**	823	478	1,301	1,137	752	418	279	194	130	98	49	30	30	2	-
1983	**4,920**	971	495	1,466	1,230	773	491	326	229	145	110	53	42	52	3	-
1984	**5,272**	1,024	602	1,626	1,257	803	511	342	238	178	118	70	61	65	3	-
1985	**5,746**	1,167	629	1,796	1,499	792	522	369	275	175	117	67	51	78	5	-
1986	**5,922**	1,245	586	1,831	1,421	891	579	393	272	181	134	68	57	93	2	-
1987	**6,417**	1,371	698	2,069	1,559	936	591	397	261	200	168	88	50	88	10	-
1988	**6,286**	1,430	695	2,125	1,433	878	597	408	265	191	159	100	54	71	5	-
1989	**6,402**	1,417	673	2,090	1,562	922	566	420	262	188	136	86	67	93	10	-
1990	**6,556**	1,356	739	2,095	1,670	928	603	378	299	201	132	83	48	110	9	-

Note: 1981 live births are based on a 10 per cent sample.

Table 5.2 Live births within 8 months of marriage: order of marriage and age of mother, 1980-90

England and Wales

Age of mother at birth	1980	1981	1982	1983	1984	1985	1986	1987	1988	1989	1990
All married women											
All ages	46,851	42,810	30,772	40,166	40,426	41,902	41,250	40,955	40,466	38,472	36,167
Under 16	6	-	6	5	9	10	2	2	-	1	1
16	1,021	780	665	583	452	465	377	320	259	209	166
17	3,549	3,000	2,556	2,175	1,831	1,685	1,426	1,191	980	783	627
18	6,543	5,240	4,785	4,308	3,732	3,456	3,052	2,626	2,257	1,944	1,590
19	6,649	5,920	5,365	4,960	4,687	4,394	4,043	3,669	3,219	2,758	2,472
Under 20	17,768	14,950	13,377	12,031	10,711	10,010	8,900	7,808	6,715	5,695	4,856
20	5,583	5,130	4,653	4,552	4,402	4,539	4,237	3,851	3,574	3,236	2,769
21	4,160	4,230	3,851	3,828	3,912	4,128	3,954	3,868	3,625	3,283	2,880
22	3,296	3,220	3,041	3,182	3,331	3,387	3,536	3,499	3,508	3,214	2,802
23	2,514	2,180	2,496	2,557	2,750	3,042	3,056	3,224	3,171	2,969	2,754
24	1,973	2,070	2,034	2,044	2,343	2,537	2,658	2,785	2,960	2,795	2,553
20-24	17,526	16,830	16,075	16,163	16,738	17,633	17,441	17,227	16,838	15,497	13,758
25-29	6,650	6,470	6,430	6,920	7,469	8,549	8,899	9,393	10,069	10,134	10,274
30-34	3,472	3,310	3,325	3,418	3,612	3,821	4,009	4,410	4,702	4,815	4,999
35-39	1,189	1,080	1,336	1,361	1,645	1,602	1,669	1,773	1,762	1,906	1,891
40 and over	246	180	229	273	251	287	332	344	380	425	389
Women married once only											
All ages	39,798	36,170	33,994	33,347	33,231	34,328	33,838	33,269	32,779	31,233	29,114
Under 16	6	-	6	5	9	10	2	2	-	1	1
16	1,019	780	665	579	450	465	377	318	259	209	165
17	3,537	3,000	2,555	2,172	1,827	1,682	1,424	1,189	980	782	624
18	6,535	5,210	4,778	4,302	3,729	3,453	3,041	2,624	2,253	1,939	1,587
19	6,638	5,910	5,353	4,946	4,679	4,385	4,027	3,654	3,205	2,750	2,465
Under 20	17,735	14,900	13,357	12,004	10,694	9,995	8,871	7,787	6,697	5,681	4,842
20	5,535	5,070	4,627	4,526	4,380	4,507	4,185	3,816	3,542	3,209	2,741
21	4,063	4,060	3,757	3,713	3,822	4,024	3,856	3,768	3,546	3,205	2,826
22	3,021	2,910	2,806	2,984	3,130	3,206	3,321	3,297	3,330	3,076	2,696
23	2,089	1,920	2,172	2,251	2,396	2,727	2,770	2,924	2,875	2,714	2,569
24	1,500	1,530	1,608	1,638	1,941	2,065	2,238	2,371	2,567	2,470	2,257
20-24	16,208	15,490	14,970	15,112	15,669	16,529	16,370	16,176	15,860	14,674	13,089
25-29	4,000	3,950	3,866	4,324	4,719	5,656	6,110	6,559	7,189	7,504	7,646
30-34	1,428	1,380	1,356	1,459	1,605	1,611	1,878	2,080	2,330	2,590	2,690
35-39	357	430	396	378	488	471	530	579	589	673	742
40 and over	70	20	49	70	56	66	79	88	114	111	105
Remarried women											
All ages	7,053	6,650	6,778	6,819	7,195	7,574	7,412	7,686	7,687	7,239	7,053
Under 16	-	-	-	-	-	-	-	-	-	-	-
16	2	-	-	4	2	-	-	2	-	-	1
17	12	10	1	3	4	3	2	2	-	1	3
18	8	30	7	6	3	3	11	2	4	5	3
19	11	10	12	14	8	9	16	15	14	8	7
Under 20	33	50	20	27	17	15	29	21	18	14	14
20	48	60	26	26	22	32	52	35	32	27	28
21	97	170	94	115	90	104	98	100	79	78	54
22	275	310	235	198	201	181	215	202	178	138	106
23	425	260	324	306	354	315	286	300	296	255	185
24	473	540	426	406	402	472	420	414	393	325	296
20-24	1,318	1,340	1,105	1,051	1,069	1,104	1,071	1,051	978	823	669
25-29	2,650	2,520	2,564	2,596	2,750	2,893	2,789	2,834	2,880	2,630	2,628
30-34	2,044	1,930	1,969	1,959	2,007	2,210	2,131	2,330	2,372	2,225	2,309
35-39	832	650	940	983	1,157	1,131	1,139	1,194	1,173	1,233	1,149
40 and over	176	150	180	203	195	221	253	256	266	314	284

Table 5.3 Live births within 8 months of marriage: duration and order of marriage and age of mother, 1990 **England and Wales**

Age of mother at birth	Duration of current marriage - completed months								
	0-7	0	1	2	3	4	5	6	7
All Married women									
All Ages	36,167	933	1,721	2,770	4,234	7,029	8,427	6,573	4,480
Under 16	1	-	-	-	-	-	1	-	-
16	166	12	14	25	34	28	29	15	9
17	627	30	58	71	101	127	131	88	21
18	1,590	65	114	176	268	323	342	187	115
19	2,472	81	147	233	345	558	518	383	207
Under 20	4,856	188	333	505	748	1,036	1,021	673	352
20	2,769	76	141	237	374	590	656	413	282
21	2,880	71	129	202	375	606	716	472	309
22	2,802	59	115	195	289	557	717	502	368
23	2,754	58	116	189	299	572	654	542	324
24	2,553	49	96	175	259	540	598	502	334
20-24	13,758	313	597	998	1,596	2,865	3,341	2,431	1,617
25-29	10,274	230	394	699	1,091	1,887	2,451	2,024	1,498
30-34	4,999	128	253	363	523	869	1,109	1,028	726
35-39	1,891	57	104	163	224	316	421	361	245
40 and over	389	17	40	42	52	56	84	56	42
Women married once only									
All Ages	29,114	701	1,320	2,126	3,457	5,882	6,945	5,207	3,476
Under 16	1	-	-	-	-	-	1	-	-
16	165	12	14	25	34	28	29	14	9
17	624	30	58	71	99	127	131	87	21
18	1,587	65	114	176	268	323	339	187	115
19	2,465	81	146	233	343	556	517	383	206
Under 20	4,842	188	332	505	744	1,034	1,017	671	351
20	2,741	74	139	232	369	589	645	412	281
21	2,826	67	124	194	369	601	711	459	301
22	2,696	53	109	182	279	544	693	483	353
23	2,569	49	103	171	276	542	612	517	299
24	2,257	41	78	147	225	474	542	445	305
20-24	13,089	284	553	926	1,518	2,750	3,203	2,316	1,539
25-29	7,646	148	261	458	806	1,443	1,893	1,532	1,105
30-34	2,690	58	122	172	277	511	634	540	376
35-39	742	20	38	54	95	124	180	136	95
40 and over	105	3	14	11	17	20	18	12	10
Re-married women									
All Ages	7,053	232	401	644	777	1,147	1,482	1,366	1,004
Under 16	-	-	-	-	-	-	-	-	-
16	1	-	-	-	-	-	-	1	-
17	3	-	-	-	2	-	-	1	-
18	3	-	-	-	-	-	3	-	-
19	7	-	1	-	2	2	1	-	1
Under 20	14	-	1	-	4	2	4	2	1
20	28	2	2	5	5	1	11	1	1
21	54	4	5	8	6	5	5	13	8
22	106	6	6	13	10	13	24	19	15
23	185	9	13	18	23	30	42	25	25
24	296	8	18	28	34	66	56	57	29
20-24	669	29	44	72	78	115	138	115	78
25-29	2,628	82	133	241	285	444	558	492	393
30-34	2,309	70	131	191	246	358	475	488	350
35-39	1,149	37	66	109	129	192	241	225	150
40 and over	284	14	26	31	35	36	66	44	32

Table 6.1   Maternities with multiple births: occurrence inside/outside marriage   **England and Wales**
             and age of mother, 1980-1990
             a. numbers

Year	Age of mother at birth							
	All ages	Under 20	20-24	25-29	30-34	35-39	40-44	45 and over
	All maternities with multiple births							
1980	**6,404**	345	1,572	2,315	1,609	487	72	4
1982	**6,277**	336	1,512	2,246	1,532	575	69	7
1983	**6,387**	312	1,616	2,243	1,559	592	61	4
1984	**6,406**	282	1,583	2,270	1,518	655	94	4
1985	**6,803**	320	1,677	2,375	1,628	707	85	11
1986	**7,105**	372	1,633	2,503	1,754	754	85	4
1987	**7,320**	339	1,589	2,671	1,847	766	102	6
1988	**7,622**	337	1,689	2,714	1,966	790	122	4
1989	**7,774**	344	1,641	2,754	2,118	796	118	3
1990	**8,145**	333	1,600	2,892	2,287	920	108	5
	Maternities within marriage							
1980	**5,742**	213	1,357	2,178	1,502	428	61	3
1982	**5,471**	173	1,245	2,044	1,427	519	56	7
1983	**5,535**	147	1,309	2,049	1,436	538	53	3
1984	**5,494**	124	1,259	2,064	1,386	578	79	4
1985	**5,622**	118	1,249	2,104	1,444	621	76	10
1986	**5,755**	124	1,164	2,172	1,564	656	71	4
1987	**5,878**	92	1,131	2,289	1,632	647	81	6
1988	**5,984**	81	1,131	2,279	1,720	667	102	4
1989	**5,988**	75	1,039	2,284	1,844	653	91	2
1990	**6,181**	76	956	2,347	1,940	767	90	5
	Maternities outside marriage							
1980	**662**	132	215	137	107	59	11	1
1982	**806**	163	267	202	105	56	13	-
1983	**852**	165	307	194	123	54	8	1
1984	**912**	158	324	206	132	77	15	-
1985	**1,181**	202	428	271	184	86	9	1
1986	**1,350**	248	469	331	190	98	14	-
1987	**1,442**	247	458	382	215	119	21	-
1988	**1,638**	256	558	435	246	123	20	-
1989	**1,786**	269	602	470	274	143	27	1
1990	**1,964**	257	644	545	347	153	18	-

Notes: 1. The figures include maternities where stillbirths occurred.
        2. Figures for 1981 are not available.

Table 6.1   **Maternities with multiple births: occurrence inside/outside marriage and age of mother, 1980-1990**
b. rates

Year	Age of mother at birth							
	All ages	Under 20	20-24	25-29	30-34	35-39	40-44	45 and over
	All maternities with multiple births per 1,000 all maternities							
1980	**9.8**	5.7	7.8	10.4	12.5	14.4	11.8	6.3
1982	**10.1**	6.1	7.9	10.7	12.8	14.8	11.7	10.9
1983	**10.2**	5.8	8.4	10.5	13.0	14.4	9.8	6.0
1984	**10.1**	5.2	8.3	10.5	12.5	15.4	14.4	7.1
1985	**10.4**	5.6	8.7	10.5	13.0	16.1	12.4	18.9
1986	**10.8**	6.5	8.5	11.0	13.7	16.8	12.1	7.5
1987	**10.8**	5.9	8.3	11.3	13.6	16.6	12.6	11.3
1988	**11.1**	5.7	8.8	11.2	14.1	16.8	14.4	7.8
1989	**11.4**	6.2	8.9	11.4	14.7	16.3	13.4	6.1
1990	**11.6**	6.0	8.9	11.5	14.8	17.9	11.7	9.9
	Maternities within marriage with multiple births per 1,000 maternities within marriage							
1980	**9.9**	6.1	7.8	10.4	12.3	13.9	11.4	5.1
1982	**10.2**	6.5	7.8	10.5	12.8	14.8	10.9	12.0
1983	**10.5**	6.2	8.5	10.5	13.0	14.6	9.8	4.8
1984	**10.5**	5.8	8.4	10.5	12.4	15.2	13.9	7.7
1985	**10.7**	5.9	8.6	10.4	12.7	16.0	12.9	18.8
1986	**11.1**	7.0	8.5	10.9	13.6	16.7	12.0	8.1
1987	**11.3**	5.9	8.6	11.2	13.6	16.3	12.0	12.3
1988	**11.7**	5.8	9.0	11.2	14.1	16.7	14.6	8.7
1989	**12.0**	6.2	9.1	11.5	14.9	15.9	12.9	4.6
1990	**12.3**	6.9	9.0	11.6	14.7	18.0	12.4	11.5
	Maternities outside marriage with multiple births per 1,000 maternities outside marriage							
1980	**8.6**	5.1	8.1	10.2	14.2	19.5	14.4	21.3
1982	**9.0**	5.7	8.2	12.7	13.0	15.3	16.8	-
1983	**8.6**	5.4	8.4	10.9	13.4	13.2	10.1	20.4
1984	**8.3**	4.8	7.9	10.0	13.1	17.0	17.0	-
1985	**9.4**	5.5	9.0	11.2	16.4	16.9	9.0	20.8
1986	**9.6**	6.3	8.7	12.0	14.6	17.3	13.1	-
1987	**9.1**	5.9	7.6	11.7	14.2	18.7	15.4	-
1988	**9.3**	5.7	8.2	11.5	14.1	17.1	13.5	-
1989	**9.7**	6.2	8.5	11.3	13.9	18.2	15.3	16.4
1990	**9.9**	5.8	8.7	11.5	15.3	17.7	9.4	-

Notes: 1. The figures include maternities where stillbirths occurred.
        2. Figures for 1981 are not available.

Table 6.2 Maternities with multiple births: live/still births, age of mother and sex, 1990 — England and Wales

Age of mother at birth	Maternities	Births						
	Total	Total						
		Live				Still		
		Total	Male only	Female only		Total	Male only	Female only
All maternities with multiple births								
All ages	**8,145**	16,274	8,173	8,101		237	122	115
under 20	**333**	656	317	339		15	7	8
20-24	**1,600**	3,188	1,649	1,539		36	22	14
25-29	**2,892**	5,745	2,889	2,856		96	52	44
30-34	**2,287**	4,612	2,295	2,317		55	24	31
35-39	**920**	1,849	906	943		31	16	15
40-44	**108**	214	112	102		4	1	3
45 and over	**5**	10	5	5		-	-	-
Twins only								
All ages	**7,934**	15,648	7,851	7,797		220	113	107
under 20	**328**	641	306	335		15	7	8
20-24	**1,578**	3,120	1,616	1,504		36	22	14
25-29	**2,836**	5,583	2,800	2,783		89	50	39
30-34	**2,200**	4,352	2,171	2,181		48	19	29
35-39	**881**	1,734	846	888		28	14	14
40-44	**106**	208	107	101		4	1	3
45 and over	**5**	10	5	5		-	-	-
Triplets and over								
All ages	**211**	626	322	304		17	9	8
under 20	**5**	15	11	4		-	-	-
20-24	**22**	68	33	35		-	-	-
25-29	**56**	162	89	73		7	2	5
30-34	**87**	260	124	136		7	5	2
35-39	**39**	115	60	55		3	2	1
40-44	**2**	6	5	1		-	-	-
45 and over	**-**	-	-	-		-	-	-

Table 6.3 Maternities within marriage with multiple births: age of mother and previous liveborn children, 1990 — England and Wales

Number of previous liveborn children	Age of mother at birth							
	All ages	Under 20	20-24	25-29	30-34	35-39	40-44	45 and over
Numbers								
Total	**6,181**	76	956	2,347	1,940	767	90	5
0	**2,555**	62	497	1,032	720	221	21	2
1	**2,103**	13	341	835	649	244	21	-
2	**990**	1	96	332	366	173	22	-
3	**332**	-	15	108	129	70	10	-
4 and over	**201**	-	7	40	76	59	16	3
Rates: maternities with multiple births per 1,000 maternities within marriage								
Total	**12.3**	6.9	9.0	11.6	14.7	18.0	12.4	11.5
0	**12.9**	7.4	8.8	12.0	19.1	24.8	17.5	44.4
1	**11.4**	5.4	9.4	10.8	12.5	17.2	11.6	-
2	**12.6**	4.9	9.5	11.7	13.4	16.5	12.9	-
3	**12.9**	-	7.1	12.9	13.8	14.5	9.1	-
4 and over	**13.1**	-	17.6	11.6	13.6	14.0	11.0	13.1

Note: The figures include maternities where stillbirths occurred.

Table 6.4   All maternities: age of mother and type of outcome, 1990 **England and Wales**

Outcome	All maternities							
	All ages	Under 20	20-24	25-29	30-34	35-39	40-44	45 and over
All maternities	**701,030**	**55,535**	**179,317**	**250,670**	**154,553**	**51,259**	**9,193**	**503**
Singleton Births	**692,885**	**55,202**	**177,717**	**247,778**	**152,266**	**50,339**	**9,085**	**498**
1 LM	353,239	28,207	90,738	126,314	77,491	25,669	4,568	252
1 LF	336,627	26,678	86,210	120,518	74,161	24,387	4,438	235
1 SM	1,631	173	419	506	316	163	51	3
1 SF	1,388	144	350	440	298	120	28	8
All Multiple Births	**8,145**	**333**	**1,600**	**2,892**	**2,287**	**920**	**108**	**5**
Twins	**7,934**	**328**	**1,578**	**2,836**	**2,200**	**881**	**106**	**5**
2 LM	2,717	120	609	982	710	255	39	2
1 LM and 1 LF	2,341	62	390	801	735	324	28	1
2 LF	2,689	135	550	977	713	277	35	2
1 LM and 1 SM	61	3	7	30	11	9	1	-
1 LM and 1 SF	15	1	1	5	5	3	-	-
1 LF and 1 SM	16	-	3	6	4	3	-	-
1 LF and 1 SF	62	3	11	22	16	7	3	-
2 SM	18	2	6	7	2	1	-	-
1 SM and 1 SF	-	-	-	-	-	-	-	-
2 SF	15	2	1	6	4	2	-	-
Triplets	**201**	**5**	**20**	**55**	**81**	**38**	**2**	**-**
3 LM	41	3	4	8	17	8	1	-
2 LM and 1 LF	56	1	6	22	14	12	1	-
1 LM and 2 LF	53	-	6	15	24	8	-	-
3 LF	37	1	4	5	19	8	-	-
2 LM and 1 SM	3	-	-	-	3	-	-	-
2 LM and 1 SF	1	-	-	-	1	-	-	-
1 LM, 1 LF and 1 SM	5	-	-	2	2	1	-	-
1 LM, 1 LF and 1 SF	2	-	-	1	-	1	-	-
2 LF and 1 SM	-	-	-	-	-	-	-	-
2 LF and 1 SF	1	-	-	-	1	-	-	-
1 LM and 2 SM	-	-	-	-	-	-	-	-
1 LM, 1 SM and 1 SF	-	-	-	-	-	-	-	-
1 LM and 2 SF	-	-	-	-	-	-	-	-
1 LF and 2 SM	-	-	-	-	-	-	-	-
1 LF, 1 SM and 1 SF	-	-	-	-	-	-	-	-
1 LF and 2 SF	2	-	-	2	-	-	-	-
3 SM	-	-	-	-	-	-	-	-
2 SM and 1 SF	-	-	-	-	-	-	-	-
1 SM and 2 SF	-	-	-	-	-	-	-	-
3 SF	-	-	-	-	-	-	-	-
Quads and above	**10**	**-**	**2**	**1**	**6**	**1**	**-**	**-**
4 LM	1	-	-	-	1	-	-	-
3 LM and 1 LF	1	-	-	1	-	-	-	-
2 LM and 2 LF	4	-	1	-	3	-	-	-
2 LM, 1 LF and 1 SM	1	-	-	-	-	1	-	-
1 LM and 3 LF	2	-	1	-	1	-	-	-
4 LF	1	-	-	-	1	-	-	-

LM-Liveborn male   SM-Stillborn male   LF-Liveborn female   SF-Stillborn female

Table 7.1 Live and still births: area of usual residence, occurrence inside/outside marriage, general and total period fertility rates, 1990

England and Wales, England, Wales, standard regions, Greater London, metropolitan counties, regional health authorities

Area of usual residence	Estimated number of women aged 15-44 (thousands)	Live births			Stillbirths			Live births outside marriage per 1,000 live births	Stillbirths per 1,000 live and still births	General fertility rate (GFR)	Total period fertility (TPFR)
		Total	Within marriage	Outside marriage	Total	Within marriage	Outside marriage				
England and Wales	**10,984,451**	**706,140**	**506,141**	**199,999**	**3,256**	**2,176**	**1,080**	**283**	**5**	**64.3**	**1.84**
England	10,375,620	666,920	478,372	188,548	3,068	2,045	1,023	283	5	64.3	1.84
Wales	608,831	38,866	27,466	11,400	180	124	56	293	5	63.8	1.83
Outside England and Wales	N/P	354	303	51	8	7	1	144	22	N/P	N/P
Standard regions											
North	658,058	40,657	27,327	13,330	185	113	72	328	5	61.8	1.78
Yorkshire and Humberside	1,071,103	68,920	47,822	21,098	308	204	104	306	4	64.3	1.85
East Midlands	874,092	54,808	39,489	15,319	241	161	80	280	4	62.7	1.81
East Anglia	438,576	26,587	20,524	6,063	95	73	22	228	4	60.6	1.75
South East	3,860,274	249,627	184,869	64,758	1,168	806	362	259	5	64.7	1.87
South West	977,076	58,971	44,627	14,344	235	171	64	243	5	60.4	1.76
West Midlands	1,119,847	75,092	53,234	21,858	390	243	147	291	5	67.1	1.94
North West	1,376,594	92,260	60,481	31,779	446	274	172	344	5	67.0	1.93
Metropolitan counties											
Greater London	1,570,995	105,702	73,501	32,201	531	347	184	305	5	67.3	1.92
Greater Manchester	567,276	38,694	24,676	14,018	204	111	93	362	5	68.2	1.95
Merseyside	308,168	20,834	12,640	8,194	98	60	38	393	5	67.6	1.94
South Yorkshire	281,117	17,733	11,999	5,734	90	57	33	323	5	63.1	1.80
Tyne and Wear	240,715	15,010	9,565	5,445	79	43	36	363	5	62.4	1.79
West Midlands	554,188	40,074	27,037	13,037	238	141	97	325	6	72.3	2.07
West Yorkshire	450,340	30,460	21,051	9,409	137	90	47	309	4	67.6	1.94
Regional health authorities											
Northern	658,058	40,656	27,327	13,329	185	113	72	328	5	61.8	1.78
Yorkshire	789,988	51,187	35,823	15,364	218	147	71	300	4	64.8	1.87
Trent	1,018,732	63,571	44,907	18,664	288	192	96	294	5	62.4	1.79
East Anglian	438,572	26,590	20,525	6,065	95	73	22	228	4	60.6	1.75
North West Thames	797,359	50,793	38,690	12,103	217	149	68	238	4	63.7	1.84
North East Thames	854,866	57,999	41,640	16,359	315	215	100	282	5	67.8	1.94
South East Thames	784,206	52,086	35,736	16,350	258	155	103	314	5	66.4	1.92
South West Thames	639,610	40,101	31,043	9,058	152	113	39	226	4	62.7	1.84
Wessex	619,751	38,571	29,459	9,112	162	121	41	236	4	62.2	1.81
Oxford	586,941	36,424	28,368	8,056	181	136	45	221	5	62.1	1.79
South Western	683,846	41,090	30,783	10,307	161	114	47	251	4	60.1	1.75
West Midlands	1,119,846	75,092	53,234	21,858	390	243	147	291	5	67.1	1.94
Mersey	518,668	33,771	22,111	11,660	154	98	56	345	5	65.1	1.88
North Western	865,177	58,989	38,726	20,263	292	176	116	344	5	68.2	1.96

Note: The figures relate to usual area of residence of the mother. Births to mothers usually resident outside England and Wales are included in the total for England and Wales.

Table 7.2 Live births: area of usual residence and age of mother, 1990

Area of usual residence	Age of mother at birth							Age of mother at birth						
	All ages	Under 20	20-24	25-29	30-34	35-39	40 and over	All ages	Under 20	20-24	25-29	30-34	35-39	40 and over
	Numbers							Rates per 1,000 women in age-group						
England and Wales	706,140	55,541	180,136	252,577	156,264	51,905	9,717	**64.3**	33.3	91.7	122.4	87.3	31.2	5.3
Outside England and Wales	354	19	89	113	85	42	6	:	:	:	:	:	:	:
England	666,920	51,725	169,080	238,821	148,586	49,426	9,282	**64.3**	32.9	91.1	122.7	87.7	31.4	5.4
Wales	38,866	3,797	·10,967	13,643	7,593	2,437	429	**63.8**	39.2	102.0	116.5	79.8	26.8	4.2
Standard regions														
North	40,657	4,295	11,490	14,410	7,854	2,224	384	**61.8**	43.2	98.4	115.7	72.7	22.4	3.5
Yorkshire and Humberside	68,920	7,004	19,829	24,179	13,102	4,050	756	**64.3**	42.4	102.4	120.4	75.1	25.2	4.3
East Midlands	54,808	4,607	15,122	19,916	11,145	3,429	589	**62.7**	35.2	97.3	120.9	77.8	25.8	4.0
East Anglia	26,587	1,856	6,958	9,923	5,704	1,793	353	**60.6**	27.8	90.5	122.7	78.3	26.5	4.8
South East	249,627	14,006	55,036	90,182	63,549	22,617	4,237	**64.7**	24.5	79.1	124.2	100.5	38.5	6.6
South West	58,971	3,817	14,462	21,911	13,551	4,389	841	**60.4**	25.1	85.7	122.2	84.7	29.2	5.1
West Midlands	75,092	6,799	20,894	26,315	15,097	5,005	982	**67.1**	39.3	104.2	125.6	83.8	29.7	5.2
North West	92,260	9,342	25,290	31,985	18,584	5,919	1,140	**67.0**	44.1	101.8	122.9	83.3	28.8	5.0
Metropolitan counties														
Greater London	105,702	5,892	23,184	36,355	27,485	10,630	2,156	**67.3**	26.2	76.5	119.6	107.5	45.7	8.6
Greater Manchester	38,694	4,295	10,924	13,192	7,409	2,404	470	**68.2**	48.9	103.2	122.0	81.5	28.9	5.1
Merseyside	20,834	1,994	5,497	7,338	4,358	1,398	249	**67.6**	41.5	100.1	126.1	85.9	30.3	5.0
South Yorkshire	17,733	1,818	5,322	6,291	3,164	955	183	**63.1**	42.6	103.8	117.6	69.5	22.8	4.0
Tyne and Wear	15,010	1,673	4,225	5,141	2,966	860	145	**62.4**	45.3	97.6	112.2	74.9	23.9	3.7
West Midlands	40,074	3,990	11,813	13,616	7,597	2,538	520	**72.3**	45.6	114.8	129.4	85.8	31.5	5.8
West Yorkshire	30,460	3,256	8,925	10,297	5,807	1,815	360	**67.6**	46.7	108.2	122.0	79.3	27.0	4.9
Regional health authorities														
Northern	40,656	4,294	11,490	14,410	7,854	2,224	384	**61.8**	43.2	98.4	115.7	72.7	22.4	3.5
Yorkshire	51,187	5,186	14,507	17,888	9,938	3,095	573	**64.8**	42.3	102.0	121.4	77.1	26.0	4.4
Trent	63,571	5,725	18,076	22,851	12,435	3,800	684	**62.4**	37.3	99.0	118.7	74.8	24.7	4.0
East Anglian	26,590	1,856	6,960	9,924	5,704	1,793	353	**60.6**	27.8	90.5	122.7	78.3	26.5	4.8
North West Thames	50,793	2,457	10,333	18,307	13,699	5,052	945	**63.7**	21.1	70.6	122.2	104.9	41.6	7.1
North East Thames	57,999	3,624	14,000	20,522	13,764	5,033	1,056	**67.8**	29.2	87.0	124.8	99.6	39.5	7.5
South East Thames	52,086	3,312	12,306	19,160	12,342	4,206	760	**66.4**	27.9	87.1	130.0	96.5	35.6	5.8
South West Thames	40,101	1,763	7,385	14,047	11,764	4,326	816	**62.7**	18.9	67.2	118.5	111.9	43.1	7.3
Wessex	38,571	2,466	9,474	14,463	8,829	2,826	513	**62.2**	25.9	88.4	126.4	86.8	29.6	4.9
Oxford	36,424	2,112	8,128	13,514	9,103	3,069	498	**62.1**	23.6	78.6	122.8	93.0	34.2	5.2
South Western	41,090	2,746	10,088	15,281	9,353	3,050	572	**60.1**	26.1	85.2	122.2	83.3	28.8	4.9
West Midlands	75,092	6,799	20,894	26,315	15,097	5,005	982	**67.1**	39.3	104.2	125.6	83.8	29.7	5.2
Mersey	33,771	3,100	8,706	11,960	7,264	2,320	421	**65.1**	39.0	95.2	121.9	85.5	29.7	4.9
North Western	58,989	6,285	16,733	20,179	11,440	3,627	725	**68.2**	47.1	105.6	123.3	82.1	28.3	5.1

Note: The rates for women of all ages, under 20 and 40 and over are based on women aged 15-44, 15-19 and 40-44 respectively.

Table 7.3   Livebirths: area of usual residence by birthweight, 1990

England and Wales, England, Wales, standard
regions, Greater London, metropolitan
counties,regional health authorities

Area of usual residence	Birthweight (gramms)												
	All weights	Under 1,500	1,500-1,999	2,000-2,499	2,500-2,999	3,000-3,499	3,500 and over	All weights	Under 1,500	1,500-1,999	2,000-2,499	2,500-2,999	3,000-3,499	3,500 and over
	a. Numbers							b. Percentages						
England and Wales	706,140	6,500	8,924	30,631	116,754	252,688	262,877	100.0	0.9	1.3	4.3	16.5	35.8	37.2
England	666,920	6,166	8,461	29,062	110,537	238,753	247,521	100.0	0.9	1.3	4.4	16.6	35.8	37.1
Wales	38,866	326	452	1,551	6,166	13,814	15,231	100.0	0.8	1.2	4.0	15.9	35.5	39.2
Standard regions													
North	40,657	360	540	1,790	6,833	15,020	15,617	100.0	0.9	1.3	4.4	16.8	36.9	38.4
Yorkshire and Humberside	68,920	652	894	3,190	12,332	25,209	24,890	100.0	0.9	1.3	4.6	17.9	36.6	36.1
East Midlands	54,808	541	649	2,634	8,876	19,992	20,391	100.0	1.0	1.2	4.8	16.2	36.5	37.2
East Anglia	26,587	207	310	1,026	4,051	9,475	10,717	100.0	0.8	1.2	3.9	15.2	35.6	40.3
South East	249,627	2,232	3,124	10,379	40,843	87,881	90,913	100.0	0.9	1.3	4.2	16.4	35.2	36.4
South West	58,971	505	659	2,309	9,053	21,181	23,563	100.0	0.9	1.1	3.9	15.4	35.9	40.0
West Midlands	75,092	784	1,050	3,544	13,025	27,469	27,536	100.0	1.0	1.4	4.7	17.3	36.6	36.7
North West	92,260	885	1,235	4,190	15,524	32,528	33,894	100.0	1.0	1.3	4.5	16.8	35.3	36.7
Metropolitan counties													
Greater London	105,702	1,118	1,426	4,909	18,762	36,944	35,076	100.0	1.1	1.3	4.6	17.7	35.0	33.2
Greater Manchester	38,694	387	542	1,925	7,063	13,906	13,725	100.0	1.0	1.4	5.0	18.3	35.9	35.5
Merseyside	20,834	188	264	893	3,064	6,794	7,531	100.0	0.9	1.3	4.3	14.7	32.6	36.1
South Yorkshire	17,733	168	220	817	2,965	6,457	6,450	100.0	0.9	1.2	4.6	16.7	36.4	36.4
Tyne and Wear	15,010	130	213	665	2,625	5,531	5,758	100.0	0.9	1.4	4.4	17.5	36.8	38.4
West Midlands	40,074	453	580	2,094	7,592	14,769	13,552	100.0	1.1	1.4	5.2	18.9	36.9	33.8
West Yorkshire	30,460	324	450	1,525	5,931	11,217	10,406	100.0	1.1	1.5	5.0	19.5	36.8	34.2
Regional health authorities													
Northern	40,656	360	540	1,790	6,833	15,019	15,617	100.0	0.9	1.3	4.4	16.8	36.9	38.4
Yorkshire	51,187	484	674	2,373	9,367	18,752	18,440	100.0	0.9	1.3	4.6	18.3	36.6	36.0
Trent	63,571	630	776	3,078	10,374	23,187	23,339	100.0	1.0	1.2	4.8	16.3	36.5	36.7
East Anglian	26,590	207	310	1,027	4,051	9,475	10,719	100.0	0.8	1.2	3.9	15.2	35.6	40.3
North West Thames	50,793	482	623	2,202	8,327	17,153	16,969	100.0	0.9	1.2	4.3	16.4	33.8	33.4
North East Thames	57,999	527	741	2,510	10,068	20,632	20,420	100.0	0.9	1.3	4.3	17.4	35.6	35.2
South East Thames	52,086	472	696	2,123	8,249	18,320	18,893	100.0	0.9	1.3	4.1	15.8	35.2	36.3
South West Thames	40,101	357	460	1,562	6,427	14,532	15,852	100.0	0.9	1.1	3.9	16.0	36.2	39.5
Wessex	38,571	362	471	1,584	6,088	13,932	15,420	100.0	0.9	1.2	4.1	15.8	36.1	40.0
Oxford	36,424	268	459	1,456	5,909	12,871	13,816	100.0	0.7	1.3	4.0	16.2	35.3	37.9
South Western	41,090	344	424	1,605	6,226	14,724	16,382	100.0	0.8	1.0	3.9	15.2	35.8	39.9
West Midlands	75,092	784	1,050	3,544	13,025	27,469	27,536	100.0	1.0	1.4	4.7	17.3	36.6	36.7
Mersey	33,771	310	405	1,358	4,947	11,459	12,885	100.0	0.9	1.2	4.0	14.6	33.9	38.2
North Western	58,989	579	832	2,850	10,646	21,228	21,233	100.0	1.0	1.4	4.8	18.0	36.0	36.0

Note: Occurrences where the birthweight was not stated are included in the all weights column only.

Table 7.4   Stillbirths: area of usual residence by birthweight, 1990

Area of usual residence	Birthweight (gramms)												
	All weights	Under 1,500	1,500- 1,999	2,000- 2,499	2,500- 2,999	3,000- 3,499	3,500 and over	All weights	Under 1,500	1,500- 1,999	2,000- 2,499	2,500- 2,999	3,000- 3,499	3,500 and over
	a. Numbers							b. Percentages						
England and Wales	**3,256**	897	542	465	455	442	303	**100.0**	27.5	16.6	14.3	14.0	13.6	9.3
England	**3,068**	848	510	437	432	413	279	**100.0**	27.6	16.6	14.2	14.1	13.5	9.1
Wales	**180**	45	31	27	23	28	24	**100.0**	25.0	17.2	15.0	12.8	15.6	13.3
Standard regions														
North	**185**	48	29	28	28	29	17	**100.0**	25.9	15.7	15.1	15.1	15.7	9.2
Yorkshire and Humberside	**308**	81	52	53	45	38	34	**100.0**	26.3	16.9	17.2	14.6	12.3	11.0
East Midlands	**241**	82	40	29	31	31	16	**100.0**	34.0	16.6	12.0	12.9	12.9	6.6
East Anglia	**95**	24	21	7	10	14	13	**100.0**	25.3	22.1	7.4	10.5	14.7	13.7
South East	**1,168**	298	189	167	166	170	109	**100.0**	25.5	16.2	14.3	14.2	14.6	9.3
South West	**235**	56	37	35	30	37	28	**100.0**	23.8	15.7	14.9	12.8	15.7	11.9
West Midlands	**390**	120	75	58	52	44	29	**100.0**	30.8	19.2	14.9	13.3	11.3	7.4
North West	**446**	139	67	60	70	50	33	**100.0**	31.2	15.0	13.5	15.7	11.2	7.4
Metropolitan counties														
Greater London	**531**	135	91	71	79	80	50	**100.0**	25.4	17.1	13.4	14.9	15.1	9.4
Greater Manchester	**204**	66	29	30	30	20	14	**100.0**	32.4	14.2	14.7	14.7	9.8	6.9
Merseyside	**98**	20	21	20	9	10	9	**100.0**	20.4	21.4	20.4	9.2	10.2	9.2
South Yorkshire	**90**	24	16	17	14	12	7	**100.0**	26.7	17.8	18.9	15.6	13.3	7.8
Tyne and Wear	**79**	21	16	10	10	13	8	**100.0**	26.6	20.3	12.7	12.7	16.5	10.1
West Midlands	**238**	66	53	38	32	26	16	**100.0**	27.7	22.3	16.0	13.4	10.9	6.7
West Yorkshire	**137**	31	26	24	21	12	20	**100.0**	22.6	19.0	17.5	15.3	8.8	14.6
Regional health authorities														
Northern	**185**	48	29	28	28	29	17	**100.0**	25.9	15.7	15.1	15.1	15.7	9.2
Yorkshire	**218**	57	36	36	31	26	27	**100.0**	26.1	16.5	16.5	14.2	11.9	12.4
Trent	**288**	93	47	42	36	41	18	**100.0**	32.3	16.3	12.5	14.2	6.3
East Anglian	**95**	24	21	7	10	14	13	**100.0**	25.3	22.1	7.4	10.5	14.7	13.7
North West Thames	**217**	58	30	30	34	28	23	**100.0**	26.7	13.8	13.8	15.7	12.9	10.6
North East Thames	**315**	69	54	55	40	49	35	**100.0**	21.9	17.1	17.5	12.7	15.6	11.1
South East Thames	**258**	70	44	32	34	40	24	**100.0**	27.1	17.1	12.4	13.2	15.5	9.3
South West Thames	**152**	40	25	17	30	21	12	**100.0**	26.3	16.4	11.2	19.7	13.8	7.9
Wessex	**162**	38	22	22	19	31	20	**100.0**	23.5	13.6	13.6	11.7	19.1	12.3
Oxford	**181**	52	38	25	26	17	9	**100.0**	28.7	21.0	13.8	14.4	9.4	5.0
South Western	**161**	40	22	25	22	23	19	**100.0**	24.8	13.7	15.5	13.7	14.3	11.8
West Midlands	**390**	120	75	58	52	44	29	**100.0**	30.8	19.2	14.9	13.3	11.3	7.4
Mersey	**154**	42	26	24	20	18	12	**100.0**	27.3	16.9	15.6	13.0	11.7	7.8
North Western	**292**	97	41	36	50	32	21	**100.0**	33.2	14.0	12.3	17.1	11.0	7.2

Note: Occurrences where the birthweight was not stated are included in the all weights column only.

Table 8.1 Maternities: place of confinement, age of mother, occurrence   **England and Wales**
inside/outside marriage and previous liveborn children, 1990

	Place of confinement	Age of mother at birth							
		All ages	Under 20	20-24	25-29	30-34	35-39	40-44	45 and over
Total	Total	701,030	55,535	179,317	250,670	154,553	51,259	9,193	503
	NHS Hospital 'A'	11,112	567	2,933	4,456	2,564	540	51	1
	NHS Hospital 'B'	674,793	54,407	173,617	240,937	147,521	48,968	8,850	493
	Other Hospitals	7,210	228	1,441	2,503	2,031	840	162	5
	At home	7,346	272	1,145	2,596	2,324	882	123	4
	Elsewhere	569	61	181	178	113	29	7	-
All maternities within Marriage	Total	501,942	10,947	105,664	203,092	131,906	42,627	7,272	434
	NHS Hospital 'A'	8,722	129	1,952	3,855	2,279	465	41	1
	NHS Hospital 'B'	481,081	10,643	101,775	194,792	125,774	40,672	6,999	426
	Other Hospitals	6,478	120	1,213	2,329	1,896	772	144	4
	At home	5,364	43	654	2,010	1,875	696	83	3
	Elsewhere	297	12	70	106	82	22	5	-

Number of previous liveborn children within marriage:

	Place of confinement	All ages	Under 20	20-24	25-29	30-34	35-39	40-44	45 and over
0	Total	198,675	8,324	56,749	85,761	37,686	8,908	1,202	45
	NHS Hospital 'A'	2,078	73	738	946	286	31	3	1
	NHS Hospital 'B'	193,390	8,130	55,228	83,572	36,632	8,632	1,154	42
	Other Hospitals	2,735	100	689	1,048	631	223	42	2
	At home	448	19	89	187	130	20	3	-
	Elsewhere	24	2	5	8	7	2	-	-
1	Total	183,785	2,409	36,321	77,035	51,967	14,192	1,816	45
	NHS Hospital 'A'	4,169	47	966	1,951	1,047	148	10	-
	NHS Hospital 'B'	174,724	2,316	34,530	73,166	49,377	13,546	1,744	45
	Other Hospitals	2,405	20	424	880	771	266	44	-
	At home	2,356	20	360	990	740	228	18	-
	Elsewhere	131	6	41	48	32	4	-	-
2	Total	78,391	204	10,085	28,482	27,352	10,502	1,712	54
	NHS Hospital 'A'	1,835	8	212	767	666	175	7	-
	NHS Hospital 'B'	73,919	190	9,602	26,800	25,705	9,915	1,653	54
	Other Hospitals	942	-	91	307	338	180	26	-
	At home	1,615	3	163	581	620	224	24	-
	Elsewhere	80	3	17	27	23	8	2	-
3	Total	25,788	9	2,112	8,360	9,331	4,822	1,093	61
	NHS Hospital 'A'	518	1	32	155	236	80	14	-
	NHS Hospital 'B'	24,304	6	2,031	7,936	8,694	4,529	1,048	60
	Other Hospitals	268	-	9	68	109	64	17	1
	At home	661	1	34	185	282	145	14	-
	Elsewhere	37	1	6	16	10	4	-	-
4 and over	Total	15,303	1	397	3,454	5,570	4,203	1,449	229
	NHS Hospital 'A'	122	-	4	36	44	31	7	-
	NHS Hospital 'B'	14,744	1	384	3,318	5,366	4,050	1,400	225
	Other Hospitals	128	-	-	26	47	39	15	1
	At home	284	-	8	67	103	79	24	3
	Elsewhere	25	-	1	7	10	4	3	-
Outside Marriage	Total	199,088	44,588	73,653	47,578	22,647	8,632	1,921	69
	NHS Hospital 'A'	2,390	438	981	601	285	75	10	-
	NHS Hospital 'B'	193,712	43,764	71,842	46,145	21,747	8,296	1,851	67
	Other Hospitals	732	108	228	174	135	68	18	1
	At home	1,982	229	491	586	449	186	40	1
	Elsewhere	272	49	111	72	31	7	2	-

Note: For detailed description of the categories - NHS hospital 'A' etc - see Introduction.

Table 8.2 Maternities: place of confinement, area of usual residence and area of occurrence, 1990

Regional and district health authorities

Area of usual residence	Place of confinement						Health authority of occurrence		
	Total	NHS hospital A	NHS hospital B	Other hospitals	At home	Elsewhere	Same as usual residence	Other than usual residence	Not identified
England, Wales and Elsewhere	**701,030**	**11,112**	**674,793**	**7,210**	**7,346**	**569**	**700,674**	**356**	-
England and Wales	**700,674**	**11,090**	**674,490**	**7,183**	**7,346**	**565**	**700,674**	-	-
Northern	**40,435**	1,212	39,007	3	184	29	39,943	279	213
Hartlepool	**1,283**	-	1,282	-	1	-	1,256	26	1
North Tees	**2,612**	2	2,596	-	13	1	2,147	451	14
South Tees	**4,173**	129	4,012	-	26	6	4,105	36	32
East Cumbria	**2,131**	258	1,855	1	14	3	2,047	67	17
South Cumbria	**2,103**	568	1,522	2	10	1	1,911	181	11
West Cumbria	**1,814**	-	1,795	-	17	2	1,664	131	19
Darlington	**1,657**	-	1,645	-	10	2	1,411	234	12
Durham	**3,071**	-	3,054	-	12	5	1,637	1,417	17
North West Durham	**1,086**	-	1,082	-	4	-	960	122	4
South West Durham	**2,043**	-	2,037	-	6	-	1,714	323	6
Northumberland	**3,535**	254	3,260	-	19	2	2,950	564	21
Gateshead	**2,549**	-	2,536	-	13	-	1,630	906	13
Newcastle	**3,748**	-	3,730	-	15	3	3,675	55	18
North Tyneside	**2,429**	-	2,418	-	9	2	1,746	672	11
South Tyneside	**2,060**	1	2,054	-	4	1	1,959	96	5
Sunderland	**4,141**	-	4,129	-	11	1	3,727	402	12
Yorkshire	**50,816**	1,323	49,010	3	438	42	49,521	815	480
Hull	**4,856**	1	4,812	-	39	4	3,983	830	43
East Yorkshire	**2,124**	1	2,101	-	21	1	1,514	588	22
Grimsby	**2,397**	595	1,777	-	24	1	2,362	10	25
Scunthorpe	**2,602**	568	2,016	-	15	3	1,739	845	18
Northallerton	**1,461**	2	1,450	-	8	1	1,256	196	9
York	**3,369**	12	3,322	1	28	6	3,030	305	34
Scarborough	**1,708**	130	1,559	-	18	1	1,578	111	19
Harrogate	**1,479**	1	1,473	-	5	-	1,398	76	5
Bradford	**5,815**	-	5,759	1	46	9	5,597	163	55
Airedale	**2,338**	12	2,316	-	10	-	1,981	347	10
Calderdale	**2,804**	-	2,783	-	20	1	2,450	333	21
Huddersfield	**2,948**	-	2,930	-	18	-	2,809	121	18
Dewsbury	**2,653**	-	2,638	-	12	3	2,497	141	15
Leeds Western	**4,855**	1	4,779	-	69	6	3,682	1,098	75
Leeds Eastern	**4,920**	-	4,870	1	46	3	4,012	859	49
Wakefield	**1,979**	-	1,943	-	34	2	1,697	246	36
Pontefract	**2,508**	-	2,482	-	25	1	2,077	405	26
Trent	**63,166**	1,049	61,479	1	584	53	58,446	4,083	637
North Derbyshire	**4,513**	182	4,292	-	35	4	2,933	1,541	39
Southern Derbyshire	**7,594**	5	7,524	-	58	7	5,009	2,520	65
Leicestershire	**12,660**	541	11,979	-	126	14	10,720	1,800	140
North Lincolnshire	**3,384**	204	3,135	1	40	4	2,525	815	44
South Lincolnshire	**3,640**	115	3,492	-	30	3	2,722	885	33
Bassetlaw Central	**1,322**	1	1,311	-	10	-	973	339	10
Nottinghamshire	**3,777**	-	3,730	-	44	3	2,884	846	47
Nottingham	**8,604**	1	8,521	-	79	3	8,441	81	82
Barnsley	**3,087**	-	3,064	-	20	3	2,627	437	23
Doncaster	**4,250**	-	4,238	-	11	1	3,978	260	12
Rotherham	**3,689**	-	3,668	-	19	2	3,085	583	21
Sheffield	**6,646**	-	6,525	-	112	9	6,454	71	121
East Anglian	**26,384**	73	24,690	1,183	421	17	25,750	196	438
Cambridge	**3,429**	-	3,057	344	26	2	3,033	368	28
Peterborough	**3,153**	-	3,033	104	15	1	2,728	409	16
West Suffolk	**3,275**	4	2,842	393	33	3	2,875	364	36
East Suffolk	**4,311**	41	4,039	178	51	2	3,799	459	53
Norwich	**5,549**	28	5,301	7	209	4	4,999	337	213
Great Yarmouth and Waveney	**2,428**	-	2,387	2	38	1	2,211	178	39
West Norfolk and Wisbech	**2,231**	-	2,107	95	26	3	2,000	202	29
Huntingdon	**2,008**	-	1,924	60	23	1	1,842	142	24

Note: For detailed description of the categories - NHS hospital 'A' etc - see Introduction

Table 8.2 - *continued*

Area of usual residence	Place of confinement						Health authority of occurrence		
	Total	NHS hospital A	NHS hospital B	Other hospitals	At home	Elsewhere	Same as usual residence	Other than usual residence	Not identified
North West Thames	**50,373**	5	48,319	1,537	490	22	43,405	6,456	512
North Bedfordshire	**3,325**	-	3,253	43	26	3	2,245	1,051	29
South Bedfordshire	**4,880**	1	4,777	21	78	3	4,188	611	81
North Hertfordshire	**2,666**	1	2,634	5	26	-	2,321	319	26
East Hertfordshire	**3,872**	-	3,824	15	31	2	2,296	1,543	33
North West Hertfordshire	**3,462**	-	3,194	206	60	2	2,414	986	62
South West Hertfordshire	**3,376**	-	3,275	76	24	1	2,568	783	25
Barnet	**4,034**	1	3,699	297	35	2	2,160	1,837	37
Harrow	**2,765**	1	2,715	41	8	-	2,074	683	8
Hillingdon	**3,504**	-	3,428	44	31	1	2,839	633	32
Hounslow and Spelthorne	**4,393**	-	4,320	36	35	2	3,120	1,236	37
Ealing	**4,438**	-	4,373	37	26	2	2,099	2,311	28
Riverside	**3,776**	-	3,190	515	68	3	2,745	960	71
Parkside	**5,882**	1	5,637	201	42	1	3,399	2,440	43
North East Thames	**57,576**	1,228	54,913	652	747	36	55,112	1,681	783
Basildon and Thurrock	**4,494**	2	4,462	3	26	1	4,240	227	27
Mid Essex	**4,039**	638	3,290	10	97	4	3,586	352	101
North East Essex	**3,799**	371	3,381	1	44	2	3,543	210	46
West Essex	**3,363**	24	3,282	29	26	2	2,484	851	28
Southend	**4,058**	-	3,956	2	96	4	3,809	149	100
Barking,Havering and Brentwood	**6,187**	2	6,118	12	53	2	4,621	1,511	55
Hampstead	**1,385**	-	1,199	162	22	2	787	574	24
Bloomsbury	**1,660**	-	1,443	183	33	1	1,183	443	34
Islington	**2,803**	-	2,711	51	40	1	1,351	1,411	41
City and Hackney	**3,886**	-	3,750	50	83	3	3,080	720	86
Newham	**4,413**	187	4,188	3	29	6	3,894	484	35
Tower Hamlets	**3,212**	-	3,149	10	50	3	2,954	205	53
Enfield	**3,897**	-	3,839	35	21	2	2,407	1,467	23
Haringey	**3,491**	-	3,354	72	65	-	1,576	1,850	65
Redbridge	**3,237**	2	3,183	24	27	1	1,934	1,275	28
Waltham Forest	**3,652**	2	3,608	5	35	2	3,146	469	37
South East Thames	**51,669**	74	50,514	141	898	42	49,158	1,571	940
Brighton	**3,710**	1	3,625	1	80	3	3,228	399	83
Eastbourne	**2,543**	71	2,420	6	43	3	1,715	782	46
Hastings	**1,924**	-	1,886	1	34	3	1,664	223	37
South East Kent	**3,546**	-	3,497	2	45	2	3,285	214	47
Canterbury and Thanet	**3,659**	-	3,625	-	33	1	3,565	60	34
Dartford and Gravesham	**3,196**	-	3,148	4	41	3	2,809	343	44
Maidstone	**2,810**	-	2,777	2	29	2	2,498	281	31
Medway	**5,262**	-	5,137	3	114	8	4,523	617	122
Tunbridge Wells	**2,399**	2	2,353	8	35	1	2,127	236	36
Bexley	**3,244**	-	3,219	1	22	2	2,474	746	24
Greenwich	**3,485**	-	3,418	6	59	2	2,716	708	61
Bromley	**3,590**	-	3,473	52	61	4	2,823	702	65
West Lambeth	**2,771**	-	2,690	24	54	3	2,185	529	57
Camberwell	**3,943**	-	3,829	13	97	4	3,044	798	101
Lewisham and North Southwark	**5,587**	-	5,417	18	151	1	4,384	1,051	152
South West Thames	**39,739**	7	37,300	1,961	448	23	35,524	3,744	471
North West Surrey	**2,837**	-	2,742	73	20	2	2,485	330	22
West Surrey and North East Hampshire D	**3,968**	-	2,455	1,480	31	2	3,586	349	33
South West Surrey	**2,086**	-	1,950	109	27	-	1,848	211	27
Mid Surrey	**1,878**	-	1,845	20	12	1	1,572	293	13
East Surrey	**2,317**	-	2,264	22	28	3	1,975	311	31
Chichester	**1,898**	5	1,859	2	30	2	1,712	154	32
Mid Downs	**3,791**	-	3,731	3	57	-	3,493	241	57
Worthing	**2,796**	-	2,755	2	39	-	2,237	520	39
Croydon	**4,962**	-	4,834	46	78	4	3,988	892	82
Kingston and Esher	**2,281**	1	2,244	21	14	1	1,828	438	15
Richmond,Twickenham and Roehampton	**2,913**	-	2,813	58	40	2	1,001	1,870	42
Wandsworth	**3,022**	-	2,906	86	29	1	2,036	956	30
Merton and Sutton	**4,990**	1	4,902	39	43	5	3,322	1,620	48

Note: For detailed description of the categories - NHS hospital 'A' etc - see Introduction.

Table 8.2 - *continued*

Area of usual residence	Place of confinement						Health authority of occurrence		
	Total	NHS hospital A	NHS hospital B	Other hospitals	At home	Elsewhere	Same as usual residence	Other than usual residence	Not identified
Wessex	38,251	2,274	34,846	686	412	33	36,617	1,189	445
East Dorset	5,017	-	4,971	2	37	7	4,574	399	44
West Dorset	2,428	3	2,382	1	38	4	1,838	548	42
Portsmouth and South East Hampshire DH	7,182	356	6,757	7	56	6	6,534	586	62
Southampton and South West Hampshire D	5,871	180	5,641	1	47	2	5,437	385	49
Winchester	2,725	123	2,528	17	54	3	2,266	402	57
Basingstoke and North Hampshire	3,159	51	2,831	250	26	1	2,314	818	27
Salisbury	1,520	2	1,492	4	19	3	1,424	74	22
Swindon	3,702	11	3,303	357	28	3	3,400	271	31
Bath	5,264	1,548	3,598	47	68	3	4,788	405	71
Isle of Wight	1,383	-	1,343	-	39	1	1,335	8	40
Oxford	36,126	211	34,580	969	338	28	34,107	1,653	366
East Berkshire	5,446	-	5,258	164	19	5	4,714	708	24
West Berkshire	6,253	20	6,068	120	44	1	5,286	922	45
Aylesbury Vale	2,121	-	1,918	175	25	3	1,682	411	28
Wycombe	3,494	-	3,328	129	34	3	3,012	445	37
Milton Keynes	2,930	-	2,889	3	35	3	2,783	109	38
Kettering	3,753	-	3,721	2	27	3	3,358	365	30
Northampton	4,664	2	4,537	67	53	5	3,958	648	58
Oxfordshire	7,465	189	6,861	309	101	5	7,049	310	106
South Western	40,781	1,310	38,691	41	688	51	39,237	805	739
Bristol and Weston	4,720	13	4,617	-	78	12	3,702	928	90
Frenchay	3,104	3	3,066	-	31	4	2	3,067	35
Southmead	3,031	-	2,996	1	33	1	2,628	369	34
Cornwall and Isles of Scilly	5,579	250	5,216	1	101	11	4,252	1,215	112
Exeter	3,568	529	2,936	-	100	3	3,306	159	103
North Devon	1,679	23	1,634	-	20	2	1,595	62	22
Plymouth	4,377	65	4,207	-	104	1	4,166	106	105
Torbay	2,730	-	2,685	2	40	3	2,470	217	43
Cheltenham and District	2,651	19	2,574	31	24	3	2,169	455	27
Gloucester	4,369	258	4,040	4	62	5	3,880	422	67
Somerset	4,973	150	4,720	2	95	6	4,370	502	101
West Midlands	74,608	1,103	72,773	4	660	68	72,968	912	728
Bromsgrove and Redditch	2,335	1	2,316	-	18	-	1,921	396	18
Herefordshire	2,090	6	2,044	-	34	6	1,839	211	40
Kidderminster and District	1,284	285	991	-	6	2	285	991	8
Worcester and District	3,063	-	3,029	2	31	1	2,625	406	32
Shropshire	5,394	559	4,760	2	63	10	4,875	446	73
Mid Staffordshire	4,159	13	4,104	-	35	7	2,515	1,602	42
North Staffordshire	6,276	5	6,227	-	37	7	6,102	130	44
South East Staffordshire	3,784	226	3,510	-	47	1	2,474	1,262	48
Rugby	1,068	-	1,051	-	15	2	901	150	17
North Warwickshire	2,627	-	2,594	-	32	1	2,200	394	33
South Warwickshire	2,633	2	2,611	-	19	1	2,148	465	20
Central Birmingham	2,999	-	2,972	-	24	3	1,773	1,199	27
East Birmimgham	3,752	-	3,717	-	27	8	-	3,717	35
North Birmingham	2,101	-	2,078	-	23	-	1,746	332	23
South Birmingham	3,718	-	3,684	-	31	3	1,868	1,816	34
West Birmingham	3,984	-	3,915	-	68	1	2,687	1,228	69
Coventry	4,647	-	4,602	-	41	4	4,514	88	45
Dudley	4,086	1	4,062	-	20	3	3,591	472	23
Sandwell	4,442	-	4,411	-	27	4	2,819	1,592	31
Solihull	2,557	1	2,543	-	13	-	2,461	83	13
Walsall	3,850	3	3,829	-	17	1	3,084	748	18
Wolverhampton	3,759	1	3,723	-	32	3	3,593	131	35

Note: For detailed description of the categories - NHS hospital 'A' etc - see Introduction.

Table 8.2 - *continued*

Area of usual residence	Place of confinement						Health authority of occurrence		
	Total	NHS hospital A	NHS hospital B	Other hospitals	At home	Elsewhere	Same as usual residence	Other than usual residence	Not identified
Mersey	**33,523**	-	33,311	1	193	18	31,443	1,869	211
Chester	**2,338**	-	2,316	-	21	1	2,254	62	22
Crewe	**3,469**	-	3,447	1	20	1	2,886	562	21
Halton	**2,082**	-	2,060	-	20	2	-	2,060	22
Macclesfield	**2,103**	-	2,090	-	11	2	1,334	756	13
Warrington	**2,612**	-	2,598	-	13	1	2,404	194	14
Liverpool	**7,199**	-	7,160	-	35	4	5,704	1,456	39
St Helens and Knowsley	**5,015**	-	4,977	-	34	4	2,516	2,461	38
Southport and Formby	**1,286**	-	1,282	-	4	-	1,136	146	4
South Sefton	**2,556**	-	2,533	-	22	1	1,887	646	23
Wirral	**4,863**	-	4,848	-	13	2	4,610	238	15
North Western	**58,601**	514	57,593	1	452	41	57,318	790	493
Lancaster	**1,542**	13	1,526	-	2	1	1,508	31	3
Blackpool,Wyre and Fylde	**3,811**	2	3,779	-	28	2	3,522	259	30
Preston	**2,120**	1	2,097	-	21	1	2,075	23	22
Blackburn,Hyndburn and Ribble Valley D	**4,128**	240	3,867	-	19	2	3,805	302	21
Burnley,Pendle and Rossendale	**3,615**	14	3,574	-	23	4	2,819	769	27
West Lancashire	**1,483**	-	1,474	-	8	1	1,110	364	9
Chorley and South Ribble	**2,857**	240	2,599	-	17	1	240	2,599	18
Bolton	**3,966**	2	3,935	-	27	2	3,826	111	29
Bury	**2,578**	-	2,567	-	9	2	1,763	804	11
North Manchester	**2,469**	-	2,440	-	26	3	1,690	750	29
Central Manchester	**2,128**	-	2,097	-	28	3	1,720	377	31
South Manchester	**2,696**	-	2,667	-	28	1	2,169	498	29
Oldham	**3,412**	-	3,350	-	60	2	3,032	318	62
Rochdale	**3,418**	-	3,377	-	40	1	2,138	1,239	41
Salford	**3,487**	-	3,464	-	19	4	3,063	401	23
Stockport	**3,832**	-	3,797	1	33	1	3,171	627	34
Tameside and Glossop	**3,780**	1	3,751	-	25	3	3,055	697	28
Trafford	**2,968**	-	2,945	-	21	2	1,138	1,807	23
Wigan	**4,311**	1	4,287	-	18	5	3,276	1,012	23
Wales	**38,624**	707	37,462	-	393	62	36,696	1,473	455
Clwyd	**5,305**	2	5,267	-	32	4	4,480	789	36
East Dyfed	**2,719**	2	2,663	-	49	5	1,689	976	54
Pembrokeshire	**1,433**	-	1,414	-	16	3	1,346	68	19
Gwent	**6,355**	-	6,261	-	82	12	5,990	271	94
Gwynedd	**3,001**	123	2,820	-	42	16	2,418	525	58
Mid Glamorgan	**7,777**	2	7,712	-	55	8	7,338	376	63
Powys	**1,463**	577	866	-	14	6	586	857	20
South Glamorgan	**5,832**	1	5,759	-	68	4	5,524	236	72
West Glamorgan	**4,739**	-	4,700	-	35	4	4,665	35	39

Note: For detailed description of the categories - NHS hospital 'A' etc - see Introduction.

Table 8.3   **Maternities in hospitals: area of occurrence and whether live or still births, 1990**

**England and Wales, England, Wales,
standard regions and regional health authorities**

Area of occurrence	Total maternities	Live births	Stillbirths	Stillbirths per 1,000 live and still births
England and Wales	**692,763**	**697,917**	**3,186**	**4.54**
England	**655,801**	**660,724**	**3,023**	**4.55**
Wales	**36,962**	**37,193**	**163**	**4.36**
Standard Regions				
North	**40,227**	40,446	181	4.46
Yorkshire and Humberside	**69,013**	69,464	302	4.33
East Midlands	**48,417**	48,785	211	4.31
East Anglia	**27,978**	28,206	98	3.46
South East	**243,394**	245,421	1,157	4.69
South West*	**58,375**	58,844	235	3.98
West Midlands	**75,613**	76,103	392	5.12
North West*	**92,784**	93,455	447	4.76
Regional Health Authorities				
Northern	**40,227**	40,446	181	4.46
Yorkshire	**50,697**	51,084	210	4.09
Trent	**59,019**	59,399	268	4.49
East Anglian	**27,978**	28,206	98	3.46
North West Thames	**46,910**	47,332	202	4.25
North East Thames	**60,060**	60,536	318	5.23
South East Thames	**50,748**	51,168	260	5.06
South West Thames	**37,881**	38,183	144	3.76
Wessex	**37,817**	38,137	160	4.18
Oxford	**35,912**	36,211	181	4.97
South Western	**40,155**	40,464	162	3.99
West Midlands	**75,613**	76,103	392	5.12
Mersey	**32,744**	33,008	148	4.46
North Western	**60,040**	60,447	299	4.92

* Region of occurrence is not comparable to region of usual address as defined in tables 7.1, 7.2 and 8.2.

Table 9.1 Live births: country of birth of mother, 1980-1990 — England and Wales

Country of birth of mother	1980	1985	1986	1987	1988	1989	1990
a. Numbers							
Total	**656,234**	**656,417**	**661,018**	**681,511**	**693,577**	**687,725**	**706,140**
United Kingdom*	569,069	575,220	579,322	600,734	612,530	607,228	624,160
Total outside United Kingdom	**86,833**	**81,063**	**81,591**	**80,688**	**80,987**	**80,434**	**81,946**
Irish Republic	9,154	6,311	6,188	6,000	6,483	6,561	6,424
Australia, Canada and New Zealand	2,497	2,361	2,470	2,498	2,653	2,772	2,998
New Commonwealth	**55,478**	**52,733**	**52,705**	**51,574**	**50,570**	**49,532**	**49,790**
India	13,458	11,110	10,650	9,991	9,542	8,830	8,570
Pakistan	13,844	13,643	13,559	12,919	12,500	12,249	12,359
Bangladesh	2,736	4,238	4,717	4,845	4,799	5,085	5,618
East Africa	6,625	7,281	7,142	7,181	6,995	6,742	6,590
Rest of Africa	3,415	3,422	3,700	3,965	4,175	4,721	4,954
Caribbean	7,064	4,851	4,674	4,565	4,219	4,032	3,809
Far East†	3,348	3,795	3,934	3,805	4,139	3,847	3,963
Mediterranean≠	3,219	2,802	2,795	2,715	2,621	2,511	2,345
Remainder of New Commonwealth	1,769	1,591	1,534	1,588	1,580	1,515	1,582
West Germany§	2,681	3,376	3,489	3,654	3,732	3,880	4,102
Other European Community**	2,344	1,639	1,610	1,523	1,547	1,610	1,757
Other Europe (including USSR)	4,499	3,495	3,336	3,395	3,484	3,491	3,448
United States of America	2,474	3,109	3,136	3,206	3,272	3,301	3,338
Rest of the World	7,706	8,039	8,657	8,838	9,246	9,287	10,089
Not stated	332	134	105	89	60	63	34
b. Percentage of all live births							
Total	**100.0**	**100.0**	**100.0**	**100.0**	**100.0**	**100.0**	**100.0**
United Kingdom*	86.7	87.7	88.3	91.5	93.3	92.5	95.1
Total outside United Kingdom	**13.2**	**12.4**	**12.4**	**12.3**	**12.3**	**12.3**	**12.5**
Irish Republic	1.4	1.0	0.9	0.9	1.0	1.0	1.0
Australia, Canada and New Zealand	0.4	0.4	0.4	0.4	0.4	0.4	0.5
New Commonwealth	**8.5**	**8.0**	**8.0**	**7.9**	**7.7**	**7.5**	**7.6**
India	2.1	1.7	1.6	1.5	1.5	1.3	1.3
Pakistan	2.1	2.1	2.1	2.0	1.9	1.9	1.9
Bangladesh	0.4	0.6	0.7	0.7	0.7	0.8	0.9
East Africa	1.0	1.1	1.1	1.1	1.1	1.0	1.0
Rest of Africa	0.5	0.5	0.6	0.6	0.6	0.7	0.8
Caribbean	1.1	0.7	0.7	0.7	0.6	0.6	0.6
Far East†	0.5	0.6	0.6	0.6	0.6	0.6	0.6
Mediterranean≠	0.5	0.4	0.4	0.4	0.4	0.4	0.4
Remainder of New Commonwealth	0.3	0.2	0.2	0.2	0.2	0.2	0.2
West Germany§	0.4	0.5	0.5	0.6	0.6	0.6	0.6
Other European Community**	0.4	0.2	0.2	0.2	0.2	0.2	0.3
Other Europe (including USSR)	0.7	0.5	0.5	0.5	0.5	0.5	0.5
United States of America	0.4	0.5	0.5	0.5	0.5	0.5	0.5
Rest of the World	1.2	1.2	1.3	1.3	1.4	1.4	1.5
Not stated	0.0	0.0	0.0	0.0	0.0	0.0	0.0

* Including Isle of Man and Channel Islands.
† Hong Kong, Malaysia and Singapore.
≠ Cyprus, Gibraltar and Malta.
** As now constituted.
§ Including German Democratic Republic.

Table 9.2 Live births: country of birth of mother and area of usual residence, 1990

England and Wales, metropolitan counties, Greater London, London boroughs, selected metropolitan and non-metropolitan districts (where 15% or more of the total live births in 1990 were to mothers born outside the United Kingdom)

| Area of usual residence of mother | All live births | Birthplace of mother outside United Kingdom | | | | | | | | |
| | | Irish Republic | | New Commonwealth | | Rest of the World | | All outside United Kingdom | |
		Number	%	Number	%	Number	%	Number	%
England and Wales	705,786	6,420	1	49,756	7	25,677	4	81,853	12
Greater London	105,702	3,123	3	20,854	20	9,617	9	33,594	32
Inner London	43,012	1,265	3	10,350	24	5,453	13	17,068	40
Camden	2,410	105	4	479	20	496	21	1,080	45
Hackney	3,875	121	3	985	25	555	14	1,661	43
Hammersmith and Fulham	2,197	90	4	271	12	413	19	774	35
Haringey	3,535	161	5	912	26	475	13	1,548	44
Islington	2,823	144	5	434	15	305	11	883	31
Kensington and Chelsea	1,842	26	1	222	12	714	39	962	52
Lambeth	4,354	110	3	949	22	444	10	1,503	35
Lewisham	3,994	90	2	678	17	250	6	1,018	25
Newham	4,434	76	2	1,820	41	209	5	2,105	47
Southwark	4,058	142	4	930	23	297	7	1,369	34
Tower Hamlets	3,230	26	1	1,543	48	193	6	1,762	55
Wandsworth	3,868	87	2	645	17	367	9	1,099	28
Westminster City†	2,392	87	4	482	20	735	31	1,304	55
Outer London	62,648	1,856	3	10,493	17	4,163	7	16,512	26
Barking and Dagenham	2,437	32	1	189	8	31	1	252	10
Barnet	4,075	158	4	714	18	600	15	1,472	36
Bexley	3,272	28	1	189	6	82	3	299	9
Brent	3,971	358	9	1,474	37	453	11	2,285	58
Bromley	3,624	45	1	164	5	194	5	403	11
Croydon	4,990	79	2	810	16	247	5	1,136	23
Ealing	4,462	220	5	1,266	28	449	10	1,935	43
Enfield	3,924	120	3	670	17	211	5	1,001	26
Greenwich	3,520	73	2	361	10	172	5	606	17
Harrow	2,792	151	5	791	28	183	7	1,125	40
Havering	2,919	26	1	81	3	38	1	145	5
Hillingdon	3,545	90	3	468	13	183	5	741	21
Hounslow	3,228	98	3	781	24	234	7	1,113	34
Kingston-upon-Thames	1,772	39	2	122	7	135	8	296	17
Merton	2,610	54	2	452	17	252	10	758	29
Redbridge	3,270	105	3	799	24	132	4	1,036	32
Richmond-upon-Thames	2,130	40	2	124	6	288	14	452	21
Sutton	2,436	34	1	137	6	116	5	287	12
Waltham Forest	3,671	106	3	901	25	163	4	1,170	32
Metropolitan districts*									
Greater Manchester	38,694	365	1	2,770	7	767	2	3,902	10
Manchester	7,344	164	2	701	10	244	3	1,109	15
Oldham	3,432	10	0	547	16	45	1	602	18
Merseyside	20,834	98	0	217	1	336	2	651	3
South Yorkshire	17,733	37	0	628	4	266	2	931	5
Tyne and Wear	15,010	25	0	408	3	263	2	696	5
West Midlands	40,074	371	1	5,492	14	582	1	6,445	16
Birmingham	16,626	228	1	3,418	21	290	2	3,936	24
West Yorkshire	30,460	141	0	3,306	11	504	2	3,951	13
Bradford	7,638	32	0	1,643	22	112	1	1,787	23

* Where 15 per cent or more of the total live births were to mothers born outside the United Kingdom.
† Includes City of London.

Table 9.2 - *continued*

Area of usual residence of mother	All live births	Birthplace of mother outside United Kingdom							
		Irish Republic		New Commonwealth		Rest of the World		All outside United Kingdom	
		Number	%	Number	%	Number	%	Number	%
Non-metropolitan districts*									
Bedfordshire	**8,263**	**172**	**2**	**916**	**11**	**313**	**4**	**1,401**	**17**
North Bedfordshire	1,825	18	1	183	10	94	5	295	16
Luton	3,272	115	4	667	20	52	2	834	25
Berkshire	**11,028**	**148**	**1**	**1,097**	**10**	**564**	**5**	**1,809**	**16**
Reading	2,058	45	2	199	10	103	5	347	17
Slough	1,895	48	3	561	30	61	3	670	35
Windsor and Maidenhead	1,629	20	1	143	9	116	7	279	17
Buckinghamshire	**9,070**	**94**	**1**	**690**	**8**	**443**	**5**	**1,227**	**14**
South Buckinghamshire	676	16	2	30	4	62	9	108	16
Wycombe	2,215	27	1	277	13	116	5	420	19
Cambridgeshire	**9,069**	**45**	**0**	**437**	**5**	**577**	**6**	**1,059**	**12**
Cambridge	1,175	13	1	75	6	129	11	217	18
Hertfordshire	**13,493**	**150**	**1**	**669**	**5**	**528**	**4**	**1,347**	**10**
St Ablbans	1,619	30	2	118	7	96	6	244	15
Watford	1,222	31	3	141	12	44	4	216	18
Lancashire	**19,795**	**81**	**0**	**1,507**	**8**	**287**	**1**	**1,875**	**9**
Blackburn	2,398	11	0	533	22	34	1	578	24
Pendle	1,310	4	0	250	19	17	1	271	21
Leicestershire	**12,750**	**49**	**0**	**1,707**	**13**	**291**	**2**	**2,047**	**16**
Leicester	4,833	21	0	1,365	28	122	3	1,508	31
Oxfordshire	**7,856**	**53**	**1**	**305**	**4**	**613**	**8**	**971**	**12**
Cherwell	1,830	13	1	59	3	230	13	302	17
Oxford	1,337	13	1	136	10	131	10	280	21
Suffolk	**8,551**	**34**	**0**	**169**	**2**	**809**	**9**	**1,012**	**12**
Forest Heath	963	6	1	13	1	340	35	359	37
Suffolk Coastal	1,315	7	1	28	2	228	17	263	20
Surrey	**12,639**	**140**	**1**	**559**	**4**	**795**	**6**	**1,494**	**12**
Elmbridge	1,363	19	1	45	3	145	11	209	15
Woking	1,254	18	1	110	9	78	6	206	16
West Sussex	**8,569**	**47**	**1**	**366**	**4**	**326**	**4**	**739**	**9**
Crawley	1,362	12	1	167	12	57	4	236	17

* Where 15 per cent or more of the total live births were to mothers born outside the United Kingdom.

Table 9.3 Live births: country of birth of mother and father, 1990   **England and Wales**

Country of birth of father	Country of birth of mother					New Commonwealth				
	Total	United Kingdom*	**Total outside United Kingdom**	Irish Republic	Australia, Canada and New Zealand	**Total**	India	Pakistan	Bangladesh	East Africa
Total	**706,140**	**624,160**	**81,946**	**6,424**	**2,998**	**49,790**	**8,570**	**12,359**	**5,618**	**6,590**
United Kingdom *	**566,568**	540,276	**26,264**	3,140	2,170	10,057	1,444	1,308	106	1,165
Total outside United Kingdom	**84,660**	32,350	**52,310**	2,681	668	37,952	7,077	10,976	5,498	5,285
Irish Republic	**6,414**	3,871	**2,543**	2,229	42	94	16	3	-	17
Australia, Canada and New Zealand	**2,426**	1,787	**639**	19	401	67	7	1	1	9
New Commonwealth	**53,859**	15,456	**38,403**	194	83	36,866	6,893	10,937	5,494	5,105
India	**8,746**	2,458	**6,288**	24	8	6,082	4,636	190	15	1,094
Pakistan	**13,354**	2,373	**10,981**	13	8	10,877	84	10,482	29	235
Bangladesh	**5,766**	249	**5,517**	1	-	5,495	29	11	5,443	2
East Africa	**7,822**	1,507	**6,315**	30	14	6,059	1,983	234	1	3,664
Rest of Africa	**4,941**	1,508	**3,433**	27	6	3,270	26	2	-	50
Caribbean	**5,003**	3,063	**1,940**	26	14	1,784	12	3	2	21
Far East †	**3,674**	1,727	**1,947**	24	18	1,547	83	9	-	14
Mediterranean ≠	**2,844**	2,111	**733**	21	9	596	6	1	2	8
Remainder of New Commonwealth	**1,709**	460	**1,249**	28	6	1,156	34	5	2	17
Other European Community	**6,586**	5,021	**1,565**	64	41	181	11	-	-	29
Other Europe (including USSR)	**1,998**	816	**1,182**	21	27	76	2	1	-	8
United States of America	**3,527**	1,460	**2,067**	32	33	69	7	1	-	17
Rest of the World	**9,850**	3,939	**5,911**	122	41	599	141	33	3	100
Not stated	**54,912**	51,534	**3,372**	603	160	1,781	49	75	14	140

Country of birth of father	Country of birth of mother									
	New Commonwealth - *continued*					Other European Community	Other Europe (including USSR)	United States of America	Rest of the World	Not stated
	Rest of Africa	Caribbean	Far East†	Mediterranean≠	Remainder of New Commonwealth					
Total	**4,954**	**3,809**	**3,963**	**2,345**	**1,582**	**7,527**	**2,461**	**3,338**	**9,408**	**34**
United Kingdom *	975	1,219	1,980	1,528	332	5,318	1,135	1,249	3,195	28
Total outside United Kingdom	3,361	1,950	1,870	719	1,216	1,747	1,274	1,990	5,998	-
Irish Republic	11	15	15	12	5	65	22	33	58	-
Australia, Canada and New Zealand	13	7	16	7	6	59	20	33	40	-
New Commonwealth	3,228	1,843	1,605	589	1,172	300	108	53	799	-
India	14	17	81	7	28	32	15	8	119	-
Pakistan	2	6	22	3	14	16	12	3	52	-
Bangladesh	1	5	-	2	2	6	1	1	13	-
East Africa	73	27	33	8	36	36	16	9	151	-
Rest of Africa	3,073	102	8	3	6	34	11	7	78	-
Caribbean	57	1,647	15	4	23	52	9	13	42	-
Far East †	4	10	1,406	5	16	54	8	9	287	-
Mediterranean ≠	2	4	13	556	4	45	28	1	33	-
Remainder of New Commonwealth	2	25	27	1	1,043	25	8	2	24	-
Other European Community	22	20	46	40	13	970	68	67	174	-
Other Europe (including USSR)	4	8	12	33	8	50	926	24	58	-
United States of America	6	16	12	7	3	94	27	1,694	118	-
Rest of the World	77	41	164	31	9	209	103	86	4,751	-
Not stated	618	640	113	98	34	462	52	99	215	6

* Including Isle of Man and Channel Islands.
† Hong Kong, Malaysia and Singapore.
≠ Cyprus, Gibraltar and Malta.

**Table 9.4   Live births: country of birth
            and age of mother, 1990**

England and Wales

Country of birth of mother	Age of mother at birth								Total period fertility rate (TPFR)
	All ages	Under 20	20-24	25-29	30-34	35-39	40-44	45 and over	
a. Number of live births									
Total*	**706,140**	**55,541**	**180,136**	**252,577**	**156,264**	**51,905**	**9,220**	**497**	
United Kingdom+	**624,160**	52,295	163,239	225,675	133,609	41,857	7,238	247	
Total outside United Kingdom	**81,946**	**3,243**	**16,885**	**26,896**	**22,644**	**10,046**	**1,982**	**250**	
New Commonwealth	**49,790**	**1,896**	**10,834**	**16,515**	**13,536**	**5,743**	**1,049**	**217**	
India	**8,570**	155	2,063	3,420	2,043	768	108	13	
Pakistan and Bangladesh	**17,977**	1,332	5,688	4,734	3,629	1,919	489	186	
East Africa	**6,590**	83	843	2,570	2,281	717	96	-	
Rest of Africa	**4,954**	83	698	2,084	1,476	520	88	5	
Caribbean	**3,809**	62	247	896	1,658	808	129	9	
Far East#	**3,963**	69	662	1,457	1,206	518	51	-	
Mediterranean**	**2,345**	97	451	837	702	222	36	-	
Remainder New Commonwealth	1,582	15	182	517	541	271	52	4	
Rest of the World	**32,156**	1,347	6,051	10,381	9,108	4,303	933	33	
b. Age-specific fertility rates: all live births per 1,000 women in age-group									
Total	**64**	**33**	**92**	**122**	**87**	**31**	**5**	**0**	**1.86**
United Kingdom+	**63**	33	90	121	85	28	4	0	1.8
Total outside United Kingdom	**80**	**40**	**120**	**140**	**100**	**50**	**10**	**0**	**2.3**
New Commonwealth	**90**	**50**	**160**	**140**	**100**	**60**	**10**	**0**	**2.6**
India	**70**	40	160	140	70	30	0	0	2.2
Pakistan and Bangladesh	**170**	90	320	210	150	110	40	20	4.7
East Africa	**80**	10	70	130	100	50	10	0	1.8
Rest of Africa	**160**	50	230	250	170	90	20	0	4.1
Caribbean	**50**	30	90	60	80	50	10	0	1.6
Far East#	**70**	10	50	100	110	60	10	0	1.7
Mediterranean**	**60**	30	80	120	80	30	0	0	1.7
Remainder New Commonwealth	**70**	10	110	150	110	50	10	0	2.2
Rest of the World	**70**	30	80	120	100	50	10	0	2.0

Note: The rates for women of all ages, under 20 and 45 and over are based upon the estimated population of women aged 15-44,
       15-19 and 45-49 respectively.
* Includes 34 births to women whose country of birth was not stated.
+ Including Isle of Man and Channel Islands.
# Hong Kong, Malaysia and Singapore.
** Cyprus, Gibraltar and Malta.

Table 9.5 Total period fertility rates by country of birth of mother, 1981-1990   **England and Wales**

Country of birth of mother	1981	1985	1986	1987	1988	1989	1990
Total	**1.80**	**1.78**	**1.77**	**1.81**	**1.83**	**1.80**	**1.86**
United Kingdom*	1.7	1.7	1.7	1.8	1.8	1.8	1.8
Total outside United Kingdom	**2.5**	**2.5**	**2.4**	**2.4**	**2.4**	**2.3**	**2.3**
New Commonwealth	**2.9**	**2.9**	**2.9**	**2.8**	**2.8**	**2.7**	**2.6**
India	3.1	2.9	2.9	2.7	2.8	2.4	2.2
Pakistan and Bangladesh	6.5	5.6	5.6	5.2	4.9	4.7	4.7
East Africa	2.1	2.1	2.0	2.0	2.0	1.9	1.8
Rest of Africa	3.4	3.0	2.8	3.2	3.6	4.2	4.1
Caribbean	2.0	1.8	1.8	1.9	1.8	1.6	1.6
Far East†	1.7	2.0	1.9	1.8	1.9	1.7	1.7
Mediterranean≠	2.1	2.2	2.1	2.0	2.0	1.9	1.7
Remainder of New Commonwealth	2.3	2.3	2.3	2.5	2.7	2.4	2.2
Rest of the World	2.0	2.0	1.9	1.9	2.0	1.9	2.0

* Including Isle of Man and Channel Islands.
† Hong Kong, Malaysia and Singapore.
≠ Cyprus, Gibraltar and Malta.

F*

Table 9.6 Live births: country of birth of mother, occurrence inside/outside marriage and previous liveborn children, 1980-1990

England and Wales

Country of birth of mother	Year	All live births (= 100%)	All births within marriage	Number of previous liveborn children within marriage						Births outside marriage
				0	1	2	3	4	5 and over	
Total*	**1980**	**656,234**	**88.2**	**36.7**	**31.9**	**13.2**	**4.2**	**1.3**	**0.9**	**11.8**
	1985	**656,417**	**80.8**	**32.3**	**29.4**	**12.6**	**4.1**	**1.4**	**1.0**	**19.2**
	1989	**687,725**	**73.0**	**29.2**	**26.6**	**11.3**	**3.8**	**1.2**	**0.9**	**27.0**
	1990	**706,140**	**71.7**	**28.4**	**26.2**	**11.2**	**3.7**	**1.2**	**1.0**	**28.3**
United Kingdom†	1980	569,069	87.8	37.1	32.3	12.9	3.8	1.0	0.6	12.2
	1985	575,220	79.4	32.6	29.6	12.1	3.6	1.0	0.5	20.6
	1989	607,228	71.1	29.1	26.5	10.8	3.3	0.9	0.5	28.9
	1990	624,160	69.7	28.0	26.2	10.8	3.3	0.9	0.5	30.3
Irish Republic	1980	9,154	85.7	27.3	27.6	17.4	7.8	3.0	2.5	14.3
	1985	6,311	79.8	23.9	25.9	17.2	6.8	3.2	2.7	20.2
	1989	6,561	70.2	24.1	22.3	13.1	5.8	2.4	2.6	29.8
	1990	6,424	69.7	26.7	21.5	12.1	4.6	2.1	2.7	30.3
New Commonwealth Total	**1980**	**55,478**	**91.1**	**32.4**	**27.5**	**15.2**	**7.7**	**4.0**	**4.4**	**8.9**
	1985	**52,733**	**91.8**	**27.5**	**27.0**	**16.8**	**9.3**	**5.4**	**5.8**	**8.2**
	1989	**49,532**	**90.0**	**27.9**	**26.2**	**16.2**	**8.8**	**4.9**	**5.9**	**10.0**
	1990	**49,790**	**89.8**	**28.5**	**26.4**	**15.6**	**8.2**	**4.9**	**6.1**	**10.2**
India	1980	13,458	98.8	36.4	31.3	16.9	8.0	3.4	2.8	1.2
	1985	11,110	98.2	30.8	33.4	19.7	8.7	3.2	2.4	1.8
	1989	8,830	97.9	31.4	32.9	20.1	8.3	3.0	2.1	2.1
	1990	8,570	97.6	32.3	33.6	18.8	7.6	3.0	2.3	2.4
Pakistan	1980	13,844	99.4	24.1	24.2	20.9	12.9	8.1	9.3	0.6
	1985	13,643	99.3	20.2	19.2	18.9	16.2	11.6	13.1	0.7
	1989	12,249	98.9	23.0	19.8	18.1	15.0	10.5	12.6	1.1
	1990	12,359	98.7	24.7	20.8	16.9	13.4	10.2	12.8	1.3
Bangladesh	1980	2,736	99.5	21.3	20.6	17.4	12.6	9.9	17.7	0.5
	1985	4,238	99.7	18.6	15.7	16.6	15.2	13.4	20.2	0.3
	1989	5,085	99.2	21.2	18.7	15.1	13.3	11.0	20.0	0.8
	1990	5,618	99.5	24.2	19.5	13.9	12.5	10.7	18.8	0.5
East Africa	1980	6,625	98.0	49.1	34.6	10.1	2.8	0.9	0.4	2.0
	1985	7,281	96.6	38.1	37.2	15.9	4.2	0.9	0.4	3.4
	1989	6,742	94.4	36.2	34.9	16.8	4.9	1.2	0.5	5.6
	1990	6,590	93.8	35.1	35.2	16.8	4.6	1.4	0.6	6.2
Rest of Africa	1980	3,415	87.0	31.3	28.1	14.0	8.2	3.1	2.2	13.0
	1985	3,422	80.2	26.3	25.0	15.8	7.3	3.7	2.0	19.8
	1989	4,721	73.0	27.5	22.9	13.1	6.1	2.0	1.4	27.0
	1990	4,954	68.9	25.9	21.9	12.9	5.1	2.1	0.9	31.1
Caribbean	1980	7,064	49.1	15.8	16.3	9.0	4.2	1.8	1.9	50.9
	1985	4,851	51.4	16.1	17.2	10.9	4.2	1.8	1.2	48.6
	1989	4,032	51.9	14.7	18.4	10.6	5.0	2.0	1.2	48.1
	1990	3,809	52.2	15.8	16.9	11.7	4.9	1.5	1.4	47.8
Far East≠	1980	3,348	94.6	48.6	29.5	11.1	3.6	1.2	0.6	5.4
	1985	3,795	91.3	40.4	32.5	13.0	4.1	1.2	0.1	8.7
	1989	3,847	86.7	37.6	31.0	13.0	3.6	1.0	0.5	13.3
	1990	3,963	88.4	37.7	31.8	13.2	4.0	1.2	0.6	11.6
Mediterranean**	1980	3,219	93.5	39.1	33.9	14.4	4.1	1.3	0.8	6.5
	1985	2,802	90.3	34.0	35.7	14.9	4.5	0.9	0.3	9.7
	1989	2,511	84.4	29.7	32.1	16.5	4.6	1.3	0.3	15.6
	1990	2,345	85.0	29.9	31.6	16.5	5.2	1.2	0.6	15.0
Remainder New Commonwealth	1980	1,769	94.5	46.0	36.2	9.5	2.0	0.7	0.1	5.5
	1985	1,591	93.1	37.9	37.7	14.6	2.3	0.4	0.3	6.9
	1989	1,515	92.0	41.4	34.9	12.1	2.8	0.7	0.2	8.0
	1990	1,582	91.5	40.1	34.4	12.7	3.0	0.9	0.3	8.5
Rest of the World	1980	22,201	92.6	41.4	32.8	12.5	3.8	1.1	1.0	7.4
	1985	22,019	89.6	37.6	31.9	13.2	4.3	1.3	1.3	10.4
	1989	24,341	85.9	37.0	30.0	12.3	4.0	1.4	1.2	14.1
	1990	25,732	84.5	37.0	28.7	11.6	4.3	1.4	1.5	15.5

*   Including births to women whose country of birth was not stated.
†   Including Isle of Man and Channel Islands.
≠   Hong Kong, Malaysia and Singapore.
**   Cyprus, Gibraltar and Malta.

**Table 10.1 Age-specific fertility rates: age and
year of birth of woman, 1920-1975**

Year of birth of woman/female birth cohort	Age of woman														
	15	16	17	18	19	20	21	22	23	24	25	26	27	28	29
1920	0	3	10	23	40	59	84	105	117	131	119	159	164	136	123
1921	0	3	10	23	40	61	90	109	127	123	158	183	147	134	121
1922	0	3	9	21	39	64	91	113	118	152	181	152	138	129	118
1923	0	2	8	21	40	65	95	108	143	182	159	149	136	129	119
1924	1	2	8	21	42	69	93	123	173	164	153	143	135	127	121
1925	1	3	9	22	43	67	101	147	157	156	148	141	134	131	118
1926	1	3	9	23	44	72	124	142	151	150	148	148	142	133	121
1927	1	3	10	24	45	86	124	138	144	149	148	152	142	134	128
1928	1	3	11	24	54	88	123	134	146	153	155	150	143	143	135
1929	1	4	10	27	59	91	117	132	146	158	156	151	148	148	137
1930	1	3	11	30	60	87	117	138	155	162	162	165	160	154	141
1931	1	3	12	32	58	85	119	143	156	162	169	170	162	153	147
1932	1	3	14	31	57	87	123	142	154	171	175	173	160	157	147
1933	1	4	13	32	58	90	125	146	167	180	183	178	172	165	151
1934	1	3	12	32	61	92	128	157	175	188	190	189	179	173	155
1935	1	3	13	33	61	94	137	162	180	190	198	193	181	173	158
1936	1	4	13	35	63	103	141	168	179	191	201	196	184	174	151
1937	1	3	14	35	70	107	147	168	184	198	206	199	188	167	142
1938	1	3	15	40	75	112	150	174	194	204	210	202	181	162	136
1939	1	4	18	44	79	116	156	180	200	208	213	193	174	154	131
1940	1	5	20	48	83	123	162	189	204	214	208	191	169	152	127
1941	1	5	22	52	91	128	169	193	209	210	201	182	162	144	123
1942	1	6	24	54	91	132	169	192	202	202	193	178	159	139	121
1943	1	7	27	57	95	132	167	187	197	191	187	172	154	139	112
1944	1	8	31	63	98	135	166	183	188	189	180	168	155	128	105
1945	2	11	35	66	103	136	166	176	181	181	178	168	145	121	101
1946	2	12	36	67	104	136	161	172	175	179	178	159	139	119	100
1947	2	12	36	66	99	128	151	158	165	169	159	145	130	111	97
1948	3	13	38	67	102	127	147	161	167	160	153	142	127	114	100
1949	3	13	38	71	101	124	144	155	152	148	144	134	125	113	106
1950	3	14	41	73	101	124	142	141	142	141	137	131	123	118	114
1951	3	15	43	75	103	125	129	131	133	130	131	126	126	127	115
1952	3	16	45	77	104	115	121	126	125	128	129	132	136	129	114
1953	3	17	46	78	97	107	115	118	121	122	133	141	138	125	114
1954	4	17	47	73	89	100	105	112	114	127	139	142	133	123	113
1955	4	18	47	68	83	92	101	107	119	134	144	135	129	123	114
1956	4	19	43	62	76	86	95	110	127	136	138	133	129	124	117
1957	4	18	41	57	70	81	98	115	128	131	133	134	130	127	116
1958	4	16	35	50	63	81	100	116	119	127	132	133	132	124	119
1959	4	13	30	46	64	84	102	107	116	125	129	133	128	126	120
1960	3	12	28	45	66	85	96	105	114	122	129	127	130	124	116
1961	3	12	27	47	66	78	90	102	110	119	124	129	127	121	120
1962	3	11	28	47	61	74	86	98	108	115	123	126	123	124	
1963	3	11	27	42	58	71	83	95	105	114	122	122	126		
1964	3	11	24	41	55	68	83	93	104	114	117	123			
1965	3	10	24	39	55	69	81	93	104	109	119				
1966	2	10	24	40	58	70	83	95	102	110					
1967	2	10	25	43	59	72	85	92	103						
1968	3	11	27	45	62	75	84	92							
1969	3	12	28	46	63	72	82								
1970	3	12	28	47	61	71									
1971	3	12	30	45	61										
1972	3	13	29	47											
1973	3	13	31												
1974	4	14													
1975	4														

* Includes births at ages 45 and over achieved up to the end of 1989.

Notes: 1. The age-specific fertility rates refer to 'all live births per 1,000 women' at the ages shown.

2. Live births to women aged under 15 are not included in the calculation of the rate for age 15.

3. Figures for the 1920-22 female birth cohorts at the younger ages are estimated; information on births by age of mother at birth was not available before 1938.

4. Figures along a diagonal line represent fertility experience of different female birth cohorts in a particular calendar year; for example, the bottom diagonal represents the fertility experience of women by age in the calendar year 1989.

England and Wales

30	31	32	33	34	35	36	37	38	39	40	41	42	43	44	45*	Year of birth of woman/female birth cohort
109	93	87	76	68	58	52	43	38	32	25	17	13	8	5	4	1920
109	94	89	75	66	59	52	44	38	31	24	17	13	8	4	4	1921
108	95	86	73	67	61	52	43	40	32	24	16	13	8	4	4	1922
112	94	86	77	71	63	53	46	41	32	24	17	13	7	4	4	1923
109	91	89	78	72	62	55	47	41	32	25	17	11	7	4	3	1924
108	97	90	79	72	65	56	47	40	32	23	15	11	6	3	3	1925
113	100	94	80	76	68	58	48	43	31	22	15	10	6	3	3	1926
120	103	95	85	77	67	57	49	40	29	21	13	9	5	3	2	1927
123	104	101	86	79	67	59	47	38	28	20	13	8	5	2	2	1928
125	109	102	86	79	68	56	43	36	26	18	11	7	4	2	2	1929
136	117	109	91	83	68	54	43	35	24	17	11	7	4	2	2	1930
134	117	107	91	77	63	51	39	31	21	16	10	6	3	2	2	1931
133	116	111	88	72	60	47	36	28	20	13	8	5	3	2	2	1932
137	117	105	85	70	57	44	34	26	18	12	7	5	2	2	2	1933
140	112	97	80	67	53	42	32	22	15	10	6	4	2	1	2	1934
134	104	92	73	62	50	39	28	19	13	9	6	4	3	2	2	1935
128	101	88	70	57	47	34	24	17	12	8	5	4	2	2	3	1936
121	97	83	66	54	41	29	21	16	11	7	5	4	2	1	2	1937
117	94	78	64	47	35	25	19	14	11	8	6	4	2	1	2	1938
112	90	75	56	41	31	24	18	14	10	8	6	4	2	1	2	1939
108	88	67	50	38	29	23	17	14	11	8	7	4	2	2	2	1940
107	80	60	46	36	28	22	19	15	12	8	6	4	2	2	2	1941
96	72	57	43	34	28	23	20	16	12	8	6	4	2	1	2	1942
89	68	54	43	35	30	25	21	15	11	8	6	4	2	1	2	1943
85	66	53	43	37	33	27	21	15	11	8	6	4	2	1	2	1944
83	66	56	47	42	34	26	21	16	12	9	6	4	2	1	2	1945
85	69	60	54	45	34	28	22	17	13	9	6	4	2	1		1946
83	73	64	53	41	34	27	22	16	12	9	6	4	2			1947
92	82	69	56	45	36	29	23	18	13	10	6	4				1948
100	85	69	55	46	37	31	24	19	14	10	7					1949
103	85	68	56	47	39	32	26	20	15	11						1950
100	83	71	59	49	42	34	27	21	16							1951
100	86	72	62	51	44	35	28	22								1952
102	89	76	64	54	45	37	30									1953
103	90	78	67	57	47	39										1954
106	91	81	68	58	49											1955
106	94	82	69	61												1956
109	95	82	73													1957
109	97	87														1958
109	100															1959
113																1960
																1961
																1962
																1963
																1964
																1965
																1966
																1967
																1968
																1969
																1970
																1971
																1972
																1973
																1974
																1975

Table 10.2   Average number of liveborn children: age and year of birth of woman, 1920-1975

Year of birth of woman/female birth cohort	Age of woman - completed years														
	15	16	17	18	19	20	21	22	23	24	25	26	27	28	29
1920	0.00	0.00	0.01	0.04	0.08	0.13	0.22	0.32	0.44	0.57	0.69	0.85	1.01	1.15	1.27
1921	0.00	0.00	0.01	0.04	0.08	0.14	0.23	0.34	0.46	0.58	0.74	0.93	1.07	1.21	1.33
1922	0.00	0.00	0.01	0.03	0.07	0.14	0.23	0.34	0.46	0.61	0.79	0.94	1.08	1.21	1.33
1923	0.00	0.00	0.01	0.03	0.07	0.14	0.23	0.34	0.48	0.67	0.82	0.97	1.11	1.24	1.36
1924	0.00	0.00	0.01	0.03	0.07	0.14	0.24	0.36	0.53	0.69	0.85	0.99	1.13	1.25	1.37
1925	0.00	0.00	0.01	0.03	0.08	0.14	0.24	0.39	0.55	0.70	0.85	0.99	1.13	1.26	1.37
1926	0.00	0.00	0.01	0.04	0.08	0.15	0.28	0.42	0.57	0.72	0.87	1.01	1.16	1.29	1.41
1927	0.00	0.00	0.01	0.04	0.08	0.17	0.29	0.43	0.58	0.72	0.87	1.02	1.17	1.30	1.43
1928	0.00	0.00	0.02	0.04	0.09	0.18	0.30	0.44	0.58	0.74	0.89	1.04	1.18	1.33	1.46
1929	0.00	0.00	0.01	0.04	0.10	0.19	0.31	0.44	0.59	0.75	0.90	1.05	1.20	1.35	1.49
1930	0.00	0.00	0.01	0.04	0.10	0.19	0.31	0.45	0.60	0.76	0.93	1.09	1.25	1.41	1.55
1931	0.00	0.00	0.02	0.05	0.11	0.19	0.31	0.45	0.61	0.77	0.94	1.11	1.27	1.42	1.57
1932	0.00	0.00	0.02	0.05	0.11	0.19	0.32	0.46	0.61	0.78	0.96	1.13	1.29	1.45	1.59
1933	0.00	0.00	0.02	0.05	0.11	0.20	0.32	0.47	0.63	0.81	1.00	1.18	1.35	1.51	1.66
1934	0.00	0.00	0.02	0.05	0.11	0.20	0.33	0.49	0.66	0.85	1.04	1.23	1.41	1.58	1.73
1935	0.00	0.00	0.02	0.05	0.11	0.20	0.34	0.50	0.68	0.87	1.07	1.26	1.45	1.62	1.78
1936	0.00	0.00	0.02	0.05	0.12	0.22	0.36	0.53	0.71	0.90	1.10	1.29	1.48	1.65	1.80
1937	0.00	0.00	0.02	0.05	0.12	0.23	0.38	0.54	0.73	0.93	1.13	1.33	1.52	1.69	1.83
1938	0.00	0.00	0.02	0.06	0.13	0.25	0.40	0.57	0.76	0.97	1.18	1.38	1.56	1.72	1.86
1939	0.00	0.00	0.02	0.07	0.14	0.26	0.42	0.60	0.80	1.00	1.22	1.41	1.58	1.74	1.87
1940	0.00	0.01	0.03	0.07	0.16	0.28	0.44	0.63	0.83	1.05	1.26	1.45	1.61	1.77	1.89
1941	0.00	0.01	0.03	0.08	0.17	0.30	0.47	0.66	0.87	1.08	1.28	1.46	1.63	1.77	1.89
1942	0.00	0.01	0.03	0.08	0.18	0.31	0.48	0.67	0.87	1.07	1.27	1.44	1.60	1.74	1.86
1943	0.00	0.01	0.04	0.09	0.19	0.32	0.49	0.67	0.87	1.06	1.25	1.42	1.57	1.71	1.83
1944	0.00	0.01	0.04	0.10	0.20	0.34	0.50	0.69	0.87	1.06	1.24	1.41	1.56	1.69	1.80
1945	0.00	0.01	0.05	0.11	0.22	0.35	0.52	0.69	0.88	1.06	1.23	1.40	1.55	1.67	1.77
1946	0.00	0.01	0.05	0.12	0.22	0.36	0.52	0.69	0.86	1.04	1.22	1.38	1.52	1.64	1.74
1947	0.00	0.01	0.05	0.12	0.22	0.34	0.49	0.65	0.82	0.99	1.14	1.29	1.42	1.53	1.63
1948	0.00	0.02	0.05	0.12	0.22	0.35	0.50	0.66	0.83	0.99	1.14	1.28	1.41	1.52	1.62
1949	0.00	0.02	0.05	0.13	0.23	0.35	0.50	0.65	0.80	0.95	1.09	1.23	1.35	1.47	1.57
1950	0.00	0.02	0.06	0.13	0.23	0.36	0.50	0.64	0.78	0.92	1.06	1.19	1.31	1.43	1.54
1951	0.00	0.02	0.06	0.14	0.24	0.36	0.49	0.62	0.76	0.89	1.02	1.14	1.27	1.40	1.51
1952	0.00	0.02	0.07	0.14	0.25	0.36	0.48	0.61	0.73	0.86	0.99	1.12	1.26	1.39	1.50
1953	0.00	0.02	0.07	0.14	0.24	0.35	0.46	0.58	0.70	0.82	0.96	1.10	1.24	1.36	1.48
1954	0.00	0.02	0.07	0.14	0.23	0.33	0.44	0.55	0.66	0.79	0.93	1.07	1.20	1.32	1.44
1955	0.00	0.02	0.07	0.14	0.22	0.31	0.41	0.52	0.64	0.77	0.92	1.05	1.18	1.31	1.42
1956	0.00	0.02	0.07	0.13	0.20	0.29	0.39	0.50	0.62	0.76	0.90	1.03	1.16	1.28	1.40
1957	0.00	0.02	0.06	0.12	0.19	0.27	0.37	0.49	0.61	0.74	0.88	1.01	1.14	1.27	1.38
1958	0.00	0.02	0.06	0.11	0.17	0.25	0.35	0.47	0.58	0.71	0.84	0.98	1.11	1.23	1.35
1959	0.00	0.02	0.05	0.09	0.16	0.24	0.34	0.45	0.56	0.69	0.82	0.95	1.08	1.20	1.32
1960	0.00	0.02	0.04	0.09	0.15	0.24	0.34	0.44	0.55	0.68	0.81	0.93	1.06	1.19	1.30
1961	0.00	0.02	0.04	0.09	0.16	0.23	0.32	0.42	0.53	0.65	0.78	0.90	1.03	1.15	1.27
1962	0.00	0.01	0.04	0.09	0.15	0.23	0.31	0.41	0.52	0.63	0.75	0.88	1.00	1.13	
1963	0.00	0.01	0.04	0.08	0.14	0.21	0.30	0.39	0.50	0.61	0.73	0.85	0.98		
1964	0.00	0.01	0.04	0.08	0.13	0.20	0.29	0.38	0.48	0.60	0.71	0.84			
1965	0.00	0.01	0.04	0.08	0.13	0.20	0.28	0.38	0.48	0.59	0.71				
1966	0.00	0.01	0.04	0.08	0.14	0,21	0.29	0.38	0.48	0.59					
1967	0.00	0.01	0.04	0.08	0.14	0.21	0.30	0.39	0.49						
1968	0.00	0.01	0.04	0.09	0.15	0.22	0.31	0.40							
1969	0.00	0.02	0.04	0.09	0.15	0.22	0.31								
1970	0.00	0.02	0.04	0.09	0.15	0.22									
1971	0.00	0.02	0.05	0.09	0.15										
1972	0.00	0.02	0.05	0.09											
1973	0.00	0.02	0.05												
1974	0.00	0.02													
1975	0.00														

* Includes births at ages 45 and over achieved up to the end of 1989 by woman born in 1944 and earlier years.

England and Wales

30	31	32	33	34	35	36	37	38	39	40	41	42	43	44	45*	Year of birth of woman/female birth cohort
1.38	1.47	1.56	1.64	1.70	1.76	1.81	1.86	1.90	1.93	1.95	1.97	1.98	1.99	2.00	2.00	1920
1.44	1.53	1.62	1.69	1.76	1.82	1.87	1.92	1.95	1.98	2.01	2.03	2.04	2.05	2.05	2.05	1921
1.44	1.53	1.62	1.69	1.76	1.82	1.87	1.91	1.95	1.98	2.01	2.02	2.04	2.05	2.05	2.05	1922
1.47	1.56	1.65	1.73	1.80	1.86	1.91	1.96	2.00	2.03	2.05	2.07	2.08	2.09	2.09	2.10	1923
1.48	1.57	1.66	1.74	1.81	1.87	1.93	1.98	2.02	2.05	2.07	2.09	2.10	2.11	2.11	2.11	1924
1.48	1.58	1.67	1.75	1.82	1.88	1.94	1.99	2.03	2.06	2.08	2.10	2.11	2.11	2.12	2.12	1925
1.52	1.62	1.72	1.80	1.87	1.94	2.00	2.05	2.09	2.12	2.14	2.16	2.17	2.17	2.18	2.18	1926
1.55	1.65	1.74	1.83	1.91	1.97	2.03	2.08	2.12	2.15	2.17	2.18	2.19	2.19	2.20	2.20	1927
1.58	1.69	1.79	1.88	1.95	2.02	2.08	2.13	2.16	2.19	2.21	2.22	2.23	2.24	2.24	2.24	1928
1.61	1.72	1.82	1.91	1.99	2.05	2.11	2.15	2.19	2.21	2.23	2.24	2.25	2.25	2.26	2.26	1929
1.68	1.80	1.91	2.00	2.08	2.15	2.20	2.25	2.28	2.30	2.32	2.33	2.34	2.34	2.34	2.35	1930
1.70	1.82	1.93	2.02	2.10	2.16	2.21	2.25	2.28	2.30	2.32	2.33	2.33	2.34	2.34	2.34	1931
1.73	1.84	1.95	2.04	2.11	2.17	2.22	2.26	2.28	2.30	2.32	2.33	2.33	2.33	2.33	2.34	1932
1.80	1.92	2.02	2.11	2.18	2.23	2.28	2.31	2.34	2.36	2.37	2.37	2.38	2.38	2.38	2.38	1933
1.88	1.99	2.08	2.16	2.23	2.28	2.33	2.36	2.38	2.40	2.41	2.41	2.42	2.42	2.42	2.42	1934
1.91	2.01	2.11	2.18	2.24	2.29	2.33	2.36	2.38	2.39	2.40	2.41	2.41	2.41	2.41	2.42	1935
1.93	2.03	2.12	2.19	2.25	2.29	2.33	2.35	2.37	2.38	2.39	2.39	2.40	2.40	2.40	2.40	1936
1.95	2.05	2.13	2.20	2.25	2.29	2.32	2.34	2.35	2.37	2.37	2.38	2.38	2.38	2.39	2.39	1937
1.98	2.07	2.15	2.21	2.26	2.29	2.32	2.34	2.35	2.36	2.37	2.38	2.38	2.38	2.38	2.39	1938
1.98	2.07	2.15	2.20	2.24	2.27	2.30	2.32	2.33	2.34	2.35	2.35	2.36	2.36	2.36	2.36	1939
2.00	2.09	2.16	2.21	2.24	2.27	2.30	2.31	2.33	2.34	2.35	2.36	2.36	2.36	2.36	2.36	1940
2.00	2.08	2.14	2.19	2.22	2.25	2.27	2.29	2.31	2.32	2.32	2.33	2.33	2.34	2.34	2.34	1941
1.96	2.03	2.09	2.13	2.16	2.19	2.21	2.23	2.25	2.26	2.27	2.28	2.28	2.28	2.28	2.29	1942
1.91	1.98	2.04	2.08	2.12	2.15	2.17	2.19	2.21	2.22	2.23	2.23	2.24	2.24	2.24	2.24	1943
1.88	1.95	2.00	2.04	2.08	2.11	2.14	2.16	2.18	2.19	2.20	2.20	2.20	2.21	2.21	2.21	1944
1.85	1.92	1.97	2.02	2.06	2.10	2.12	2.14	2.16	2.17	2.18	2.19	2.19	2.19	2.19	2.19	1945
1.82	1.89	1.95	2.00	2.05	2.08	2.11	2.13	2.15	2.16	2.17	2.18	2.18	2.18	2.18		1946
1.71	1.78	1.85	1.90	1.94	1.98	2.00	2.02	2.04	2.05	2.06	2.07	2.07	2.07			1947
1.71	1.80	1.86	1.92	1.97	2.00	2.03	2.05	2.07	2.08	2.09	2.10	2.10				1948
1.67	1.76	1.82	1.88	1.93	1.96	1.99	2.02	2.04	2.05	2.06	2.07					1949
1.65	1.73	1.80	1.86	1.91	1.94	1.98	2.00	2.02	2.04	2.05						1950
1.61	1.69	1.77	1.82	1.87	1.91	1.95	1.98	2.00	2.01							1951
1.60	1.69	1.76	1.82	1.87	1.92	1.95	1.98	2.00								1952
1.58	1.67	1.74	1.81	1.86	1.91	1.94	1.97									1953
1.54	1.63	1.71	1.77	1.83	1.88	1.92										1954
1.53	1.62	1.70	1.77	1.82	1.87											1955
1.51	1.60	1.68	1.75	1.81												1956
1.49	1.59	1.67	1.74													1957
1.46	1.56	1.64														1958
1.43	1.53															1959
1.42																1960
																1961
																1962
																1963
																1964
																1965
																1966
																1967
																1968
																1969
																1970
																1971
																1972
																1973
																1974
																1975

Table 10.3 Average number of first liveborn children:
age and year of birth of woman, 1920-1975

Year of birth of woman/female birth cohort	Age of woman - completed years														
	15	16	17	18	19	20	21	22	23	24	25	26	27	28	29
1920	0.00	0.00	0.01	0.03	0.07	0.11	0.17	0.24	0.32	0.39	0.45	0.53	0.60	0.64	0.67
1921	0.00	0.00	0.01	0.03	0.07	0.11	0.18	0.26	0.34	0.40	0.49	0.58	0.63	0.67	0.70
1922	0.00	0.00	0.01	0.03	0.06	0.11	0.18	0.26	0.33	0.42	0.52	0.58	0.63	0.67	0.70
1923	0.00	0.00	0.01	0.03	0.06	0.12	0.19	0.26	0.35	0.46	0.54	0.59	0.64	0.68	0.71
1924	0.00	0.00	0.01	0.03	0.07	0.12	0.19	0.28	0.39	0.48	0.54	0.60	0.64	0.68	0.71
1925	0.00	0.00	0.01	0.03	0.07	0.12	0.20	0.30	0.40	0.47	0.54	0.59	0.64	0.68	0.71
1926	0.00	0.00	0.01	0.03	0.07	0.13	0.22	0.32	0.40	0.47	0.54	0.59	0.64	0.68	0.71
1927	0.00	0.00	0.01	0.03	0.07	0.14	0.23	0.32	0.40	0.47	0.54	0.60	0.64	0.68	0.72
1928	0.00	0.00	0.01	0.04	0.08	0.15	0.24	0.32	0.40	0.48	0.54	0.60	0.65	0.69	0.73
1929	0.00	0.00	0.01	0.04	0.09	0.16	0.24	0.32	0.40	0.48	0.54	0.60	0.65	0.69	0.73
1930	0.00	0.00	0.01	0.04	0.09	0.16	0.23	0.32	0.41	0.48	0.55	0.62	0.67	0.71	0.75
1931	0.00	0.00	0.01	0.04	0.09	0.15	0.23	0.32	0.41	0.49	0.56	0.62	0.67	0.71	0.75
1932	0.00	0.00	0.02	0.04	0.09	0.15	0.24	0.32	0.41	0.49	0.57	0.63	0.68	0.72	0.75
1933	0.00	0.00	0.02	0.04	0.09	0.16	0.24	0.33	0.42	0.51	0.58	0.64	0.70	0.74	0.77
1934	0.00	0.00	0.02	0.04	0.09	0.16	0.25	0.34	0.44	0.53	0.60	0.66	0.71	0.76	0.79
1935	0.00	0.00	0.02	0.04	0.09	0.16	0.26	0.36	0.45	0.53	0.61	0.67	0.72	0.76	0.79
1936	0.00	0.00	0.02	0.05	0.10	0.17	0.27	0.37	0.46	0.54	0.62	0.68	0.73	0.77	0.80
1937	0.00	0.00	0.02	0.05	0.10	0.18	0.28	0.38	0.47	0.55	0.62	0.69	0.73	0.77	0.80
1938	0.00	0.00	0.02	0.05	0.11	0.19	0.29	0.39	0.48	0.57	0.64	0.70	0.75	0.78	0.81
1939	0.00	0.00	0.02	0.06	0.12	0.20	0.30	0.40	0.50	0.58	0.65	0.71	0.75	0.79	0.81
1940	0.00	0.01	0.02	0.07	0.13	0.22	0.31	0.42	0.51	0.59	0.66	0.72	0.76	0.79	0.82
1941	0.00	0.01	0.03	0.07	0.14	0.23	0.33	0.43	0.52	0.60	0.67	0.73	0.77	0.80	0.82
1942	0.00	0.01	0.03	0.07	0.14	0.23	0.33	0.43	0.52	0.60	0.67	0.72	0.76	0.79	0.82
1943	0.00	0.01	0.03	0.08	0.15	0.24	0.33	0.43	0.52	0.60	0.66	0.71	0.75	0.79	0.81
1944	0.00	0.01	0.04	0.09	0.16	0.25	0.34	0.44	0.52	0.60	0.66	0.71	0.76	0.79	0.82
1945	0.00	0.01	0.05	0.10	0.17	0.26	0.35	0.44	0.53	0.60	0.66	0.71	0.76	0.79	0.82
1946	0.00	0.01	0.05	0.10	0.18	0.26	0.35	0.44	0.52	0.59	0.66	0.71	0.75	0.79	0.82
1947	0.00	0.01	0.05	0.10	0.17	0.25	0.34	0.42	0.49	0.56	0.63	0.68	0.72	0.75	0.78
1948	0.00	0.02	0.05	0.10	0.18	0.26	0.34	0.42	0.49	0.56	0.62	0.67	0.72	0.75	0.78
1949	0.00	0.02	0.05	0.11	0.18	0.26	0.34	0.41	0.48	0.54	0.60	0.65	0.69	0.73	0.76
1950	0.00	0.02	0.05	0.11	0.19	0.26	0.34	0.40	0.47	0.53	0.58	0.63	0.67	0.71	0.75
1951	0.00	0.02	0.06	0.12	0.19	0.26	0.33	0.39	0.45	0.51	0.56	0.61	0.65	0.70	0.73
1952	0.00	0.02	0.06	0.12	0.20	0.26	0.32	0.38	0.44	0.49	0.55	0.60	0.65	0.69	0.72
1953	0.00	0.02	0.06	0.13	0.19	0.26	0.31	0.37	0.42	0.48	0.53	0.59	0.64	0.68	0.71
1954	0.00	0.02	0.06	0.12	0.18	0.24	0.30	0.35	0.40	0.46	0.52	0.57	0.62	0.66	0.69
1955	0.00	0.02	0.06	0.12	0.18	0.23	0.28	0.34	0.39	0.45	0.51	0.56	0.61	0.65	0.68
1956	0.00	0.02	0.06	0.11	0.16	0.22	0.27	0.32	0.38	0.44	0.50	0.55	0.59	0.63	0.67
1957	0.00	0.02	0.06	0.10	0.15	0.20	0.26	0.32	0.38	0.43	0.48	0.54	0.58	0.63	0.66
1958	0.00	0.02	0.05	0.09	0.14	0.19	0.25	0.30	0.36	0.41	0.47	0.52	0.57	0.61	0.65
1959	0.00	0.02	0.04	0.08	0.13	0.18	0.24	0.29	0.35	0.40	0.45	0.50	0.55	0.60	0.64
1960	0.00	0.02	0.04	0.08	0.13	0.18	0.24	0.29	0.34	0.39	0.45	0.50	0.54	0.59	0.63
1961	0.00	0.01	0.04	0.08	0.13	0.18	0.23	0.28	0.33	0.38	0.43	0.48	0.53	0.58	0.62
1962	0.00	0.01	0.04	0.08	0.12	0.17	0.22	0.27	0.32	0.37	0.42	0.47	0.52	0.57	
1963	0.00	0.01	0.04	0.07	0.12	0.16	0.21	0.26	0.31	0.36	0.41	0.46	0.51		
1964	0.00	0.01	0.04	0.07	0.11	0.16	0.20	0.25	0.30	0.36	0.41	0.46			
1965	0.00	0.01	0.04	0.07	0.11	0.16	0.20	0.25	0.30	0.35	0.40				
1966	0.00	0.01	0.03	0.07	0.11	0.16	0.21	0.26	0.31	0.36					
1967	0.00	0.01	0.04	0.07	0.12	0.17	0.22	0.27	0.31						
1968	0.00	0.01	0.04	0.08	0.13	0.18	0.23	0.27							
1969	0.00	0.01	0.04	0.08	0.13	0.18	0.23								
1970	0.00	0.02	0.04	0.08	0.13	0.18									
1971	0.00	0.02	0.04	0.08	0.13										
1972	0.00	0.02	0.04	0.08											
1973	0.00	0.02	0.05												
1974	0.00	0.02													
1975	0.00														

* Includes births at ages 45 and over achieved up to the end of 1989 by woman born in 1944 and earlier years.

England and Wales

30	31	32	33	34	35	36	37	38	39	40	41	42	43	44	45*	Year of birth of woman/female birth cohort
0.70	0.72	0.73	0.75	0.76	0.76	0.77	0.78	0.78	0.78	0.79	0.79	0.79	0.79	0.79	0.79	1920
0.73	0.75	0.76	0.77	0.78	0.79	0.80	0.81	0.81	0.81	0.81	0.82	0.82	0.82	0.82	0.82	1921
0.72	0.74	0.76	0.77	0.78	0.79	0.80	0.80	0.81	0.81	0.81	0.81	0.81	0.81	0.81	0.81	1922
0.73	0.76	0.77	0.79	0.80	0.81	0.81	0.82	0.82	0.83	0.83	0.83	0.83	0.83	0.83	0.83	1923
0.74	0.76	0.77	0.79	0.80	0.81	0.81	0.82	0.82	0.82	0.83	0.83	0.83	0.83	0.83	0.83	1924
0.73	0.75	0.77	0.78	0.79	0.80	0.81	0.82	0.82	0.82	0.82	0.83	0.83	0.83	0.83	0.83	1925
0.74	0.76	0.78	0.79	0.80	0.81	0.82	0.82	0.83	0.83	0.83	0.83	0.83	0.83	0.83	0.83	1926
0.74	0.76	0.78	0.79	0.81	0.81	0.82	0.83	0.83	0.83	0.83	0.84	0.84	0.84	0.84	0.84	1927
0.75	0.77	0.79	0.80	0.82	0.82	0.83	0.84	0.84	0.84	0.84	0.84	0.84	0.85	0.85	0.85	1928
0.76	0.78	0.79	0.81	0.82	0.82	0.83	0.84	0.84	0.84	0.84	0.84	0.84	0.84	0.84	0.84	1929
0.77	0.79	0.81	0.82	0.83	0.84	0.85	0.85	0.86	0.86	0.86	0.86	0.86	0.86	0.86	0.86	1930
0.77	0.79	0.81	0.82	0.83	0.84	0.84	0.85	0.85	0.85	0.85	0.86	0.86	0.86	0.86	0.86	1931
0.78	0.80	0.81	0.82	0.83	0.84	0.84	0.85	0.85	0.85	0.85	0.86	0.86	0.86	0.86	0.86	1932
0.79	0.81	0.83	0.84	0.85	0.85	0.86	0.86	0.87	0.87	0.87	0.87	0.87	0.87	0.87	0.87	1933
0.81	0.83	0.84	0.85	0.86	0.87	0.87	0.88	0.88	0.88	0.88	0.88	0.88	0.88	0.88	0.88	1934
0.82	0.83	0.85	0.86	0.86	0.87	0.88	0.88	0.88	0.88	0.88	0.88	0.88	0.89	0.89	0.89	1935
0.82	0.84	0.85	0.86	0.87	0.87	0.88	0.88	0.88	0.88	0.88	0.88	0.88	0.88	0.89	0.89	1936
0.82	0.84	0.85	0.86	0.86	0.87	0.87	0.88	0.88	0.88	0.88	0.88	0.88	0.88	0.88	0.88	1937
0.83	0.84	0.86	0.86	0.87	0.88	0.88	0.88	0.88	0.89	0.89	0.89	0.89	0.89	0.89	0.89	1938
0.83	0.84	0.86	0.86	0.87	0.88	0.88	0.88	0.88	0.88	0.89	0.89	0.89	0.89	0.89	0.89	1939
0.84	0.85	0.86	0.87	0.87	0.88	0.88	0.88	0.89	0.89	0.89	0.89	0.89	0.89	0.89	0.89	1940
0.84	0.85	0.86	0.87	0.88	0.88	0.88	0.89	0.89	0.89	0.89	0.89	0.89	0.89	0.89	0.89	1941
0.83	0.85	0.86	0.86	0.87	0.87	0.88	0.88	0.88	0.88	0.89	0.89	0.89	0.89	0.89	0.89	1942
0.83	0.84	0.85	0.86	0.87	0.87	0.88	0.88	0.88	0.88	0.88	0.88	0.88	0.88	0.88	0.88	1943
0.84	0.85	0.86	0.87	0.87	0.88	0.88	0.89	0.89	0.89	0.89	0.89	0.89	0.89	0.89	0.89	1944
0.84	0.85	0.86	0.87	0.88	0.88	0.89	0.89	0.89	0.90	0.90	0.90	0.90	0.90	0.90	0.90	1945
0.84	0.85	0.87	0.88	0.88	0.89	0.89	0.90	0.90	0.90	0.90	0.90	0.90	0.90	0.90		1946
0.80	0.82	0.83	0.84	0.85	0.86	0.86	0.86	0.87	0.87	0.87	0.87	0.87	0.87			1947
0.80	0.82	0.84	0.85	0.86	0.86	0.87	0.87	0.87	0.88	0.88	0.88	0.88				1948
0.79	0.81	0.82	0.83	0.84	0.85	0.85	0.86	0.86	0.86	0.86	0.86					1949
0.77	0.80	0.81	0.82	0.83	0.84	0.84	0.85	0.85	0.85	0.85						1950
0.76	0.78	0.79	0.80	0.81	0.82	0.83	0.83	0.84	0.84							1951
0.75	0.77	0.78	0.80	0.81	0.82	0.82	0.83	0.83								1952
0.74	0.76	0.78	0.79	0.81	0.81	0.82	0.83									1953
0.72	0.74	0.76	0.78	0.79	0.80	0.81										1954
0.71	0.74	0.76	0.78	0.79	0.80											1955
0.70	0.73	0.75	0.77	0.78												1956
0.70	0.72	0.74	0.76													1957
0.68	0.71	0.73														1958
0.67	0.70															1959
0.66																1960
																1961
																1962
																1963
																1964
																1965
																1966
																1967
																1968
																1969
																1970
																1971
																1972
																1973
																1974
																1975

Table 10.4 Components of average family size: age and year of birth of woman, occurrence inside/outside marriage and birth order, 1920-1971   **England and Wales**

Mother's year of birth	All live births	Outside marriage	Within marriage – All	First	Second	Third	Fourth	Fifth and later
All ages of mother at birth								
1920	**2.00**	0.13	1.87	0.77	0.55	0.28	0.13	0.15
1921	**2.05**	0.13	1.93	0.79	0.57	0.29	0.14	0.15
1922	**2.05**	0.13	1.92	0.79	0.56	0.29	0.14	0.15
1923	**2.10**	0.13	1.97	0.80	0.58	0.30	0.14	0.15
1924	**2.11**	0.13	1.98	0.80	0.58	0.30	0.15	0.16
1925	**2.12**	0.12	2.00	0.80	0.58	0.30	0.15	0.17
1926	**2.18**	0.12	2.05	0.80	0.60	0.32	0.16	0.17
1927	**2.20**	0.12	2.08	0.81	0.61	0.32	0.16	0.18
1928	**2.24**	0.12	2.13	0.82	0.62	0.33	0.17	0.18
1929	**2.26**	0.11	2.14	0.82	0.63	0.34	0.17	0.18
1930	**2.35**	0.12	2.23	0.84	0.66	0.36	0.18	0.19
1931	**2.34**	0.12	2.22	0.84	0.66	0.36	0.18	0.19
1932	**2.34**	0.12	2.22	0.84	0.66	0.36	0.18	0.18
1933	**2.39**	0.12	2.26	0.85	0.69	0.37	0.18	0.17
1934	**2.42**	0.13	2.30	0.86	0.70	0.38	0.18	0.17
1935	**2.42**	0.13	2.29	0.86	0.71	0.38	0.18	0.16
1936	**2.40**	0.13	2.27	0.86	0.71	0.38	0.17	0.15
1937	**2.39**	0.14	2.25	0.85	0.71	0.38	0.17	0.13
1938	**2.39**	0.14	2.24	0.86	0.72	0.38	0.17	0.13
1939	**2.36**	0.15	2.21	0.86	0.72	0.37	0.16	0.11
1940	**2.36**	0.16	2.21	0.86	0.73	0.37	0.15	0.11
1941	**2.34**	0.16	2.18	0.86	0.73	0.36	0.14	0.09
1942	**2.29**	0.16	2.12	0.85	0.72	0.34	0.13	0.08
1943	**2.24**	0.16	2.08	0.85	0.72	0.32	0.12	0.07
1944	**2.21**	0.16	2.04	0.85	0.72	0.31	0.11	0.06
1945	**2.20**	1.17	2.02	0.85	0.72	0.30	0.10	0.05
Under 20								
1920	**0.08**	0.01	0.06	0.06	0.01	0.00		
1921	**0.08**	0.01	0.06	0.06	0.01	0.00		
1922	**0.07**	0.01	0.06	0.05	0.01	0.00		
1923	**0.07**	0.02	0.06	0.05	0.01	0.00		
1924	**0.07**	0.02	0.06	0.05	0.00	0.00		
1925	**0.08**	0.02	0.06	0.05	0.00	0.00		
1926	**0.08**	0.02	0.06	0.05	0.00	0.00		
1927	**0.08**	0.02	0.06	0.05	0.00	0.00		
1928	**0.09**	0.02	0.07	0.06	0.01	0.00		
1929	**0.10**	0.02	0.08	0.07	0.01	0.00		
1930	**0.10**	0.02	0.09	0.08	0.01	0.00		
1931	**0.11**	0.02	0.09	0.08	0.01	0.00		
1932	**0.11**	0.02	0.09	0.08	0.01	0.00		
1933	**0.11**	0.02	0.09	0.08	0.01	0.00		
1934	**0.11**	0.02	0.09	0.08	0.01	0.00		
1935	**0.11**	0.02	0.09	0.08	0.01	0.00		
1936	**0.12**	0.02	0.10	0.08	0.01	0.00		
1937	**0.12**	0.02	0.10	0.09	0.01	0.00		
1938	**0.13**	0.02	0.11	0.10	0.01	0.00		
1939	**0.14**	0.02	0.12	0.10	0.02	0.00		
1940	**0.16**	0.03	0.13	0.11	0.02	0.00		
1941	**0.17**	0.03	0.14	0.12	0.02	0.00		
1942	**0.18**	0.03	0.14	0.12	0.02	0.00		
1943	**0.19**	0.03	0.15	0.13	0.02	0.00		
1944	**0.20**	0.04	0.16	0.13	0.03	0.00		
1945	**0.22**	0.04	0.17	0.14	0.03	0.00		
1946	**0.22**	0.05	0.17	0.14	0.03	0.00		
1947	**0.22**	0.05	0.17	0.13	0.03	0.00		
1948	**0.22**	0.05	0.17	0.13	0.03	0.00		
1949	**0.23**	0.06	0.17	0.14	0.03	0.00		
1950	**0.23**	0.06	0.17	0.14	0.03	0.00		
1951	**0.24**	0.06	0.18	0.14	0.03	0.00		
1952	**0.25**	0.06	0.18	0.15	0.03	0.00		
1953	**0.24**	0.06	0.18	0.14	0.03	0.00		
1954	**0.23**	0.06	0.17	0.14	0.03	0.00		
1955	**0.22**	0.06	0.16	0.13	0.03	0.00		

Mother's year of birth	All live births	Outside marriage	Within marriage – All	First	Second	Third	Fourth	Fifth and later
Under 20 - *continued*								
1956	**0.20**	0.06	0.14	0.12	0.03	0.00		
1957	**0.19**	0.06	0.13	0.10	0.02	0.00		
1958	**0.17**	0.06	0.11	0.09	0.02	0.00		
1959	**0.16**	0.06	0.10	0.08	0.02	0.00		
1960	**0.15**	0.06	0.09	0.08	0.02	0.00		
1961	**0.15**	0.06	0.09	0.08	0.02	0.00		
1962	**0.15**	0.06	0.09	0.07	0.02	0.00		
1963	**0.14**	0.07	0.07	0.06	0.01	0.00		
1964	**0.13**	0.07	0.06	0.05	0.01	0.00		
1965	**0.13**	0.08	0.06	0.05	0.01	0.00		
1966	**0.13**	0.08	0.05	0.04	0.01	0.00		
1967	**0.14**	0.09	0.05	0.04	0.01	0.00		
1968	**0.15**	0.10	0.04	0.03	0.01	0.00		
1969	**0.15**	0.11	0.04	0.03	0.01	0.00		
1970	**0.15**	0.12	0.04	0.03	0.01	0.00		
1971	**0.15**	0.12	0.03	0.02	0.01	0.00		
20-24								
1920	**0.49**	0.04	0.45	0.31	0.11	0.03	0.01	0.00
1921	**0.51**	0.05	0.46	0.32	0.11	0.03	0.01	0.00
1922	**0.54**	0.05	0.49	0.33	0.12	0.03	0.01	0.00
1923	**0.59**	0.06	0.54	0.37	0.13	0.03	0.01	0.00
1924	**0.62**	0.05	0.57	0.39	0.14	0.03	0.01	0.00
1925	**0.63**	0.05	0.58	0.39	0.15	0.04	0.01	0.00
1926	**0.64**	0.04	0.60	0.39	0.16	0.04	0.01	0.00
1927	**0.64**	0.04	0.60	0.39	0.16	0.04	0.01	0.00
1928	**0.64**	0.03	0.61	0.38	0.17	0.05	0.01	0.00
1929	**0.64**	0.03	0.61	0.38	0.17	0.05	0.01	0.00
1930	**0.66**	0.03	0.63	0.38	0.18	0.05	0.01	0.00
1931	**0.66**	0.03	0.63	0.39	0.18	0.05	0.01	0.00
1932	**0.68**	0.03	0.64	0.39	0.18	0.05	0.01	0.00
1933	**0.71**	0.03	0.67	0.41	0.19	0.06	0.01	0.00
1934	**0.74**	0.04	0.70	0.42	0.20	0.06	0.02	0.00
1935	**0.76**	0.04	0.72	0.43	0.21	0.06	0.02	0.00
1936	**0.78**	0.04	0.74	0.43	0.22	0.07	0.02	0.01
1937	**0.80**	0.04	0.76	0.43	0.23	0.07	0.02	0.01
1938	**0.83**	0.05	0.79	0.44	0.24	0.08	0.02	0.01
1939	**0.86**	0.05	0.81	0.44	0.25	0.08	0.02	0.01
1940	**0.89**	0.06	0.83	0.44	0.27	0.09	0.03	0.01
1941	**0.91**	0.06	0.84	0.44	0.28	0.09	0.03	0.01
1942	**0.90**	0.07	0.83	0.44	0.27	0.09	0.02	0.01
1943	**0.87**	0.06	0.81	0.43	0.27	0.08	0.02	0.01
1944	**0.86**	0.07	0.79	0.42	0.27	0.08	0.02	0.01
1945	**0.84**	0.07	0.77	0.41	0.27	0.08	0.02	0.01
1946	**0.82**	0.07	0.76	0.40	0.26	0.08	0.02	0.00
1947	**0.77**	0.06	0.71	0.38	0.24	0.07	0.02	0.00
1948	**0.76**	0.06	0.70	0.37	0.24	0.07	0.02	0.00
1949	**0.72**	0.06	0.66	0.35	0.23	0.06	0.01	0.00
1950	**0.69**	0.06	0.63	0.34	0.22	0.06	0.01	0.00
1951	**0.65**	0.05	0.59	0.31	0.21	0.05	0.01	0.00
1952	**0.62**	0.05	0.56	0.29	0.21	0.05	0.01	0.00
1953	**0.58**	0.05	0.53	0.28	0.20	0.04	0.01	0.00
1954	**0.56**	0.05	0.51	0.27	0.19	0.04	0.01	0.00
1955	**0.55**	0.05	0.50	0.27	0.18	0.04	0.01	0.00
1956	**0.55**	0.06	0.50	0.27	0.18	0.04	0.01	0.00
1957	**0.55**	0.06	0.49	0.26	0.17	0.04	0.01	0.00
1958	**0.54**	0.07	0.47	0.26	0.17	0.04	0.01	0.00
1959	**0.53**	0.08	0.45	0.25	0.16	0.04	0.01	0.00
1960	**0.52**	0.09	0.44	0.24	0.15	0.04	0.01	0.00
1961	**0.50**	0.09	0.41	0.22	0.14	0.04	0.01	0.00
1962	**0.48**	0.10	0.38	0.20	0.13	0.03	0.01	0.00
1963	**0.47**	0.11	0.36	0.19	0.12	0.03	0.01	0.00
1964	**0.46**	0.13	0.33	0.18	0.11	0.03	0.01	0.00
1965	**0.46**	0.15	0.31	0.17	0.11	0.03	0.01	0.00
1966	**0.46**	0.16	0.30	0.17	0.10	0.03	0.01	0.00

Note: Average family sizes are obtained by summing rates for each single year of age.

Table 10.4 - *continued*

Mother's year of birth	All live births	Outside marriage	Within marriage All	First	Second	Third	Fourth	Fifth and later
25-29								
1920	**0.70**	0.04	0.66	0.28	0.24	0.10	0.03	0.02
1921	**0.74**	0.03	0.71	0.30	0.25	0.10	0.04	0.02
1922	**0.72**	0.03	0.69	0.28	0.25	0.10	0.04	0.02
1923	**0.69**	0.03	0.66	0.25	0.25	0.11	0.04	0.02
1924	**0.68**	0.03	0.65	0.24	0.24	0.11	0.04	0.02
1925	**0.67**	0.02	0.65	0.23	0.24	0.11	0.04	0.02
1926	**0.69**	0.02	0.67	0.24	0.24	0.11	0.05	0.03
1927	**0.70**	0.02	0.68	0.25	0.24	0.11	0.05	0.03
1928	**0.73**	0.02	0.70	0.25	0.25	0.12	0.05	0.03
1929	**0.74**	0.02	0.72	0.26	0.26	0.12	0.05	0.04
1930	**0.78**	0.02	0.76	0.26	0.27	0.13	0.05	0.04
1931	**0.80**	0.03	0.77	0.26	0.28	0.13	0.06	0.04
1932	**0.81**	0.03	0.79	0.26	0.28	0.14	0.06	0.04
1933	**0.85**	0.03	0.82	0.26	0.30	0.15	0.06	0.04
1934	**0.89**	0.03	0.85	0.26	0.31	0.16	0.07	0.05
1935	**0.90**	0.04	0.87	0.26	0.32	0.17	0.07	0.05
1936	**0.91**	0.04	0.87	0.25	0.32	0.17	0.07	0.05
1937	**0.90**	0.04	0.86	0.25	0.32	0.17	0.07	0.05
1938	**0.89**	0.04	0.85	0.24	0.32	0.17	0.07	0.05
1939	**0.87**	0.04	0.83	0.23	0.31	0.17	0.07	0.04
1940	**0.85**	0.04	0.80	0.23	0.31	0.16	0.07	0.04
1941	**0.81**	0.04	0.77	0.22	0.30	0.16	0.06	0.04
1942	**0.79**	0.04	0.75	0.22	0.30	0.15	0.06	0.03
1943	**0.76**	0.04	0.73	0.22	0.29	0.14	0.05	0.03
1944	**0.73**	0.03	0.70	0.22	0.29	0.13	0.04	0.02
1945	**0.71**	0.03	0.68	0.23	0.28	0.12	0.04	0.02
1946	**0.69**	0.03	0.66	0.23	0.28	0.11	0.03	0.01
1947	**0.64**	0.03	0.62	0.22	0.26	0.09	0.03	0.01
1948	**0.64**	0.03	0.61	0.23	0.26	0.09	0.02	0.01
1949	**0.62**	0.03	0.59	0.22	0.25	0.08	0.02	0.01
1950	**0.62**	0.03	0.59	0.23	0.25	0.08	0.02	0.01
1951	**0.63**	0.03	0.59	0.23	0.25	0.08	0.02	0.01
1952	**0.64**	0.04	0.60	0.23	0.25	0.09	0.03	0.01
1953	**0.65**	0.04	0.61	0.24	0.25	0.09	0.03	0.01
1954	**0.65**	0.04	0.61	0.24	0.24	0.09	0.03	0.01
1955	**0.65**	0.05	0.60	0.23	0.24	0.09	0.03	0.01
1956	**0.64**	0.05	0.59	0.23	0.24	0.09	0.03	0.01
1957	**0.64**	0.06	0.58	0.22	0.23	0.09	0.03	0.01
1958	**0.64**	0.07	0.57	0.23	0.23	0.08	0.03	0.01
1959	**0.64**	0.07	0.56	0.22	0.22	0.08	0.02	0.01
1960	**0.63**	0.08	0.54	0.22	0.21	0.08	0.02	0.01
30-34								
1920	**0.43**	0.02	0.42	0.09	0.14	0.09	0.05	0.05
1921	**0.43**	0.02	0.42	0.09	0.14	0.10	0.05	0.05
1922	**0.43**	0.02	0.41	0.09	0.14	0.09	0.05	0.05
1923	**0.44**	0.02	0.42	0.09	0.14	0.09	0.05	0.05
1924	**0.44**	0.02	0.42	0.09	0.13	0.09	0.05	0.05
1925	**0.44**	0.02	0.43	0.09	0.14	0.09	0.05	0.06
1926	**0.46**	0.02	0.45	0.09	0.14	0.10	0.05	0.06
1927	**0.48**	0.02	0.46	0.09	0.14	0.10	0.06	0.06
1928	**0.49**	0.02	0.47	0.09	0.15	0.11	0.06	0.07
1929	**0.50**	0.02	0.48	0.09	0.15	0.11	0.06	0.07
1930	**0.53**	0.02	0.51	0.09	0.15	0.12	0.07	0.08
1931	**0.53**	0.02	0.50	0.09	0.15	0.12	0.07	0.08
1932	**0.52**	0.02	0.50	0.08	0.14	0.12	0.07	0.08
1933	**0.51**	0.03	0.49	0.08	0.14	0.12	0.07	0.07
1934	**0.50**	0.02	0.47	0.08	0.14	0.12	0.07	0.07
1935	**0.47**	0.02	0.44	0.07	0.13	0.11	0.06	0.06
30-34 - *continued*								
1936	**0.44**	0.02	0.42	0.07	0.13	0.11	0.06	0.06
1937	**0.42**	0.02	0.40	0.06	0.12	0.11	0.06	0.05
1938	**0.40**	0.02	0.38	0.06	0.12	0.10	0.05	0.05
1939	**0.37**	0.02	0.35	0.06	0.11	0.09	0.05	0.04
1940	**0.35**	0.02	0.33	0.06	0.11	0.09	0.04	0.03
1941	**0.33**	0.02	0.31	0.06	0.10	0.08	0.04	0.03
1942	**0.30**	0.02	0.29	0.06	0.10	0.07	0.03	0.02
1943	**0.29**	0.02	0.27	0.06	0.10	0.07	0.03	0.02
1944	**0.28**	0.02	0.27	0.06	0.11	0.06	0.02	0.02
1945	**0.29**	0.02	0.28	0.06	0.11	0.07	0.02	0.01
1946	**0.31**	0.02	0.29	0.07	0.12	0.07	0.02	0.01
1947	**0.31**	0.02	0.30	0.07	0.12	0.07	0.02	0.01
1948	**0.34**	0.02	0.32	0.08	0.13	0.08	0.03	0.01
1949	**0.35**	0.02	0.33	0.08	0.13	0.08	0.03	0.01
1950	**0.36**	0.02	0.34	0.08	0.14	0.08	0.03	0.01
1951	**0.36**	0.03	0.33	0.08	0.13	0.08	0.03	0.02
1952	**0.37**	0.03	0.34	0.08	0.14	0.08	0.03	0.02
1953	**0.39**	0.03	0.35	0.09	0.14	0.08	0.03	0.02
1954	**0.39**	0.04	0.36	0.09	0.14	0.08	0.03	0.02
1955	**0.40**	0.04	0.36	0.10	0.14	0.08	0.03	0.02
1956	**0.41**	0.05	0.36	0.10	0.14	0.08	0.03	0.02
35 and over								
1920	**0.30**	0.02	0.28	0.03	0.06	0.06	0.05	0.08
1921	**0.29**	0.02	0.28	0.03	0.06	0.06	0.05	0.08
1922	**0.30**	0.02	0.28	0.03	0.06	0.06	0.05	0.08
1923	**0.30**	0.02	0.28	0.03	0.06	0.06	0.05	0.08
1924	**0.30**	0.02	0.28	0.03	0.06	0.06	0.05	0.08
1925	**0.30**	0.02	0.28	0.03	0.06	0.06	0.05	0.08
1926	**0.30**	0.02	0.29	0.03	0.06	0.06	0.05	0.09
1927	**0.29**	0.02	0.28	0.03	0.05	0.06	0.05	0.08
1928	**0.29**	0.02	0.27	0.03	0.05	0.06	0.05	0.08
1929	**0.27**	0.02	0.25	0.03	0.05	0.06	0.04	0.07
1930	**0.26**	0.02	0.25	0.03	0.05	0.06	0.04	0.07
1931	**0.24**	0.02	0.23	0.03	0.04	0.05	0.04	0.06
1932	**0.22**	0.02	0.21	0.02	0.04	0.05	0.04	0.06
1933	**0.21**	0.01	0.19	0.02	0.04	0.05	0.03	0.05
1934	**0.19**	0.01	0.18	0.02	0.04	0.04	0.03	0.05
1935	**0.17**	0.01	0.16	0.02	0.03	0.04	0.03	0.04
1936	**0.16**	0.01	0.14	0.02	0.03	0.03	0.02	0.03
1937	**0.14**	0.01	0.13	0.02	0.03	0.03	0.02	0.03
1938	**0.13**	0.01	0.12	0.02	0.03	0.03	0.02	0.03
1939	**0.12**	0.01	0.11	0.02	0.03	0.03	0.02	0.02
1940	**0.12**	0.01	0.11	0.02	0.03	0.03	0.02	0.02
1941	**0.12**	0.01	0.11	0.02	0.03	0.03	0.02	0.02
1942	**0.12**	0.01	0.11	0.02	0.03	0.03	0.02	0.02
1943	**0.12**	0.01	0.11	0.02	0.03	0.03	0.02	0.02
1944	**0.13**	0.01	0.12	0.02	0.03	0.03	0.02	0.02
1945	**0.13**	0.01	0.12	0.02	0.03	0.03	0.02	0.02

Table 10.5 Percentage distribution of liveborn children: **England and Wales**
age and year of birth of woman, 1920-1970

Age of woman (completed years)	Year of birth of woman	Number of liveborn children†				
		0	1	2	3	4 or more
20	1920	89	9	2	0	0
	1925	88	10	2	0	0
	1930	84	12	3	0	0
	1935	84	13	3	0	0
	1940	79	16	4	1	0
	1945	74	18	6	1	0
	1950	74	18	7	1	0
	1955	77	16	6	1	0
	1960	82	13	4	1	0
	1965	84	12	3	0	0
	1970	82	14	3	0	0
25	1920	55	28	13	4	1
	1925	46	31	17	5	1
	1930	45	29	18	6	2
	1935	39	29	21	7	3
	1940	34	27	25	9	5
	1945	34	26	27	9	4
	1950	42	23	25	7	2
	1955	49	21	22	6	2
	1960	55	19	19	5	2
	1965	60	19	15	4	2
30	1920	30	28	26	10	6
	1925	27	28	27	11	7
	1930	23	25	30	13	9
	1935	18	21	33	16	12
	1940	16	17	35	19	12
	1945	16	18	41	17	8
	1950	23	18	39	14	6
	1955	29	17	35	13	6
	1960	34	18	31	12	6
35	1920	24	23	28	14	11
	1925	20	24	30	15	12
	1930	16	19	31	17	16
	1935	13	16	33	20	18
	1940	12	13	36	22	16
	1945	12	14	43	20	11
	1950	16	14	42	19	9
	1955	20	14	39	19	9
40	1920	21	22	28	15	15
	1925	18	22	29	16	16
	1930	14	18	31	18	19
	1935	12	15	33	21	20
	1940	11	13	36	23	17
	1945	10	13	43	21	12
	1950	15	12	43	20	10
45*	1920	21	21	28	15	15
	1925	17	22	29	16	16
	1930	14	18	31	18	20
	1935	11	15	33	21	20
	1940	11	13	36	23	17
	1945	10	13	43	21	12

* Includes birth at ages over 45.
† Estimates including births inside and outside marriage (see Introduction).

Table 11.1 Live births within marriage: estimated distribution by social class of father as defined by occupation, age of mother and previous liveborn children, 1980-1990

England and Wales
thousands

Year	Number of previous liveborn children					Year	Number of previous liveborn children				
	Total	0	1	2	3 or more		**Total**	0	1	2	3 or more
	SOCIAL CLASSES I AND II						**SOCIAL CLASS IIIN**				
	All ages of mother at birth						**All ages of mother at birth**				
1980	**164.5**	69.4	62.4	24.4	8.2	1980	**61.9**	28.3	23.1	7.6	2.9
1981	**163.3**	67.5	63.5	23.6	8.8	1981	**60.4**	26.6	23.8	7.4	2.7
1982	**158.7**	63.8	62.0	23.9	9.0	1982	**58.0**	25.2	22.6	7.3	2.8
1983	**156.0**	64.5	59.8	22.9	8.7	1983	**57.1**	25.2	22.0	7.1	2.8
1984	**154.8**	64.2	57.9	23.7	9.0	1984	**57.6**	25.5	21.9	7.4	2.9
1985	**158.4**	65.3	60.7	23.6	8.8	1985	**56.2**	24.9	20.8	7.6	2.9
1986	**160.1**	66.3	60.3	24.1	9.5	1986	**55.2**	24.2	20.9	7.4	2.8
1987	**164.6**	69.2	60.9	25.2	9.3	1987	**53.9**	23.7	20.0	7.4	2.8
1988	**167.7**	71.0	61.9	25.1	9.6	1988	**54.8**	24.8	20.1	7.2	2.8
1989	**172.1**	72.5	64.9	25.1	9.6	1989	**49.9**	21.9	18.4	6.6	3.0
1990	**177.4**	73.9	66.8	26.5	10.2	1990	**53.2**	23.8	19.5	6.8	3.1
	Under 20						**Under 20**				
1980	**2.3**	2.0	0.3	-		1980	**1.8**	1.5	0.2	0.0	
1981	**2.1**	1.8	0.3	0.0		1981	**1.8**	1.4	0.3	0.0	
1982	**1.8**	1.5	0.3	0.0		1982	**1.5**	1.3	0.2	0.0	
1983	**1.8**	1.5	0.3	0.0		1983	**1.5**	1.2	0.2	0.0	
1984	**1.6**	1.3	0.2	0.0		1984	**1.4**	1.2	0.3	-	
1985	**1.6**	1.3	0.2	0.0		1985	**1.2**	1.0	0.1	0.0	
1986	**1.4**	1.2	0.2	0.0		1986	**1.2**	0.9	0.2	0.0	
1987	**1.2**	1.1	0.2	0.0		1987	**1.1**	0.9	0.2	0.0	
1988	**1.4**	1.1	0.2	0.0		1988	**0.9**	0.6	0.2	0.0	
1989	**1.3**	1.1	0.2	0.0		1989	**0.8**	0.7	0.1	0.0	
1990	**1.3**	1.1	0.2	0.0		1990	**0.9**	0.7	0.1	0.0	
	20-24						**20-24**				
1980	**25.5**	16.7	7.4	1.2	0.2	1980	**16.5**	10.7	5.1	0.6	0.1
1981	**25.0**	16.2	7.4	1.2	0.2	1981	**15.9**	10.0	5.2	0.6	0.1
1982	**24.4**	15.6	7.4	1.2	0.2	1982	**15.0**	9.2	4.8	0.9	0.2
1983	**23.2**	14.7	7.2	1.2	0.2	1983	**14.4**	9.3	4.3	0.7	0.1
1984	**22.7**	15.0	6.3	1.4	0.1	1984	**13.9**	8.6	4.3	0.9	0.1
1985	**22.9**	14.7	6.8	1.2	0.2	1985	**13.2**	8.3	4.1	0.7	0.1
1986	**22.2**	14.4	6.4	1.2	0.2	1986	**12.5**	7.7	3.9	0.8	0.1
1987	**21.5**	13.9	6.2	1.1	0.2	1987	**11.5**	7.0	3.6	0.7	0.2
1988	**23.1**	15.0	6.6	1.4	0.2	1988	**11.3**	7.2	3.3	0.6	0.1
1989	**21.3**	13.8	6.2	1.1	0.3	1989	**9.4**	5.6	3.1	0.6	0.1
1990	**20.3**	12.9	6.3	1.0	0.2	1990	**9.7**	6.1	2.9	0.7	0.1
	25-29						**25-29**				
1980	**68.4**	33.0	27.2	6.9	1.3	1980	**25.6**	11.6	10.7	2.6	0.7
1981	**67.4**	31.6	27.9	6.2	1.8	1981	**24.9**	10.9	10.8	2.6	0.6
1982	**64.0**	29.7	26.3	6.5	1.5	1982	**24.1**	10.6	10.2	2.5	0.7
1983	**61.9**	30.0	24.1	6.2	1.5	1983	**23.7**	10.6	9.9	2.3	0.8
1984	**61.1**	29.3	24.0	6.4	1.5	1984	**24.4**	11.0	10.0	2.7	0.8
1985	**62.1**	29.9	24.9	6.0	1.4	1985	**24.3**	11.1	9.6	2.8	0.8
1986	**63.1**	30.6	24.1	6.7	1.7	1986	**23.9**	10.7	9.8	2.8	0.7
1987	**64.5**	31.9	24.1	6.8	1.6	1987	**23.8**	10.9	9.4	2.8	0.7
1988	**63.9**	31.8	23.6	6.5	2.0	1988	**23.8**	11.4	8.9	2.6	0.8
1989	**65.8**	32.4	24.6	6.9	2.0	1989	**21.7**	10.5	8.1	2.3	0.7
1990	**68.5**	33.9	25.5	7.2	1.8	1990	**22.6**	11.0	8.5	2.2	0.8
	30 and over						**30 and over**				
1980	**68.3**	17.8	27.5	16.3	6.7	1980	**18.0**	4.5	7.2	4.4	2.0
1981	**68.8**	17.8	27.9	16.2	6.9	1981	**17.8**	4.2	7.5	4.1	2.0
1982	**68.5**	17.0	28.0	16.2	7.3	1982	**17.4**	4.2	7.4	3.9	1.9
1983	**69.0**	18.3	28.1	15.6	7.0	1983	**17.6**	4.1	7.5	4.1	1.9
1984	**69.4**	18.6	27.5	16.0	7.4	1984	**17.8**	4.8	7.3	3.8	1.9
1985	**71.8**	19.4	28.7	16.4	7.2	1985	**17.5**	4.5	7.0	4.0	2.0
1986	**73.4**	20.1	29.6	16.1	7.6	1986	**17.6**	4.9	6.9	3.8	2.0
1987	**77.3**	22.2	30.4	17.2	7.5	1987	**17.5**	4.8	6.8	3.9	1.9
1988	**79.3**	23.1	31.5	17.3	7.4	1988	**18.9**	5.5	7.6	3.9	1.9
1989	**83.7**	25.2	34.0	17.1	7.3	1989	**18.0**	5.1	7.1	3.7	2.1
1990	**87.3**	26.1	34.8	18.3	8.2	1990	**20.0**	5.9	8.0	3.9	2.2

Notes: 1. For definition of social classes, see Introduction. Table based on 1980 classification of occupations.
2. For an indication of the standard errors attached to the estimates see Introduction and Appendix Tables 3 and 4.

Table 11.1 - *continued*   *thousands*

SOCIAL CLASSES IIIM

All ages of mother at birth

Year	Total	0	1	2	3 or more
1980	212.2	85.8	76.4	33.6	16.3
1981	198.2	78.4	73.3	30.6	15.8
1982	190.0	72.7	70.7	30.3	16.2
1983	188.3	72.8	69.6	29.8	16.1
1984	185.5	71.8	68.2	29.3	16.1
1985	184.3	71.2	66.9	30.2	15.9
1986	179.5	68.8	65.7	28.7	16.3
1987	180.9	70.2	66.2	28.6	15.9
1988	175.0	68.1	63.4	27.6	15.9
1989	169.7	64.7	62.0	28.0	15.0
1990	168.8	63.3	62.1	28.4	15.0

Under 20

Year	Total	0	1	2	3 or more
1980	14.5	11.6	2.8	0.1	
1981	12.1	9.6	2.4	0.2	
1982	10.5	8.3	2.0	0.2	
1983	9.5	7.6	1.8	0.1	
1984	7.9	6.4	1.4	0.1	
1985	7.5	5.8	1.5	0.2	
1986	6.9	5.4	1.4	0.1	
1987	5.8	4.4	1.4	0.1	
1988	5.2	4.1	1.0	0.1	
1989	4.5	3.5	1.0	0.1	
1990	4.2	3.1	1.0	0.1	

20-24

Year	Total	0	1	2	3 or more
1980	75.1	40.8	26.2	7.0	1.1
1981	70.5	37.2	25.9	5.9	1.5
1982	66.6	34.5	24.7	6.1	1.2
1983	64.9	33.8	24.0	5.9	1.2
1984	62.3	32.3	22.7	6.0	1.3
1985	59.4	31.3	21.0	5.8	1.3
1986	55.2	29.2	19.8	4.9	1.3
1987	54.6	28.8	19.6	5.1	1.2
1988	50.6	26.5	18.5	4.6	1.1
1989	47.1	24.6	16.5	4.9	1.1
1990	42.7	22.1	15.1	4.4	1.1

25-29

Year	Total	0	1	2	3 or more
1980	76.0	25.2	31.5	14.1	5.2
1981	70.9	23.5	29.6	12.6	5.2
1982	68.7	22.0	29.0	12.2	5.5
1983	70.3	23.4	29.2	12.5	5.1
1984	70.1	24.5	28.4	11.9	5.2
1985	72.2	25.3	29.2	12.7	5.0
1986	71.1	24.8	29.0	11.9	5.4
1987	73.7	26.8	29.4	12.1	5.4
1988	72.6	27.5	28.0	12.0	5.2
1989	71.5	26.6	28.1	11.9	4.9
1990	72.0	27.0	28.2	12.0	4.9

30 and over

Year	Total	0	1	2	3 or more
1980	46.5	8.2	15.9	12.4	10.0
1981	44.7	8.1	15.5	11.9	9.2
1982	44.2	7.9	15.0	11.8	9.6
1983	43.7	7.9	14.7	11.3	9.8
1984	45.1	8.5	15.8	11.3	9.5
1985	45.2	8.8	15.2	11.6	9.6
1986	46.2	9.4	15.5	11.8	9.6
1987	46.8	10.2	15.9	11.3	9.3
1988	46.5	10.0	16.0	10.9	9.6
1989	46.6	10.1	16.4	11.1	9.0
1990	50.0	11.2	17.8	11.9	9.0

SOCIAL CLASS IV AND V

All ages of mother at birth

Year	Total	0	1	2	3 or more
1980	120.4	47.8	40.4	18.4	13.8
1981	111.4	42.2	38.1	18.3	12.8
1982	109.2	40.3	38.4	17.5	13.0
1983	107.7	39.5	37.1	18.0	13.0
1984	106.3	38.5	37.3	17.4	13.1
1985	105.9	39.0	35.6	17.7	13.6
1986	101.1	37.1	33.8	17.6	12.6
1987	99.3	35.9	34.1	16.6	12.8
1988	94.1	34.3	31.4	16.2	12.2
1989	87.8	32.1	29.7	14.6	11.3
1990	85.3	30.2	29.3	14.3	11.5

Under 20

Year	Total	0	1	2	3 or more
1980	14.6	11.5	2.8	0.3	
1981	12.1	9.1	2.8	0.2	
1982	11.1	8.3	2.5	0.2	
1983	9.1	6.9	2.0	0.2	
1984	8.8	6.6	2.0	0.2	
1985	8.0	6.2	1.7	0.1	
1986	6.8	5.1	1.6	0.1	
1987	6.2	4.5	1.6	0.1	
1988	5.4	3.9	1.4	0.1	
1989	4.3	3.1	1.1	0.1	
1990	3.7	2.7	0.9	0.1	

20-24

Year	Total	0	1	2	3 or more
1980	50.0	23.8	19.0	5.5	1.7
1981	46.0	21.0	18.0	5.8	1.3
1982	45.5	20.1	18.3	5.6	1.6
1983	44.0	20.1	16.8	5.5	1.5
1984	42.2	19.3	16.6	4.9	1.4
1985	41.2	19.5	15.3	5.1	1.3
1986	39.1	18.3	14.3	5.1	1.3
1987	36.8	17.3	13.7	4.6	1.2
1988	32.3	15.5	11.3	4.3	1.2
1989	29.9	14.3	11.0	3.6	1.1
1990	27.4	12.6	10.3	3.5	1.0

25-29

Year	Total	0	1	2	3 or more
1980	33.5	9.2	12.7	6.8	4.8
1981	31.8	8.8	11.6	7.1	4.2
1982	32.6	8.8	12.4	6.9	4.4
1983	33.8	9.3	12.7	7.2	4.5
1984	34.4	9.6	12.9	7.2	4.7
1985	35.6	10.1	12.7	7.7	5.1
1986	34.6	10.1	12.5	7.3	4.6
1987	34.7	10.6	12.5	7.2	4.4
1988	35.6	11.4	12.7	7.3	4.2
1989	32.7	10.9	12.1	6.0	3.8
1990	33.3	11.1	12.0	6.1	4.0

30 and over

Year	Total	0	1	2	3 or more
1980	22.3	3.3	5.9	5.7	7.3
1981	21.5	3.2	5.7	5.3	7.3
1982	20.1	3.0	5.2	4.9	7.0
1983	20.8	3.1	5.5	5.1	7.1
1984	21.0	3.1	5.8	5.1	7.0
1985	21.1	3.2	5.8	4.8	7.2
1986	20.6	3.5	5.5	5.0	6.6
1987	21.6	3.5	6.3	4.7	7.2
1988	20.7	3.5	6.0	4.5	6.8
1989	20.8	3.8	5.6	4.9	6.5
1990	20.9	3.8	6.0	4.6	6.5

Notes: 1. For definition FM of social classes, see Introduction. Table based on 1980 classification of occupations.
      2. For an indication of the standard errors attached to the estimates see Introduction and Appendix Tables 3 and 4.

Table 11.1 - *continued*   *thousands*

Year	Number of previous liveborn children					Year	Number of previous liveborn children				
	Total	0	1	2	3 or more		Total	0	1	2	3 or more

SOCIAL CLASS: NON-MANUAL | | **SOCIAL CLASS: MANUAL**

All ages of mother at birth

Year	Total	0	1	2	3 or more	Year	Total	0	1	2	3 or more
1980	**226.3**	97.8	85.5	32.0	11.1	1980	**332.6**	133.7	116.8	52.0	30.2
1981	**223.7**	94.0	87.2	30.9	11.5	1981	**309.7**	120.6	111.5	49.0	28.7
1982	**216.7**	89.1	84.6	31.2	11.8	1982	**299.2**	113.0	109.2	47.9	29.2
1983	**213.1**	89.7	81.8	30.1	11.5	1983	**296.0**	112.2	106.8	47.9	29.2
1984	**212.4**	89.7	79.8	31.1	11.9	1984	**291.8**	110.4	105.6	46.7	29.1
1985	**214.6**	90.2	81.5	31.2	11.7	1985	**290.2**	110.2	102.5	47.9	29.5
1986	**215.3**	90.5	81.2	31.4	12.3	1986	**280.6**	105.9	99.5	46.3	28.8
1987	**218.5**	92.8	81.0	32.6	12.1	1987	**280.2**	106.1	100.3	45.1	28.7
1988	**222.5**	95.8	82.0	32.3	12.4	1988	**269.0**	102.3	94.8	43.8	28.1
1989	**222.0**	94.4	83.3	31.6	12.6	1989	**257.5**	96.8	91.7	42.6	26.4
1990	**230.6**	97.7	86.3	33.3	13.3	1990	**254.1**	93.5	91.4	42.7	26.5

Under 20   **Under 20**

Year	Total	0	1	2	3 or more	Year	Total	0	1	2	3 or more
1980	**4.0**	3.5	0.5	0.0		1980	**29.1**	23.2	5.6	0.4	
1981	**3.9**	3.3	0.6	0.0		1981	**24.2**	18.7	5.1	0.3	
1982	**3.3**	2.7	0.5	0.0		1982	**21.5**	16.6	4.5	0.4	
1983	**3.3**	2.7	0.5	0.0		1983	**18.6**	14.5	3.8	0.3	
1984	**3.0**	2.5	0.5	0.0		1984	**16.7**	13.0	3.4	0.3	
1985	**2.8**	2.4	0.4	0.0		1985	**15.5**	11.9	3.3	0.3	
1986	**2.6**	2.1	0.4	0.0		1986	**13.8**	10.5	3.0	0.3	
1987	**2.3**	2.0	0.3	0.0		1987	**12.0**	8.9	3.0	0.2	
1988	**2.3**	1.8	0.4	0.0		1988	**10.6**	8.0	2.4	0.2	
1989	**2.2**	1.8	0.3	0.0		1989	**8.9**	6.6	2.1	0.2	
1990	**2.2**	1.8	0.3	0.1		1990	**7.9**	5.8	1.9	0.1	

20-24   **20-24**

Year	Total	0	1	2	3 or more	Year	Total	0	1	2	3 or more
1980	**41.9**	27.4	12.5	1.8	0.3	1980	**125.1**	64.5	45.2	12.6	2.9
1981	**40.9**	26.2	12.6	1.8	0.3	1981	**116.5**	58.2	43.9	11.7	2.7
1982	**39.4**	24.8	12.1	2.1	0.4	1982	**112.1**	54.7	43.0	11.7	2.7
1983	**37.7**	23.9	11.6	1.9	0.3	1983	**108.8**	53.9	40.8	11.4	2.7
1984	**36.7**	23.6	10.6	2.3	0.3	1984	**104.5**	51.6	39.3	10.9	2.7
1985	**36.2**	22.9	10.9	1.9	0.4	1985	**100.6**	50.8	36.4	10.9	2.6
1986	**34.6**	22.1	10.3	2.0	0.3	1986	**94.3**	47.6	34.0	10.0	2.6
1987	**33.0**	20.9	9.9	1.8	0.4	1987	**91.5**	46.1	33.3	9.7	2.3
1988	**34.4**	22.2	9.9	2.0	0.3	1988	**83.0**	41.9	29.8	8.9	2.3
1989	**30.7**	19.4	9.2	1.7	0.4	1989	**77.1**	38.9	27.5	8.5	2.2
1990	**30.1**	19.0	9.1	1.7	0.3	1990	**70.1**	34.6	25.4	7.9	2.1

25-29   **25-29**

Year	Total	0	1	2	3 or more	Year	Total	0	1	2	3 or more
1980	**94.0**	44.6	37.9	9.5	2.0	1980	**109.6**	34.4	44.2	21.0	10.0
1981	**92.3**	42.5	38.7	8.7	2.4	1981	**102.7**	32.4	41.3	19.8	9.3
1982	**88.1**	40.3	36.5	9.0	2.2	1982	**101.3**	30.8	41.5	19.2	9.9
1983	**85.5**	40.6	34.1	8.5	2.3	1983	**104.0**	32.8	41.9	19.8	9.6
1984	**85.6**	40.2	34.0	9.0	2.3	1984	**104.5**	34.2	41.3	19.1	9.9
1985	**86.4**	40.9	34.5	8.8	2.1	1985	**107.8**	35.4	41.9	20.4	10.1
1986	**87.1**	41.3	33.9	9.5	2.4	1986	**105.7**	34.9	41.6	19.2	10.0
1987	**88.4**	42.9	33.6	9.6	2.3	1987	**108.3**	37.4	41.8	19.2	9.9
1988	**87.7**	43.2	32.6	9.1	2.8	1988	**108.2**	38.9	40.7	19.2	9.4
1989	**87.5**	42.8	32.7	9.2	2.7	1989	**104.2**	37.5	40.2	17.9	8.7
1990	**91.1**	44.9	34.1	9.5	2.6	1990	**105.3**	38.1	40.2	18.1	8.9

30 and over   **30 and over**

Year	Total	0	1	2	3 or more	Year	Total	0	1	2	3 or more
1980	**86.3**	22.3	34.6	20.7	8.7	1980	**68.8**	11.6	21.8	18.1	17.3
1981	**86.6**	22.0	35.4	20.3	8.9	1981	**66.2**	11.3	21.1	17.2	16.6
1982	**85.9**	21.2	35.4	20.1	9.2	1982	**64.3**	10.9	20.2	16.7	16.6
1983	**86.6**	22.4	35.6	19.7	8.9	1983	**64.6**	11.0	20.2	16.4	16.9
1984	**87.2**	23.4	34.7	19.8	9.3	1984	**66.1**	11.6	21.6	16.4	16.5
1985	**89.3**	23.9	35.7	20.4	9.2	1985	**66.3**	12.0	21.0	16.4	16.8
1986	**91.0**	25.0	36.5	20.0	9.5	1986	**66.8**	12.9	21.0	16.8	16.2
1987	**94.8**	27.1	37.2	21.1	9.4	1987	**68.3**	13.6	22.2	16.0	16.5
1988	**98.2**	28.6	39.1	21.2	9.3	1988	**67.3**	13.6	21.9	15.4	16.4
1989	**101.7**	30.3	41.1	20.7	9.5	1989	**67.4**	13.9	22.0	16.0	15.5
1990	**107.3**	32.0	42.8	22.1	10.4	1990	**70.9**	15.0	23.8	16.5	15.6

Notes: 1. For definition of social classes, see Introduction. Table based on 1980 classification of occupations.
2. For an indication of the standard errors attached to the estimates see Introduction and Appendix Tables 3 and 4.

Table 11.1 - *continued*   *thousands*

OTHERS

All ages of mother at birth

Year	Number of previous liveborn children				
	Total	0	1	2	3 or more
1980	19.9	9.5	6.9	2.4	1.1
1981	20.1	9.7	7.0	2.5	0.9
1982	20.2	9.8	6.9	2.4	1.1
1983	20.8	9.8	7.1	2.8	1.1
1984	22.2	10.4	7.7	2.8	1.2
1985	25.3	11.6	9.0	3.3	1.4
1986	23.8	10.6	8.5	3.1	1.6
1987	24.4	11.1	8.1	3.5	1.8
1988	24.7	11.2	8.7	3.3	1.5
1989	22.4	9.8	7.7	3.3	1.7
1990	21.4	9.2	7.6	3.0	1.6

Under 20

Year	Total	0	1	2 and 3 or more
1980	1.7	1.5	0.2	0.0
1981	2.1	1.7	0.4	0.0
1982	1.9	1.7	0.2	0.0
1983	1.7	1.5	0.2	0.0
1984	1.7	1.4	0.3	0.0
1985	1.8	1.5	0.3	0.0
1986	1.4	1.2	0.2	0.0
1987	1.2	1.0	0.2	0.0
1988	1.2	0.9	0.3	0.0
1989	1.0	0.8	0.2	0.0
1990	0.9	0.7	0.2	0.0

20-24

Year	Total	0	1	2	3 or more
1980	7.9	4.4	2.9	0.5	0.0
1981	8.3	5.0	2.6	0.6	0.1
1982	8.4	4.9	2.9	0.5	0.1
1983	8.7	5.0	3.0	0.7	0.1
1984	9.2	5.4	2.9	0.7	0.1
1985	9.5	5.3	3.3	0.8	0.2
1986	9.1	5.0	3.2	0.7	0.1
1987	8.4	4.9	2.7	0.7	0.1
1988	8.2	4.8	2.7	0.6	0.1
1989	6.7	3.8	2.2	0.6	0.1
1990	6.0	3.4	2.0	0.5	0.2

25-29

Year	Total	0	1	2	3 or more
1980	6.4	2.6	2.4	1.0	0.4
1981	6.4	2.4	2.8	1.0	0.3
1982	6.4	2.5	2.6	1.1	0.3
1983	6.6	2.5	2.7	1.0	0.4
1984	7.3	2.8	3.0	1.2	0.4
1985	9.1	3.5	3.7	1.3	0.5
1986	8.6	3.1	3.4	1.5	0.6
1987	9.3	3.7	3.5	1.6	0.5
1988	9.4	3.7	3.8	1.3	0.5
1989	9.3	3.6	3.5	1.5	0.6
1990	8.4	3.4	3.4	1.1	0.4

30 and over

Year	Total	0	1	2	3 or more
1980	3.9	1.0	1.4	0.9	0.7
1981	3.4	0.6	1.3	0.9	0.5
1982	3.4	0.7	1.1	0.9	0.7
1983	3.7	0.9	1.2	1.1	0.6
1984	4.0	0.8	1.5	1.0	0.7
1985	5.0	1.3	1.8	1.1	0.7
1986	4.7	1.3	1.7	0.8	0.9
1987	5.5	1.5	1.7	1.2	1.1
1988	5.8	1.7	1.9	1.3	0.8
1989	5.4	1.5	1.8	1.1	1.0
1990	6.1	1.6	2.1	1.3	1.0

ALL SOCIAL CLASSES

All ages of mother at birth

Year	Number of previous liveborn children				
	Total	0	1	2	3 or more
1980	578.9	241.0	209.2	86.3	42.4
1981	553.5	224.3	205.7	82.4	41.1
1982	536.1	211.9	200.7	81.4	42.1
1983	529.9	211.8	195.6	80.7	41.8
1984	526.4	210.4	193.1	80.6	42.2
1985	530.2	212.0	193.1	82.4	42.7
1986	519.7	206.9	189.2	80.8	42.7
1987	523.1	210.0	189.4	81.2	42.6
1988	516.2	209.3	185.6	79.4	42.0
1989	501.9	201.0	182.8	77.5	40.7
1990	506.1	200.4	185.3	79.0	41.4

Under 20

Year	Total	0	1	2 and 3 or more
1980	34.9	28.2	6.3	0.4
1981	30.1	23.6	6.1	0.4
1982	26.7	21.1	5.2	0.4
1983	23.6	18.7	4.6	0.3
1984	21.4	16.9	4.2	0.3
1985	20.1	15.8	3.9	0.3
1986	17.8	13.8	3.6	0.3
1987	15.6	11.9	3.4	0.2
1988	14.1	10.7	3.1	0.3
1989	12.0	9.2	2.6	0.3
1990	11.0	8.3	2.4	0.2

20-24

Year	Total	0	1	2	3 or more
1980	174.9	96.4	60.5	14.8	3.2
1981	165.7	89.5	59.0	14.1	3.1
1982	159.9	84.4	58.1	14.2	3.2
1983	155.2	82.8	55.4	13.9	3.1
1984	150.4	80.6	52.8	13.9	3.1
1985	146.3	79.0	50.5	13.6	3.2
1986	138.0	74.7	47.5	12.7	3.1
1987	132.8	72.0	45.8	12.2	2.8
1988	125.6	68.9	42.4	11.5	2.7
1989	114.5	62.1	38.9	10.8	2.7
1990	106.2	57.0	36.5	10.1	2.5

25-29

Year	Total	0	1	2	3 or more
1980	210.0	81.6	84.6	31.5	12.4
1981	201.5	77.2	82.7	29.5	12.0
1982	195.8	73.6	80.6	29.2	12.4
1983	196.2	75.9	78.7	29.3	12.3
1984	197.4	77.2	78.3	29.3	12.6
1985	203.3	79.9	80.0	30.5	12.8
1986	201.3	79.3	78.9	30.2	13.0
1987	206.0	83.9	78.9	30.5	12.7
1988	205.3	85.8	77.1	29.7	12.6
1989	201.0	84.0	76.4	28.6	12.0
1990	204.7	86.4	77.7	28.7	11.9

30 and over

Year	Total	0	1	2	3 or more
1980	159.1	34.8	57.8	39.7	26.8
1981	156.2	34.0	57.8	38.5	26.0
1982	153.6	32.8	56.8	37.6	26.5
1983	154.9	34.3	57.0	37.2	26.4
1984	157.2	35.8	57.8	37.2	26.5
1985	160.6	37.3	58.5	38.0	26.7
1986	162.6	39.2	59.2	37.6	26.6
1987	168.6	42.2	61.2	38.3	27.0
1988	171.3	43.8	62.9	37.9	26.6
1989	174.5	45.7	64.9	37.9	25.9
1990	184.3	48.6	68.7	40.0	26.9

Notes: 1. For definition of social classes, see Introduction. Table based on 1980 classification of occupations.
2. For an indication of the standard errors attached to the estimates see Introduction and Appendix Tables 3 and 4.

Table 11.2 Pre-maritally conceived first live births to all married women: **England and Wales**
estimated distribution by social class of father as defined by occupation and age of mother, 1980-1990

Year	All classes (including 'others')	Social class of father						All social classes (including 'others')	Social class of father					
		I and II	IIIN	IIIM	IV and V	Non-manual	Manual		I and II	IIIN	IIIM	IV and V	Non-manual	Manual
	a. Number (thousands)							**b. As a percentage of all first live births within marriage**						
	All ages of mother at birth													
1980	39.3	5.2	2.9	16.3	13.2	8.0	29.4	16.3	7.5	10.1	18.9	27.6	8.2	22.0
1981	35.8	5.4	2.8	14.4	11.0	8.2	25.4	16.0	8.0	10.6	18.4	26.1	8.8	21.1
1982	33.6	5.2	2.7	13.7	10.1	7.9	23.8	15.9	8.1	10.5	18.9	25.0	8.8	21.1
1983	32.8	5.3	2.6	13.4	9.7	8.0	23.1	15.5	8.2	10.5	18.4	24.6	8.9	20.6
1984	32.6	5.7	2.8	12.9	9.3	8.4	22.3	15.5	8.8	10.9	18.0	24.3	9.4	20.2
1985	33.7	6.0	2.7	12.7	10.2	8.7	22.9	15.9	9.1	10.9	17.9	26.1	9.6	20.8
1986	32.9	6.7	3.0	12.8	8.5	9.6	21.3	15.9	10.0	12.3	18.6	23.0	10.7	20.1
1987	32.1	6.7	2.8	12.3	8.7	9.4	21.1	15.3	9.6	11.6	17.6	24.3	10.1	19.9
1988	31.4	7.3	2.8	11.2	8.3	10.0	19.5	15.0	10.2	11.2	16.5	24.1	10.5	19.1
1989	29.3	6.7	2.3	11.3	7.4	9.1	18.6	14.6	9.3	10.7	17.4	23.0	9.6	19.3
1990	27.1	6.5	2.4	10.5	6.3	8.9	16.8	13.5	8.8	10.3	16.5	21.0	9.1	18.0
	Under 20													
1980	17.3	1.0	0.9	7.5	7.0	1.9	14.6	61.3	51.2	59.0	65.1	60.8	54.6	62.9
1981	14.4	1.0	0.8	6.0	5.6	1.8	11.6	60.9	54.8	58.0	62.8	61.5	56.2	62.1
1982	12.9	0.9	0.7	5.4	5.0	1.6	10.4	61.4	59.9	56.8	65.4	60.2	58.5	62.8
1983	11.6	0.8	0.6	5.1	4.3	1.5	9.3	61.7	55.0	51.9	66.9	61.6	53.6	64.4
1984	10.2	0.8	0.7	4.2	3.9	1.5	8.1	60.7	59.4	63.3	66.1	58.9	61.2	62.5
1985	9.5	0.7	0.5	3.6	3.9	1.3	7.5	60.1	52.2	52.3	62.3	63.5	52.3	62.9
1986	8.4	0.6	0.5	3.6	3.1	1.1	6.7	60.6	51.8	55.9	67.6	59.9	53.6	63.8
1987	7.3	0.4	0.5	2.9	3.1	0.9	6.0	61.4	42.2	53.9	66.1	68.3	47.6	67.2
1988	6.2	0.5	0.4	2.5	2.4	0.9	4.9	58.1	42.8	56.9	61.8	60.2	48.0	61.0
1989	5.2	0.5	0.4	2.1	1.9	0.9	4.0	56.9	44.4	52.0	59.4	62.4	47.2	60.9
1990	4.4	0.5	0.3	1.9	1.5	0.8	3.4	55.3	42.5	42.8	62.7	55.4	42.6	59.3
	20-24													
1980	15.4	1.9	1.3	6.5	5.0	3.2	11.5	16.0	11.3	12.0	16.0	21.0	11.6	17.8
1981	14.9	1.9	1.1	6.5	4.4	3.0	10.9	16.7	11.8	11.4	17.4	21.1	11.6	18.7
1982	14.1	2.0	1.3	6.0	4.0	3.3	10.0	16.7	12.6	14.0	17.5	19.6	13.1	18.3
1983	14.0	1.7	1.3	5.9	4.2	3.1	10.1	16.9	11.7	14.4	17.5	21.0	12.7	18.8
1984	14.4	1.9	1.1	6.0	4.4	3.0	10.4	17.9	12.7	12.8	18.6	22.7	12.7	20.2
1985	15.2	2.2	1.2	6.2	4.7	3.4	10.9	19.2	14.8	14.6	19.7	24.3	14.7	21.4
1986	14.9	2.5	1.5	5.9	4.0	4.0	9.9	19.9	17.2	19.5	20.2	21.7	18.0	20.8
1987	14.4	2.2	1.1	6.2	4.1	3.4	10.3	20.0	16.1	15.8	21.4	23.7	16.0	22.4
1988	14.0	2.5	1.2	5.3	4.0	3.7	9.3	20.2	17.0	16.3	19.9	25.9	16.8	22.1
1989	12.6	2.2	1.0	5.2	3.4	3.2	8.6	20.2	15.9	18.1	21.2	24.1	16.5	22.2
1990	11.0	1.9	4.5	4.5	3.0	2.9	7.5	19.4	14.7	16.7	20.5	23.7	15.3	21.7
	25-29													
1980	4.4	1.3	0.4	1.6	0.9	1.6	2.5	5.4	3.8	3.4	6.4	9.6	3.7	7.3
1981	4.2	1.5	0.6	1.3	0.8	2.0	2.0	5.4	4.6	5.3	5.4	8.5	4.8	6.3
1982	4.3	1.2	0.4	1.7	0.8	1.6	2.5	5.9	4.1	4.0	7.9	9.0	4.1	8.2
1983	4.8	1.5	0.4	1.7	1.0	1.9	2.7	6.3	5.1	3.6	7.4	10.5	4.7	8.3
1984	5.2	1.6	0.6	1.9	0.8	2.2	2.7	6.7	5.4	5.7	7.6	8.8	5.5	8.0
1985	6.1	1.8	0.7	2.1	1.1	2.5	3.3	7.6	5.9	6.2	8.5	11.2	6.0	9.2
1986	6.4	2.1	0.7	2.3	1.1	2.7	3.3	8.0	6.8	6.1	9.1	10.6	6.6	9.6
1987	6.8	2.1	0.8	2.2	1.3	2.9	3.5	8.1	6.7	6.9	8.3	12.2	6.8	9.4
1988	7.3	2.3	0.8	2.5	1.4	3.2	3.9	8.5	7.4	7.3	9.0	12.0	7.4	9.9
1989	7.4	2.2	0.6	2.8	1.4	2.8	4.3	8.8	6.8	5.6	10.7	13.3	6.5	11.5
1990	7.4	2.4	0.7	2.6	1.3	3.1	4.0	8.5	6.9	6.5	9.8	12.1	6.8	10.5
	30 and over													
1980	2.3	1.0	0.3	0.6	0.3	1.3	0.9	6.5	5.6	6.3	7.1	9.3	5.8	7.7
1981	2.3	1.1	0.3	0.7	0.2	1.3	0.9	6.8	6.0	6.4	8.2	6.6	6.1	7.7
1982	2.3	1.1	0.2	0.6	0.3	1.4	0.8	6.9	6.8	5.5	7.0	9.2	6.5	7.6
1983	2.5	1.2	0.3	0.7	0.3	1.5	1.0	7.3	6.5	6.6	8.6	9.1	6.6	8.7
1984	2.8	1.3	0.3	0.8	0.3	1.6	1.1	7.8	7.0	6.0	9.4	10.4	6.8	9.7
1985	3.0	1.3	0.3	0.8	0.4	1.6	1.2	7.9	6.9	5.7	9.3	12.1	6.7	10.1
1986	3.3	1.5	0.3	1.0	0.4	1.9	1.3	8.5	7.6	6.6	10.3	10.7	7.4	10.4
1987	3.7	1.8	0.4	1.1	0.3	2.2	1.4	8.7	8.0	7.9	10.5	8.7	8.0	10.0
1988	3.9	2.0	0.4	1.0	0.5	2.4	1.5	8.9	8.6	7.2	9.5	14.2	8.3	10.7
1989	4.1	1.8	0.4	1.1	0.6	2.2	1.7	9.0	7.3	7.7	11.4	14.5	7.4	12.3
1990	4.3	1.8	0.4	1.4	0.5	2.2	1.9	8.6	6.9	6.5	12.2	13.4	6.8	12.5

Notes: 1. For definition of social classes, see Introduction. Table based on the 1980 classification of occupations.
2. For an indication of the standard errors attached to the estimates see Introduction and Appendix tables 2 and 3.
3. Table includes live births at durations 0-7 completed months from marriage.

Table 11.3 Median birth intervals: social class of husband as defined by occupation* and woman's marriage order, 1980-1990

Great Britain, England and Wales

Year	Median intervals in months							
	Marriage to first birth					First to second birth	Second to third birth	Third to fourth birth
	All social classes	I and II	IIIN	IIIM	IV and V			
	Women married once only					All women†		
1980	29	41	37	25	18	32	41	41
1981	28	39	34	26	19	31	40	35
1982	29	40	35	26	19	31	40	36
1983	29	39	34	27	20	31	40	35
1984	29	38	34	27	20	31	40	34
1985	28	37	33	26	18	32	40	34
1986	27	36	32	25	19	32	39	33
1987	27	35	31	25	18	32	38	33
1988	27	34	32	25	18	32	38	32
1989	27	32	32	25	20	32	38	33
1990	27	34	30	25	21	33	37	32
	Remarried women							
1980	16	19	18	15	11			
1981	17	19	18	15	15			
1982	18	19	19	17	15			
1983	19	20	19	17	17			
1984	18	18	19	18	15			
1985	17	19	20	17	12			
1986	16	17	16	16	14			
1987	16	16	18	16	13			
1988	15	17	20	14	14			
1989	16	18	18	14	12			
1990	16	15	16	15	12			

* For description of social classes and sample used in calculation see Introduction.
† From a 4 per cent sample of child benefit returns, covering Great Britain. Based on births inside and outside marriage.

Table 11.4 Mean ages of women at live births within marriage: social class of husband as defined by occupation* and birth order, 1980-1990

England and Wales

Year	All social classes	I and II	IIIN	IIIM	IV and V	All social classes	I and II	IIIN	IIIM	IV and V
	All live births within marriage					Second live births within marriage				
1980	27.1	29.1	27.6	26.4	25.5	27.4	29.4	28.1	26.6	25.3
1981	27.3	29.3	27.8	26.6	25.7	27.5	29.5	28.3	26.6	25.3
1982	27.4	29.4	27.9	26.8	25.7	27.5	29.6	28.3	26.8	25.3
1983	27.5	29.5	28.0	26.8	26.0	27.6	29.7	28.5	26.8	25.6
1984	27.6	29.6	27.9	27.0	26.1	27.8	29.9	28.4	27.0	25.7
1985	27.8	29.7	28.1	27.1	26.1	27.9	29.8	28.5	27.1	25.9
1986	27.9	29.8	28.3	27.3	26.3	28.0	30.1	28.6	27.2	26.0
1987	28.1	29.9	28.4	27.4	26.5	28.1	30.2	28.6	27.3	26.1
1988	28.2	29.9	28.5	27.5	26.6	28.3	30.2	29.0	27.4	26.3
1989	28.4	30.4	28.0	27.2	26.9	28.5	31.3	29.0	27.8	27.1
1990	28.6	30.1	28.9	27.9	27.1	28.7	30.3	29.3	27.8	26.6
	First live births within marriage					Third live births within marriage				
1980	25.2	27.5	26.0	24.4	23.1	29.5	31.5	30.6	28.7	27.7
1981	25.4	27.6	26.1	24.5	23.4	29.6	31.7	30.6	29.0	27.7
1982	25.5	27.8	26.2	24.7	23.4	29.6	31.8	30.4	29.0	27.6
1983	25.6	27.9	26.2	24.8	23.7	29.7	32.0	31.0	29.1	27.9
1984	25.8	27.8	26.4	25.1	23.8	29.7	31.8	30.3	29.0	27.8
1985	26.0	28.0	26.5	25.2	24.0	29.8	32.1	30.6	29.0	27.7
1986	26.2	28.1	26.8	25.4	24.2	29.8	32.1	30.4	29.3	27.9
1987	26.5	28.4	27.0	25.8	24.5	29.9	32.0	30.5	29.1	27.8
1988	26.6	28.4	27.2	25.8	24.7	30.0	32.1	30.6	29.2	27.8
1989	26.9	29.0	27.0	26.0	25.3	30.1	32.8	30.9	30.4	29.8
1990	27.2	28.7	27.4	26.3	25.3	30.3	32.1	30.7	29.5	28.4

* For description of social classes and sample used in calculation see Introduction.

Table 11.5   Jointly registered live births outside marriage: social class of father as   England and Wales
             defined by occupation and age of mother, 1980-1990   thousands

Age of mother	Year	All social classes (including 'others')	Social class of father					
			I and II	IIIN	IIIM	IV and V	Non-manual	Manual
All ages	1980	44.2	5.9	2.7	19.6	14.7	8.6	34.3
	1981	47.1	6.2	3.0	20.6	15.6	9.2	36.2
	1982	53.4	7.2	3.5	22.6	18.1	10.7	40.7
	1983	60.8	8.2	3.7	25.4	21.0	11.9	46.4
	1984	69.9	9.2	4.6	29.3	23.5	13.8	52.8
	1985	81.8	10.7	5.0	34.6	27.4	15.7	62.0
	1986	93.5	13.3	5.8	38.3	31.8	19.1	70.0
	1987	108.0	15.4	6.8	44.3	36.1	22.3	80.3
	1988	123.4	18.8	8.1	51.4	39.7	26.9	91.1
	1989	132.3	22.1	7.7	56.3	40.6	29.8	96.9
	1990	145.5	23.1	9.5	62.7	44.6	32.6	107.3
Under 20	1980	11.8	0.6	0.5	5.2	5.0	1.1	10.3
	1981	12.8	0.7	0.7	5.3	5.5	1.3	10.7
	1982	14.3	0.8	0.8	5.6	6.2	1.5	11.9
	1983	16.1	0.9	0.8	6.3	6.9	1.7	13.2
	1984	18.2	1.0	1.0	7.2	7.6	2.0	14.8
	1985	21.0	1.0	1.1	8.3	8.9	2.2	17.2
	1986	23.2	1.4	1.2	8.5	10.6	2.6	19.1
	1987	25.2	1.3	1.5	9.4	10.9	2.8	20.3
	1988	27.5	1.7	1.4	11.2	11.2	3.1	22.4
	1989	27.4	1.8	1.4	11.2	11.2	3.2	22.4
	1990	28.9	1.8	1.6	12.2	11.6	3.4	23.8
20-24	1980	15.3	1.8	0.9	6.7	5.4	2.7	12.1
	1981	16.8	1.8	1.1	7.9	5.5	2.9	13.4
	1982	19.4	2.0	1.1	8.7	6.9	3.1	15.6
	1983	22.6	2.2	1.4	9.8	8.3	3.6	18.2
	1984	26.2	2.6	1.5	11.6	9.4	4.1	21.0
	1985	31.3	2.8	1.8	14.1	11.2	4.6	25.3
	1986	36.2	4.0	2.1	15.6	12.7	6.1	28.3
	1987	41.5	4.4	2.4	18.0	14.8	6.8	32.7
	1988	47.8	5.1	2.9	20.8	17.0	8.0	37.8
	1989	50.6	6.3	2.6	22.6	17.3	8.9	39.9
	1990	53.7	6.4	3.2	24.3	17.9	9.6	42.2
25-29	1980	8.9	1.6	0.7	4.2	2.2	2.3	6.4
	1981	9.5	1.6	0.7	4.3	2.6	2.3	6.9
	1982	10.7	1.9	0.8	4.7	3.0	2.7	7.7
	1983	12.1	2.4	0.8	5.2	3.4	3.2	8.6
	1984	14.2	2.4	1.1	6.0	4.2	3.6	10.2
	1985	16.9	2.8	1.2	7.4	4.8	4.0	12.2
	!986	19.5	3.6	1.4	8.1	5.6	5.0	13.8
	1987	24.0	4.6	1.6	10.3	6.7	6.2	17.0
	1988	28.0	5.3	2.1	11.9	7.7	7.4	19.7
	1989	31.5	6.4	2.0	13.8	8.0	8.4	21.8
	1990	36.4	6.9	2.5	16.1	9.7	9.4	25.8
30 and over	1980	8.1	1.9	0.6	3.4	2.0	2.5	5.4
	1981	8.0	2.1	0.5	3.2	2.0	2.6	5.2
	1982	9.0	2.5	0.8	3.6	1.9	3.3	5.5
	1983	10.1	2.8	0.6	4.1	2.3	3.4	6.4
	1984	11.2	3.2	0.9	4.5	2.3	4.1	6.8
	1985	12.7	4.1	0.9	4.8	2.6	5.0	7.3
	1986	14.7	4.3	1.1	6.0	2.9	5.4	8.9
	1987	17.3	5.1	1.3	6.6	3.7	6.5	10.3
	1988	20.1	6.6	1.7	7.5	3.8	8.3	11.2
	1989	22.8	7.6	1.7	8.8	4.0	9.3	12.8
	1990	26.5	8.0	2.2	10.0	5.4	10.2	15.5

Notes: 1. For definition of social classes, see Introduction. Table based on 1980 classification of occupations.
         2. For indication of the standard errors attatched to the estimates see Introduction and Appendix Tables 3 and 4.

G

Table 12.1 All conceptions: proportions by age of woman and (a) occurrence inside/outside marriage and (b) outcome, 1979-1989

Age of woman at conception and year of conception	Total number of conceptions (000s)	Percentage of all conceptions (a) Within marriage	(a) Outside marriage	(b) Leading to maternities	(b) Terminated by abortion	Age of woman at conception and year of conception	Total number of conceptions (000s)	Percentage of all conceptions (a) Within marriage	(a) Outside marriage	(b) Leading to maternities	(b) Terminated by abortion
All ages						**25-29**					
1979	**774.1**	73.7	26.3	83.8	16.2	1979	**234.8**	87.7	12.3	90.8	9.2
1980	**765.0**	72.7	27.3	83.5	16.5	1980	**229.1**	86.9	13.1	90.6	9.4
1981	**752.3**	71.5	28.5	82.9	17.1	1981	**221.8**	85.8	14.2	90.3	9.7
1982	**755.3**	70.0	30.0	83.0	17.0	1982	**225.0**	84.6	15.4	90.2	9.8
1983	**753.4**	68.6	31.4	83.0	17.0	1983	**226.3**	83.8	16.2	90.3	9.7
1984	**790.1**	66.7	33.3	82.7	17.3	1984	**238.6**	82.2	17.8	90.0	10.0
1985	**797.2**	64.4	35.6	82.1	17.9	1985	**242.6**	80.2	19.8	89.2	10.8
1986	**818.9**	62.8	37.2	82.0	18.0	1986	**253.8**	78.6	21.4	88.9	11.1
1987	**850.4**	60.4	39.6	81.1	18.9	1987	**264.6**	76.1	23.9	88.1	11.9
1988	**849.5**	58.6	41.4	80.3	19.7	1988	**267.1**	74.0	26.0	87.3	12.7
1989	**864.7**	57.7	42.3	80.2	19.8	1989	**278.0**	72.4	27.6	86.9	13.1
Under 16						**30-34**					
1979	**9.1**	0.5	99.5	44.8	55.2	1979	**128.1**	87.4	12.6	85.1	14.9
1980	**8.6**	0.4	99.6	45.9	54.1	1980	**126.9**	87.0	13.0	85.1	14.9
1981	**8.6**	0.6	99.4	43.1	56.9	1981	**126.2**	86.3	13.7	85.3	14.7
1982	**9.0**	0.4	99.6	43.1	56.9	1982	**121.9**	85.6	14.4	85.7	14.3
1983	**9.4**	0.3	99.7	43.2	56.8	1983	**120.9**	84.7	15.3	86.2	13.8
1984	**9.6**	0.5	99.5	44.3	55.7	1984	**126.0**	83.8	16.2	86.5	13.5
1985	**9.4**	0.3	99.7	44.3	55.7	1985	**127.8**	82.7	17.3	86.6	13.4
1986	**9.2**	0.2	99.8	45.9	54.1	1986	**133.0**	81.5	18.5	86.7	13.3
1987	**9.1**	0.3	99.7	45.8	54.2	1987	**139.0**	79.9	20.1	86.4	13.6
1988	**8.8**	0.3	99.7	46.8	53.2	1988	**143.1**	78.7	21.3	86.2	13.8
1989	**8.4**	0.4	99.6	48.0	52.0	1989	**152.5**	77.5	22.5	86.3	13.7
Under 20						**35-39**					
1979	**120.9**	26.6	73.4	69.7	30.3	1979	**38.6**	82.8	17.2	68.1	31.9
1980	**117.2**	25.3	74.7	69.0	31.0	1980	**39.3**	82.8	17.2	68.7	31.3
1981	**115.2**	24.1	75.9	68.1	31.9	1981	**40.9**	80.7	19.3	69.2	30.8
1982	**113.9**	21.2	78.8	67.6	32.4	1982	**44.2**	81.1	18.9	70.8	29.2
1983	**112.4**	19.0	81.0	66.8	33.2	1983	**46.4**	80.5	19.5	72.3	27.7
1984	**118.2**	17.2	82.8	66.6	33.4	1984	**48.5**	79.5	20.5	73.4	26.6
1985	**119.3**	15.3	84.7	66.2	33.8	1985	**48.8**	78.7	21.3	74.0	26.0
1986	**118.8**	13.7	86.3	66.6	33.4	1986	**50.3**	77.5	22.5	74.6	25.4
1987	**123.2**	12.3	87.7	65.4	34.6	1987	**50.8**	75.8	24.2	75.2	24.8
1988	**120.7**	11.0	89.0	64.2	35.8	1988	**51.2**	74.7	25.3	76.0	24.0
1989	**117.5**	10.6	89.4	64.4	35.6	1989	**53.6**	73.8	26.2	76.6	23.4
20-24						**40 and over**					
1979	**241.6**	74.7	25.3	87.3	12.7	1979	**10.1**	80.6	19.4	46.7	53.3
1980	**242.0**	72.9	27.1	86.7	13.3	1980	**10.4**	80.1	19.9	47.8	52.2
1981	**238.1**	71.2	28.8	85.8	14.2	1981	**10.0**	79.9	20.1	48.7	51.3
1982	**240.7**	69.1	30.9	85.7	14.3	1982	**9.6**	79.3	20.7	49.8	50.2
1983	**237.9**	66.8	33.2	85.3	14.7	1983	**9.5**	78.5	21.5	52.7	47.3
1984	**249.1**	63.7	36.3	84.6	15.4	1984	**9.7**	77.5	22.5	53.0	47.0
1985	**249.2**	60.0	40.0	83.1	16.9	1985	**9.6**	76.0	24.0	53.1	46.9
1986	**253.1**	56.8	43.2	82.3	17.7	1986	**9.9**	75.9	24.1	54.0	46.0
1987	**261.9**	53.1	46.9	80.7	19.3	1987	**10.9**	73.7	26.3	54.8	45.2
1988	**256.0**	50.0	50.0	79.2	20.8	1988	**11.3**	72.4	27.6	54.9	45.1
1989	**251.6**	47.5	52.5	78.3	21.7	1989	**11.6**	70.2	29.8	56.4	43.6

Table 12.2 All conceptions: numbers and rates by age of woman and outcome, 1979-1989

England and Wales
Residents

Age of woman at conception and year of conception	Number of conceptions (thousands)			Conception rates per 1,000 women in age-group			Age of woman at conception and year of conception	Number of conceptions (thousands)			Conception rates per 1,000 women in age-group		
	Total conceptions	Conceptions leading to maternities	Conceptions terminated by abortion	Total conceptions	Conceptions leading to maternities	Conceptions terminated by abortion		Total conceptions	Conceptions leading to maternities	Conceptions terminated by abortion	Total conceptions	Conceptions leading to maternities	Conceptions terminated by abortion
All ages*							**25-29**						
1979	**774.1**	648.5	125.6	**76.8**	64.4	12.5	1979	**234.8**	213.3	21.5	**138.7**	126.0	12.7
1980	**765.0**	638.4	126.5	**74.8**	62.5	12.4	1980	**229.1**	207.7	21.5	**137.0**	124.1	12.8
1981	**752.3**	623.8	128.4	**72.7**	60.3	12.4	1981	**221.8**	200.3	21.6	**132.7**	119.8	12.9
1982	**755.3**	626.8	128.5	**72.3**	60.0	12.3	1982	**225.0**	203.0	22.0	**134.2**	121.0	13.1
1983	**753.4**	625.0	128.3	**71.4**	59.3	12.2	1983	**226.3**	204.3	22.0	**133.7**	120.7	13.0
1984	**790.1**	653.8	136.3	**74.2**	61.4	12.8	1984	**238.6**	214.7	23.9	**138.1**	124.3	13.8
1985	**797.2**	654.3	142.9	**74.1**	60.8	13.3	1985	**242.6**	216.5	26.2	**136.1**	121.5	14.7
1986	**818.9**	671.3	147.7	**75.1**	61.6	13.5	1986	**253.8**	225.6	28.2	**137.4**	122.1	15.3
1987	**850.4**	689.5	160.9	**77.4**	62.8	14.7	1987	**264.6**	233.2	31.5	**138.6**	122.1	16.5
1988	**849.5**	681.8	167.7	**77.2**	61.9	15.2	1988	**267.1**	233.0	34.0	**135.8**	118.5	17.3
1989	**864.7**	693.5	171.2	**78.6**	63.0	15.6	1989	**278.0**	241.6	36.3	**137.4**	119.4	18.0
Under 16†							**30-34**						
1979	**9.1**	4.1	5.0	**7.5**	3.4	4.2	1979	**128.1**	109.0	19.1	**70.3**	59.8	10.5
1980	**8.6**	3.9	4.6	**7.2**	3.3	3.9	1980	**126.9**	108.0	18.9	**68.9**	58.6	10.3
1981	**8.6**	3.7	4.9	**7.3**	3.1	4.1	1981	**126.2**	107.6	18.6	**68.4**	58.3	10.1
1982	**9.0**	3.9	5.1	**7.8**	3.4	4.4	1982	**121.9**	104.5	17.5	**69.7**	59.8	10.0
1983	**9.4**	4.0	5.3	**8.3**	3.6	4.7	1983	**120.9**	104.2	16.7	**71.4**	61.6	9.9
1984	**9.6**	4.3	5.4	**8.6**	3.8	4.8	1984	**126.0**	109.0	17.0	**75.6**	65.4	10.2
1985	**9.4**	4.2	5.2	**8.6**	3.8	4.8	1985	**127.8**	110.6	17.2	**77.4**	67.0	10.4
1986	**9.2**	4.2	5.0	**8.7**	4.0	4.7	1986	**133.0**	115.4	17.7	**80.2**	69.6	10.7
1987	**9.1**	4.2	5.0	**9.3**	4.2	5.0	1987	**139.0**	120.1	18.9	**82.8**	71.5	11.3
1988	**8.8**	4.1	4.7	**9.4**	4.4	5.0	1988	**143.1**	123.4	19.8	**84.0**	72.4	11.6
1989	**8.4**	4.0	4.4	**9.4**	4.5	4.9	1989	**152.5**	131.6	20.9	**87.8**	75.7	12.1
Under 20≠							**35-39**						
1979	**120.9**	84.3	36.6	**61.9**	43.2	18.8	1979	**38.6**	26.3	12.3	**26.2**	17.8	8.3
1980	**117.2**	80.9	36.4	**58.7**	40.5	18.2	1980	**39.3**	27.0	12.3	**25.9**	17.8	8.1
1981	**115.2**	78.4	36.7	**57.1**	38.9	18.2	1981	**40.9**	28.3	12.6	**25.9**	17.9	8.0
1982	**113.9**	77.0	36.9	**56.4**	38.1	18.3	1982	**44.2**	31.3	12.9	**25.8**	18.3	7.5
1983	**112.4**	75.0	37.4	**56.0**	37.4	18.6	1983	**46.4**	33.6	12.8	**26.0**	18.8	7.2
1984	**118.2**	78.8	39.5	**59.9**	39.9	20.0	1984	**48.5**	35.6	12.9	**26.7**	19.6	7.1
1985	**119.3**	78.9	40.3	**61.7**	40.8	20.9	1985	**48.8**	36.1	12.7	**26.5**	19.6	6.9
1986	**118.8**	79.1	39.6	**62.3**	41.5	20.8	1986	**50.3**	37.5	12.8	**27.2**	20.3	6.9
1987	**123.2**	80.5	42.6	**66.1**	43.2	22.9	1987	**50.8**	38.2	12.6	**28.9**	21.7	7.2
1988	**120.7**	77.5	43.3	**66.6**	42.8	23.9	1988	**51.2**	39.0	12.3	**30.0**	22.8	7.2
1989	**117.5**	75.7	41.8	**67.6**	43.5	24.0	1989	**53.6**	41.0	12.5	**31.9**	24.4	7.5
20-24							**40 and over****						
1979	**241.6**	210.9	30.7	**139.2**	121.5	17.7	1979	**10.1**	4.7	5.4	**7.2**	3.4	3.9
1980	**242.0**	209.9	32.1	**135.3**	117.4	17.9	1980	**10.4**	5.0	5.4	**7.4**	3.5	3.8
1981	**238.1**	204.3	33.8	**128.9**	110.6	18.3	1981	**10.0**	4.9	5.1	**7.2**	3.5	3.7
1982	**240.7**	206.3	34.4	**127.1**	108.9	18.2	1982	**9.6**	4.8	4.8	**6.8**	3.4	3.4
1983	**237.9**	203.0	34.9	**122.1**	104.2	17.9	1983	**9.5**	5.0	4.5	**6.7**	3.5	3.2
1984	**249.1**	210.6	38.5	**124.2**	105.0	19.2	1984	**9.7**	5.1	4.5	**6.6**	3.5	3.1
1985	**249.2**	207.2	42.0	**121.4**	100.9	20.5	1985	**9.6**	5.1	4.5	**6.4**	3.4	3.0
1986	**253.1**	208.4	44.8	**122.2**	100.5	21.6	1986	**9.9**	5.4	4.6	**6.3**	3.4	2.9
1987	**261.9**	211.4	50.4	**126.6**	102.3	24.4	1987	**10.9**	6.0	4.9	**6.4**	3.5	2.9
1988	**256.0**	202.8	53.3	**125.4**	99.3	26.1	1988	**11.3**	6.2	5.1	**6.4**	3.5	2.9
1989	**251.6**	197.1	54.6	**125.2**	98.0	27.1	1989	**11.6**	6.5	5.1	**6.4**	3.6	2.8

* Rates per 1,000 women aged 15-44.
† Rates per 1,000 women aged 13-15.
≠ Rates per 1,000 women aged 15-19
** Rates per 1,000 women aged 40-44.

Table 12.3 All teenage conceptions: numbers and rates by single year of age and outcome, 1979-1989

England and Wales
Residents

Age of woman at conception and year of conception	Number of conceptions			Conception rates per 1,000 women in age-group/age			Age of woman at conception and year of conception	Number of conceptions			Conception rates per 1,000 women in age-group/age		
	Total conceptions	Conceptions leading to maternities	Conceptions terminated by abortion	Total conceptions	Conceptions leading to maternities	Conceptions terminated by abortion		Total conceptions	Conceptions leading to maternities	Conceptions terminated by abortion	Total conceptions	Conceptions leading to maternities	Conceptions terminated by abortion
Under 16*							**16**						
1979	**9,108**	4,079	5,029	**7.5**	3.4	4.2	1979	**16,106**	9,307	6,799	**40.6**	23.5	17.2
1980	**8,580**	3,935	4,645	**7.2**	3.3	3.9	1980	**15,210**	8,600	6,610	**37.4**	21.1	16.3
1981	**8,561**	3,694	4,867	**7.3**	3.1	4.1	1981	**15,410**	8,782	6,628	**37.7**	21.5	16.2
1982	**8,999**	3,875	5,124	**7.8**	3.4	4.4	1982	**15,030**	8,331	6,699	**37.6**	20.9	16.8
1983	**9,369**	4,046	5,323	**8.3**	3.6	4.7	1983	**15,229**	8,431	6,798	**38.7**	21.4	17.3
1984	**9,649**	4,278	5,371	**8.6**	3.8	4.8	1984	**15,995**	8,842	7,153	**41.9**	23.2	18.7
1985	**9,406**	4,169	5,237	**8.6**	3.8	4.8	1985	**16,146**	9,107	7,039	**42.4**	23.9	18.5
1986	**9,194**	4,222	4,972	**8.7**	4.0	4.7	1986	**15,425**	8,933	6,492	**41.9**	24.3	17.6
1987	**9,135**	4,185	4,950	**9.3**	4.2	5.0	1987	**16,512**	9,415	7,097	**44.1**	25.1	19.0
1988	**8,782**	4,110	4,672	**9.4**	4.4	5.0	1988	**15,821**	8,924	6,897	**45.1**	25.4	19.7
1989	**8,382**	4,026	4,356	**9.4**	4.5	4.9	1989	**15,176**	8,741	6,435	**46.0**	26.5	19.5
Under 14†							**17**						
1979	**381**	144	237	**1.0**	0.4	0.6	1979	**24,868**	16,694	8,174	**63.3**	42.5	20.8
1980	**352**	125	227	**0.9**	0.3	0.6	1980	**23,894**	15,791	8,103	**60.0**	39.6	20.3
1981	**435**	171	264	**1.1**	0.4	0.7	1981	**23,179**	14,990	8,189	**56.8**	36.7	20.1
1982	**428**	138	290	**1.1**	0.4	0.8	1982	**22,964**	15,049	7,915	**55.8**	36.6	19.2
1983	**367**	148	219	**1.0**	0.4	0.6	1983	**22,575**	14,452	8,123	**56.0**	35.9	20.2
1984	**378**	151	227	**1.0**	0.4	0.6	1984	**24,209**	15,642	8,567	**61.4**	39.6	21.7
1985	**325**	139	186	**0.9**	0.4	0.5	1985	**24,619**	15,922	8,697	**64.2**	41.5	22.7
1986	**292**	120	172	**0.9**	0.4	0.5	1986	**24,776**	16,101	8,675	**64.8**	42.1	22.7
1987	**346**	145	201	**1.1**	0.5	0.7	1987	**24,809**	15,915	8,894	**67.1**	43.0	24.1
1988	**305**	138	167	**1.0**	0.5	0.6	1988	**25,423**	15,872	9,551	**67.6**	42.2	25.4
1989	**250**	119	131	**0.9**	0.4	0.5	1989	**24,230**	15,248	8,982	**68.7**	43.2	25.5
14							**18**						
1979	**1,904**	760	1,144	**4.7**	1.9	2.8	1979	**32,752**	24,206	8,546	**84.8**	62.7	22.1
1980	**1,714**	669	1,045	**4.3**	1.7	2.6	1980	**32,093**	23,378	8,715	**81.2**	59.2	22.1
1981	**1,817**	684	1,133	**4.6**	1.7	2.9	1981	**30,564**	21,894	8,670	**76.2**	54.6	21.6
1982	**1,868**	702	1,166	**4.9**	1.8	3.1	1982	**30,325**	21,769	8,556	**74.0**	53.1	20.9
1983	**2,034**	790	1,244	**5.4**	2.1	3.3	1983	**29,860**	21,196	8,664	**72.2**	51.2	20.9
1984	**2,018**	794	1,224	**5.5**	2.2	3.3	1984	**31,382**	22,302	9,080	**77.9**	55.3	22.5
1985	**2,063**	836	1,227	**5.5**	2.2	3.3	1985	**31,939**	22,235	9,704	**80.7**	56.2	24.5
1986	**1,980**	809	1,171	**5.7**	2.3	3.4	1986	**32,177**	22,456	9,721	**83.6**	58.4	25.3
1987	**1,899**	736	1,163	**5.8**	2.2	3.5	1987	**33,648**	23,114	10,534	**87.7**	60.3	27.5
1988	**1,761**	711	1,050	**5.7**	2.3	3.4	1988	**32,208**	21,672	10,536	**86.9**	58.5	28.4
1989	**1,765**	783	982	**6.0**	2.6	3.3	1989	**32,591**	21,791	10,800	**86.5**	57.8	28.7
15							**19**						
1979	**6,823**	3,175	3,648	**16.8**	7.8	9.0	1979	**38,110**	30,015	8,095	**102.4**	80.6	21.7
1980	**6,513**	3,140	3,373	**16.0**	7.7	8.3	1980	**37,475**	29,187	8,288	**96.4**	75.1	21.3
1981	**6,309**	2,839	3,470	**15.8**	7.1	8.7	1981	**37,458**	29,087	8,371	**94.0**	73.0	21.0
1982	**6,703**	3,035	3,668	**17.1**	7.7	9.3	1982	**36,614**	27,961	8,653	**90.1**	68.8	21.3
1983	**6,968**	3,108	3,860	**18.3**	8.2	10.1	1983	**35,318**	26,872	8,446	**84.8**	64.5	20.3
1984	**7,253**	3,333	3,920	**19.1**	8.8	10.3	1984	**36,993**	27,691	9,302	**89.3**	66.9	22.5
1985	**7,018**	3,194	3,824	**19.1**	8.7	10.4	1985	**37,157**	27,489	9,668	**91.7**	67.9	23.9
1986	**6,922**	3,293	3,629	**18.5**	8.8	9.7	1986	**37,205**	27,419	,786	**93.5**	68.9	24.6
1987	**6,890**	3,304	3,586	**19.7**	9.4	10.2	1987	**39,048**	27,911	11,137	**101.1**	72.2	28.8
1988	**6,716**	3,261	3,455	**20.4**	9.9	10.5	1988	**38,475**	26,878	11,597	**100.0**	69.8	30.1
1989	**6,367**	3,124	3,243	**20.7**	10.2	10.5	1989	**37,120**	25,918	11,202	**99.8**	69.7	30.1

* Rates per 1,000 women aged 13-15.
† Rates per 1,000 women aged 13.

Table 12.4 Conceptions within marriage: proportions by age of woman and outcome, 1979-1989

England and Wales
Residents

Age of woman at conception and year of conception	Total number of conceptions within marriage (000s)	Percentage of conceptions within marriage				Age of woman at conception and year of conception	Total number of conceptions within marriage (000s)	Percentage of conceptions within marriage			
		Leading to maternities			Terminated by abortion			Leading to maternities			Terminated by abortion
		All marriages	First marriage	Second or later marriage				All marriages	First marriage	Second or later marriage	
All ages						**30-34**					
1979	570.6	92.2	86.8	5.4	7.8	1979	112.0	88.6	78.6	10.0	11.4
1980	556.4	92.2	86.6	5.6	7.8	1980	110.4	88.9	78.8	10.2	11.1
1981	538.0	92.1	86.2	5.9	7.9	1981	109.0	89.1	78.5	10.6	10.9
1982	528.6	92.4	86.3	6.1	7.6	1982	104.4	89.5	78.2	11.3	10.5
1983	517.0	92.6	86.3	6.3	7.4	1983	102.4	90.2	78.7	11.6	9.8
1984	526.8	92.7	86.2	6.5	7.3	1984	105.7	90.7	79.0	11.7	9.3
1985	513.7	92.6	86.1	6.6	7.4	1985	105.7	90.9	79.2	11.7	9.1
1986	514.3	92.6	85.9	6.7	7.4	1986	108.4	91.1	79.1	11.9	8.9
1987	513.3	92.4	85.7	6.7	7.6	1987	111.1	91.1	79.3	11.8	8.9
1988	498.0	92.3	85.5	6.7	7.7	1988	112.6	91.1	79.7	11.4	8.9
1989	499.2	92.4	85.7	6.7	7.6	1989	118.2	91.5	80.3	11.1	8.5
Under 20						**35-39**					
1979	32.2	96.5	96.2	0.2	3.5	1979	32.0	71.7	59.3	12.4	28.3
1980	29.7	96.4	96.1	0.3	3.6	1980	32.6	72.6	59.8	12.8	27.4
1981	27.7	96.2	96.0	0.2	3.8	1981	33.0	72.1	59.2	12.9	27.9
1982	24.1	96.2	96.0	0.2	3.8	1982	35.9	75.1	61.1	14.0	24.9
1983	21.3	96.6	96.4	0.2	3.4	1983	37.3	76.6	61.8	14.8	23.4
1984	20.4	96.1	96.0	0.1	3.9	1984	38.6	77.7	61.8	15.9	22.3
1985	18.3	96.1	95.9	0.2	3.9	1985	38.4	78.4	61.9	16.4	21.6
1986	16.3	95.7	95.4	0.3	4.3	1986	38.9	79.1	62.6	16.5	20.9
1987	15.1	95.1	94.8	0.3	4.9	1987	38.5	79.7	63.0	16.7	20.3
1988	13.3	95.1	94.8	0.2	4.9	1988	38.3	80.8	64.2	16.6	19.2
1989	12.4	95.3	95.2	0.2	4.7	1989	39.6	81.8	65.1	16.7	18.2
20-24						**40 and over**					
1979	180.4	96.1	94.3	1.8	3.9	1979	8.1	49.1	40.5	8.6	50.9
1980	176.3	96.2	94.4	1.8	3.8	1980	8.3	50.7	40.8	9.8	49.3
1981	169.6	96.0	94.1	1.9	4.0	1981	8.0	51.2	41.9	9.3	48.8
1982	166.2	96.2	94.5	1.7	3.8	1982	7.6	52.6	42.4	10.3	47.4
1983	158.8	96.2	94.6	1.6	3.8	1983	7.4	56.0	44.5	11.4	44.0
1984	158.6	96.1	94.5	1.7	3.9	1984	7.5	56.6	44.6	12.0	43.4
1985	149.4	95.8	94.2	1.6	4.2	1985	7.3	57.0	44.0	13.0	43.0
1986	143.7	95.8	94.1	1.7	4.2	1986	7.5	57.1	43.8	13.3	42.9
1987	139.1	95.5	93.8	1.7	4.5	1987	8.0	58.1	43.5	14.5	41.9
1988	127.9	95.1	93.5	1.6	4.9	1988	8.2	58.1	42.6	15.6	41.9
1989	119.6	95.0	93.4	1.6	5.0	1989	8.1	60.2	44.0	16.2	39.8
25-29											
1979	205.9	94.8	89.2	5.6	5.2						
1980	199.1	94.9	89.0	5.9	5.1						
1981	190.2	94.9	88.8	6.0	5.1						
1982	190.4	95.0	88.8	6.2	5.0						
1983	189.7	95.0	88.8	6.2	5.0						
1984	196.0	95.1	88.9	6.2	4.9						
1985	194.7	94.9	88.9	6.0	5.1						
1986	199.5	94.8	89.0	5.8	5.2						
1987	201.5	94.7	89.0	5.7	5.3						
1988	197.8	94.6	89.0	5.5	5.4						
1989	201.3	94.6	89.3	5.3	5.4						

Table 12.5 Conceptions outside marriage: proportions by age of woman and outcome, 1979-1989

England and Wales
Residents

Age of woman at conception and year of conception	Total number of conceptions outside marriage (000s)	Percentage of conceptions outside marriage				
		Leading to maternities			Within marriage	Terminated by abortion
		Outside marriage				
		Total	Sole*	Joint†		
All ages						
1979	**203.5**	36.9	16.2	20.7	23.4	39.7
1980	**208.6**	38.4	16.1	22.3	21.6	40.0
1981	**214.3**	40.5	16.7	23.7	19.3	40.2
1982	**226.7**	42.7	16.8	25.9	18.3	38.9
1983	**236.4**	44.6	16.8	27.9	17.3	38.1
1984	**263.4**	46.6	16.6	30.0	16.2	37.2
1985	**283.5**	48.1	16.5	31.5	14.9	37.0
1986	**304.6**	50.3	16.5	33.8	13.7	35.9
1987	**337.1**	51.3	15.8	35.5	12.4	36.2
1988	**351.5**	51.9	15.1	36.7	11.4	36.8
1989	**365.6**	53.2	14.9	38.3	10.4	36.4
Under 16						
1979	**9.1**	37.8	24.4	13.4	6.9	55.4
1980	**8.5**	39.5	24.6	14.8	6.3	54.3
1981	**8.5**	37.9	23.8	14.1	4.9	57.1
1982	**9.0**	39.0	23.8	15.2	3.9	57.1
1983	**9.3**	39.9	24.1	15.7	3.3	56.9
1984	**9.6**	41.3	23.9	17.4	2.9	55.9
1985	**9.4**	41.9	23.6	18.3	2.3	55.8
1986	**9.2**	43.9	23.9	20.0	1.9	54.2
1987	**9.1**	43.7	23.3	20.4	2.0	54.3
1988	**8.8**	45.1	24.3	20.8	1.5	53.3
1989	**8.3**	46.7	24.1	22.7	1.1	52.1
Under 20						
1979	**88.8**	34.4	18.8	15.6	25.6	40.0
1980	**87.6**	36.7	18.6	18.1	23.0	40.3
1981	**87.4**	38.9	19.4	19.5	20.3	40.8
1982	**89.8**	41.6	19.6	22.0	18.3	40.1
1983	**91.0**	43.7	19.5	24.3	16.0	40.2
1984	**97.9**	46.1	19.5	26.6	14.4	39.5
1985	**101.0**	48.2	19.6	28.6	12.6	39.2
1986	**102.5**	51.0	20.1	30.9	11.0	38.0
1987	**108.0**	51.8	19.3	32.5	9.4	38.8
1988	**107.4**	52.3	18.8	33.5	8.0	39.6
1989	**105.1**	53.7	18.9	34.8	7.1	39.2
20-24						
1979	**61.1**	37.7	15.5	22.1	23.7	38.7
1980	**65.7**	39.1	15.9	23.3	22.3	38.6
1981	**68.5**	40.8	16.0	24.8	19.8	39.4
1982	**74.5**	43.0	16.2	26.8	19.3	37.7
1983	**79.1**	44.8	16.3	28.6	18.7	36.5
1984	**90.4**	46.4	15.8	30.7	17.8	35.8
1985	**99.8**	47.7	15.7	32.0	16.5	35.9
1986	**109.5**	49.6	15.5	34.0	15.0	35.4
1987	**122.8**	50.4	15.0	35.4	13.7	35.9
1988	**128.1**	51.1	14.3	36.8	12.2	36.7
1989	**132.0**	52.4	14.1	38.3	10.9	36.7

Age of woman at conception and year of conception	Total number of conceptions outside marriage (000s)	Percentage of conceptions outside marriage				
		Leading to maternities			Within marriage	Terminated by abortion
		Outside marriage				
		Total	Sole*	Joint†		
25-29						
1979	**28.9**	41.5	13.8	27.8	20.9	37.5
1980	**30.0**	41.1	12.7	28.3	21.1	37.8
1981	**31.6**	44.2	15.2	29.1	18.3	37.4
1982	**34.6**	45.6	14.5	31.1	18.5	36.0
1983	**36.7**	47.3	14.7	32.6	18.4	34.3
1984	**42.6**	49.0	14.6	34.4	17.5	33.5
1985	**48.0**	49.5	14.7	34.8	16.6	33.9
1986	**54.3**	51.5	14.4	37.1	15.6	32.9
1987	**63.1**	52.6	13.8	38.8	14.4	33.0
1988	**69.3**	52.6	13.1	39.5	13.8	33.6
1989	**76.7**	54.1	12.6	41.5	12.7	33.2
30-34						
1979	**16.1**	41.3	11.8	29.5	19.4	39.3
1980	**16.5**	41.9	12.5	29.4	17.4	40.7
1981	**17.3**	42.1	12.2	29.9	18.8	39.1
1982	**17.6**	45.3	13.2	32.0	17.6	37.2
1983	**18.5**	46.5	12.7	33.7	17.2	36.3
1984	**20.4**	48.1	13.4	34.7	16.8	35.1
1985	**22.1**	49.8	13.3	36.5	15.9	34.2
1986	**24.6**	51.8	13.1	38.7	15.7	32.5
1987	**28.0**	53.2	13.2	40.0	14.6	32.2
1988	**30.5**	54.1	12.6	41.5	14.0	31.9
1989	**34.3**	55.3	12.3	43.0	13.0	31.7
35-39						
1979	**6.6**	36.4	11.1	25.3	14.6	49.0
1980	**6.7**	34.9	10.7	24.2	14.9	50.2
1981	**7.5**	39.0	11.7	27.3	12.5	48.5
1982	**8.3**	38.5	11.4	27.1	13.9	47.6
1983	**9.1**	40.3	11.7	28.6	14.5	45.1
1984	**9.9**	42.8	11.7	31.2	13.9	43.3
1985	**10.4**	44.6	12.1	32.5	13.4	42.0
1986	**11.3**	45.9	11.6	34.4	13.2	40.8
1987	**12.3**	48.8	11.0	37.8	12.2	39.0
1988	**13.0**	49.7	11.4	38.3	12.3	37.9
1989	**14.0**	50.3	11.5	38.8	11.7	38.0
40 and over						
1979	**2.0**	27.4	10.9	17.0	8.9	63.7
1980	**2.1**	30.5	9.9	20.6	7.1	62.4
1981	**2.0**	29.9	7.0	22.9	7.7	62.4
1982	**2.0**	30.7	10.5	20.2	8.3	61.0
1983	**2.0**	31.5	10.7	20.7	9.1	59.4
1984	**2.2**	30.7	9.6	21.1	9.9	59.4
1985	**2.3**	31.8	9.4	22.4	9.2	59.0
1986	**2.4**	35.7	10.6	25.1	8.7	55.5
1987	**2.9**	37.1	8.8	28.4	8.6	54.3
1988	**3.1**	37.3	9.1	28.2	9.1	53.6
1989	**3.5**	39.7	8.8	30.9	7.7	52.6

* Conceptions leading to births outside marriage registered by the mother alone.
† Conceptions leading to births outside marriage registered by both parents.

Table 12.6 Conceptions within marriage: numbers and rates by age of woman and outcome, 1979-1989

England and Wales
Residents

Age of woman at conception and year of conception		Numbers of conceptions (thousands)					Conception rates per 1,000 married women in age-group				
		Total conceptions within marriage	Conceptions leading to maternities during			Conceptions terminated by abortion	Total conceptions within marriage	Conceptions leading to maternities during			Conceptions terminated by abortion
			All marriages	First marriage	Second or later marriage			All marriages	First marriage	Second or later marriage	
All ages*	1979	**570.6**	525.8	495.0	30.8	44.8	**90.5**	83.4	78.5	4.9	7.1
	1980	**556.4**	513.2	482.0	31.2	43.1	**88.6**	81.7	76.7	5.0	6.9
	1981	**538.0**	495.7	463.9	31.8	42.3	**86.3**	79.5	74.4	5.1	6.8
	1982	**528.6**	488.3	456.0	32.3	40.3	**85.7**	79.2	73.9	5.2	6.5
	1983	**517.0**	478.8	446.1	32.6	38.3	**84.6**	78.4	73.0	5.3	6.3
	1984	**526.8**	488.5	454.2	34.2	38.3	**86.7**	80.4	74.8	5.6	6.3
	1985	**513.7**	475.8	442.1	33.7	37.9	**85.0**	78.8	73.2	5.6	6.3
	1986	**514.3**	476.1	441.7	34.4	38.1	**85.4**	79.1	73.4	5.7	6.3
	1987	**513.3**	474.6	440.0	34.6	38.8	**85.5**	79.0	73.3	5.8	6.5
	1988	**498.0**	459.6	426.0	33.6	38.5	**83.6**	77.2	71.5	5.6	6.5
	1989	**499.2**	461.1	427.6	33.6	38.0	**84.6**	78.1	72.4	5.7	6.4
Under 16	1979	**0.0**	0.0	0.0	-	0.0	:	:	:	:	:
	1980	**0.0**	0.0	0.0	-	0.0	:	:	:	:	:
	1981	**0.1**	0.0	0.0	-	0.0	:	:	:	:	:
	1982	**0.0**	0.0	0.0	-	0.0	:	:	:	:	:
	1983	**0.0**	0.0	0.0	-	0.0	:	:	:	:	:
	1984	**0.0**	0.0	0.0	0.0	0.0	:	:	:	:	:
	1985	**0.0**	0.0	0.0	-	0.0	:	:	:	:	:
	1986	**0.0**	0.0	0.0	-	0.0	:	:	:	:	:
	1987	**0.0**	0.0	0.0	-	0.0	:	:	:	:	:
	1988	**0.0**	0.0	0.0	-	0.0	:	:	:	:	:
	1989	**0.0**	0.0	0.0	-	0.0	:	:	:	:	:
16	1979	**0.8**	0.7	0.7	0.0	0.0	**329.6**	310.9	310.0	0.9	18.7
	1980	**0.6**	0.6	0.6	-	0.0	**303.0**	282.0	282.0	-	21.0
	1981	**0.6**	0.5	0.5	0.0	0.0	**373.3**	342.0	341.3	0.7	31.3
	1982	**0.5**	0.5	0.5	-	0.0	**370.0**	347.7	347.7	-	22.3
	1983	**0.5**	0.4	0.4	0.0	0.0	**409.1**	392.7	391.8	0.9	16.4
	1984	**0.5**	0.4	0.4	0.0	0.0	**479.0**	448.0	446.0	2.0	31.0
	1985	**0.5**	0.4	0.4	0.0	0.0	**459.0**	425.0	422.0	3.0	34.0
	1986	**0.4**	0.4	0.4	0.0	0.0	**422.2**	393.3	391.1	2.2	28.9
	1987	**0.3**	0.3	0.3	-	0.0	**336.0**	316.0	316.0	-	20.0
	1988	**0.3**	0.3	0.3	0.0	0.0	**392.5**	363.8	362.5	1.3	28.8
	1989	**0.3**	0.3	0.3	-	0.0	**430.0**	404.3	404.3	-	25.7
17	1979	**3.3**	3.2	3.2	0.0	0.1	**315.7**	302.1	301.5	0.6	13.6
	1980	**3.0**	2.9	2.9	0.0	0.1	**316.3**	301.4	300.2	1.1	14.9
	1981	**2.7**	2.5	2.5	-	0.1	**340.3**	323.8	323.8	-	16.4
	1982	**2.3**	2.2	2.1	0.0	0.1	**326.8**	311.9	311.0	0.9	14.9
	1983	**2.0**	1.9	1.9	0.0	0.1	**325.4**	312.8	312.6	0.2	12.6
	1984	**2.0**	1.9	1.9	0.0	0.1	**375.5**	358.9	358.5	0.4	16.6
	1985	**1.8**	1.7	1.7	0.0	0.1	**386.1**	365.2	364.3	0.9	20.9
	1986	**1.5**	1.5	1.5	0.0	0.1	**359.1**	338.6	337.9	0.7	20.5
	1987	**1.4**	1.3	1.3	0.0	0.1	**302.6**	285.0	283.7	1.3	17.6
	1988	**1.2**	1.1	1.1	0.0	0.0	**276.0**	264.5	264.3	0.2	11.4
	1989	**1.1**	1.1	1.1	0.0	0.1	**306.8**	291.1	290.0	1.1	15.7
18	1979	**10.1**	9.7	9.7	0.0	0.3	**330.0**	319.0	318.4	0.5	11.0
	1980	**9.3**	9.0	8.9	0.0	0.3	**317.5**	306.2	305.4	0.8	11.3
	1981	**8.2**	7.9	7.9	0.0	0.3	**317.8**	306.5	306.1	0.4	11.3
	1982	**7.0**	6.8	6.8	0.0	0.2	**325.7**	314.4	314.1	0.4	11.3
	1983	**6.3**	6.1	6.1	0.0	0.2	**323.8**	313.1	312.7	0.4	10.7
	1984	**6.0**	5.8	5.8	0.0	0.2	**354.8**	341.8	341.2	0.6	13.0
	1985	**5.3**	5.1	5.1	0.0	0.2	**352.6**	340.0	339.5	0.5	12.6
	1986	**4.6**	4.4	4.4	0.0	0.2	**354.8**	338.9	338.1	0.8	16.0
	1987	**4.5**	4.3	4.3	0.0	0.2	**311.9**	297.3	296.4	0.9	14.7
	1988	**3.8**	3.6	3.6	0.0	0.2	**283.2**	268.6	268.1	0.5	14.6
	1989	**3.6**	3.4	3.4	0.0	0.2	**293.4**	280.3	279.8	0.6	13.1
19	1979	**18.0**	17.4	17.3	0.0	0.6	**288.3**	278.5	277.8	0.7	9.8
	1980	**16.7**	16.1	16.1	0.1	0.5	**271.0**	262.1	261.2	0.9	8.9
	1981	**16.3**	15.7	15.7	0.0	0.6	**281.7**	271.6	271.0	0.6	10.2
	1982	**14.3**	13.8	13.8	0.0	0.5	**282.0**	271.4	270.8	0.6	10.6
	1983	**12.6**	12.2	12.2	0.0	0.4	**279.2**	270.1	269.4	0.7	9.1
	1984	**11.8**	11.4	11.4	0.0	0.4	**296.9**	285.8	285.5	0.3	11.1
	1985	**10.7**	10.3	10.3	0.0	0.4	**303.5**	292.5	291.7	0.8	10.9
	1986	**9.7**	9.3	9.3	0.0	0.4	**311.4**	299.4	298.4	1.0	12.0
	1987	**8.9**	8.5	8.4	0.0	0.4	**281.2**	267.9	267.0	0.9	13.3
	1988	**7.9**	7.6	7.5	0.0	0.4	**255.6**	243.2	242.7	0.6	12.3
	1989	**7.4**	7.0	7.0	0.0	0.3	**258.6**	246.7	246.2	0.5	11.9

* Rates per 1,000 married women aged 15-44.

Table 12.6 - *continued*

Age of woman at conception and year of conception		Numbers of conceptions (thousands)					Conception rates per 1,000 married women in age-group				
		Total conceptions within marriage	Conceptions leading to maternities during			Conceptions terminated by abortion	Total conceptions within marriage	Conceptions leading to maternities during			Conceptions terminated by abortion
			All marriages	First marriage	Second or later marriage			All marriages	First marriage	Second or later marriage	
Under 20*	1979	32.2	31.0	31.0	0.1	1.1	304.4	293.6	292.9	0.7	10.8
	1980	29.7	28.6	28.5	0.1	1.1	289.5	279.0	278.2	0.9	10.4
	1981	27.7	26.7	26.6	0.0	1.1	298.7	287.3	286.8	0.5	11.4
	1982	24.1	23.2	23.2	0.0	0.9	299.4	288.0	287.5	0.5	11.4
	1983	21.3	20.6	20.6	0.0	0.7	297.6	287.5	287.0	0.5	10.1
	1984	20.4	19.6	19.5	0.0	0.8	322.7	310.3	309.8	0.4	12.5
	1985	18.3	17.6	17.5	0.0	0.7	326.7	314.0	313.3	0.8	12.7
	1986	16.3	15.6	15.5	0.0	0.7	330.2	315.9	315.0	1.0	14.2
	1987	15.1	14.4	14.4	0.0	0.7	293.3	279.0	278.1	0.9	14.2
	1988	13.3	12.6	12.6	0.0	0.7	267.1	253.9	253.3	0.5	13.2
	1989	12.4	11.8	11.8	0.0	0.6	275.4	262.6	262.0	0.5	12.8
20-24	1979	180.4	173.4	170.1	3.3	7.0	213.7	205.3	201.4	3.9	8.3
	1980	176.3	169.6	166.4	3.1	6.7	212.5	204.4	200.6	3.8	8.1
	1981	169.6	162.8	159.6	3.2	6.8	209.1	200.7	196.7	4.0	8.4
	1982	166.2	159.9	157.0	2.9	6.3	212.5	204.4	200.8	3.7	8.1
	1983	158.8	152.7	150.2	2.6	6.1	210.6	202.5	199.1	3.4	8.0
	1984	158.6	152.5	149.9	2.6	6.1	217.5	209.1	205.5	3.6	8.4
	1985	149.4	143.2	140.8	2.4	6.2	214.0	205.1	201.7	3.4	8.9
	1986	143.7	137.6	135.2	2.5	6.0	218.5	209.3	205.6	3.8	9.2
	1987	139.1	132.8	130.4	2.3	6.3	223.3	213.2	209.4	3.7	10.2
	1988	127.9	121.6	119.6	2.1	6.3	215.7	205.1	201.6	3.5	10.6
	1989	119.6	113.5	111.6	1.9	6.0	210.0	199.4	196.0	3.4	10.6
25-29	1979	205.9	195.2	183.7	11.5	10.7	156.4	148.3	139.5	8.8	8.1
	1980	199.1	189.0	177.3	11.7	10.1	156.0	148.1	138.9	9.2	7.9
	1981	190.2	180.5	169.0	11.5	9.8	152.6	144.7	135.5	9.2	7.8
	1982	190.4	180.9	169.0	11.8	9.6	155.6	147.8	138.1	9.7	7.8
	1983	189.7	180.2	168.4	11.8	9.4	157.2	149.4	139.6	9.8	7.8
	1984	196.0	186.4	174.2	12.2	9.7	163.4	155.3	145.2	10.2	8.1
	1985	194.7	184.8	173.1	11.6	9.9	161.8	153.6	143.9	9.7	8.2
	1986	199.5	189.1	177.6	11.5	10.4	165.6	157.0	147.4	9.6	8.6
	1987	201.5	190.9	179.3	11.6	10.6	166.8	158.0	148.5	9.6	8.8
	1988	197.8	187.0	176.1	11.0	10.7	164.8	155.9	146.8	9.1	8.9
	1989	201.3	190.4	179.8	10.6	10.9	169.3	160.2	151.3	8.9	9.2
30-34	1979	112.0	99.3	88.0	11.3	12.7	71.9	63.7	56.5	7.2	8.2
	1980	110.4	98.2	86.9	11.2	12.2	70.8	62.9	55.7	7.2	7.8
	1981	109.0	97.1	85.6	11.5	11.8	70.6	62.9	55.5	7.5	7.7
	1982	104.4	93.4	81.6	11.8	10.9	72.4	64.9	56.7	8.2	7.6
	1983	102.4	92.4	80.6	11.9	10.0	74.6	67.3	58.7	8.6	7.3
	1984	105.7	95.8	83.4	12.4	9.8	79.2	71.8	62.5	9.3	7.4
	1985	105.7	96.1	83.7	12.3	9.6	81.1	73.7	64.2	9.5	7.4
	1986	108.4	98.7	85.8	13.0	9.7	83.9	76.4	66.4	10.0	7.5
	1987	111.1	101.2	88.1	13.1	9.9	86.0	78.3	68.2	10.1	7.7
	1988	112.6	102.6	89.7	12.9	10.0	87.2	79.4	69.4	10.0	7.8
	1989	118.2	108.1	95.0	13.2	10.1	91.2	83.5	73.3	10.2	7.8
35-39	1979	32.0	22.9	19.0	4.0	9.1	25.0	7.9	14.8	3.1	7.1
	1980	32.6	23.6	19.5	4.2	8.9	24.9	8.1	14.9	3.2	6.8
	1981	33.0	24.0	19.7	4.3	9.0	24.5	17.8	14.6	3.2	6.7
	1982	35.9	26.9	21.9	5.0	8.9	24.6	18.5	15.0	3.5	6.1
	1983	37.3	28.6	23.1	5.5	8.7	24.8	19.0	15.3	3.7	5.8
	1984	38.6	30.0	23.8	6.1	8.6	25.4	19.7	15.7	4.0	5.7
	1985	38.4	30.1	23.8	6.3	8.3	25.1	19.7	15.6	4.1	5.4
	1986	38.9	30.8	24.4	6.4	8.1	25.7	20.3	16.1	4.2	5.4
	1987	38.5	30.7	24.3	6.4	7.8	27.0	21.5	17.0	4.5	5.5
	1988	38.3	30.9	24.6	6.3	7.4	28.0	22.6	18.0	4.6	5.4
	1989	39.6	32.3	25.8	6.6	7.2	29.7	24.3	19.4	5.0	5.4
40 and over†	1979	8.1	4.0	3.3	0.7	4.1	6.8	3.3	2.7	0.6	3.4
	1980	8.3	4.2	3.4	0.8	4.1	6.9	3.5	2.8	0.7	3.4
	1981	7.9	4.0	3.3	0.7	3.9	6.6	3.4	2.8	0.6	3.2
	1982	7.6	4.0	3.2	0.8	3.6	6.4	3.4	2.7	0.7	3.0
	1983	7.4	4.2	3.3	0.9	3.3	6.2	3.5	2.8	0.7	2.7
	1984	7.5	4.2	3.3	0.9	3.3	6.1	3.5	2.7	0.7	2.7
	1985	7.3	4.2	3.2	0.9	3.1	5.8	3.3	2.6	0.8	2.5
	1986	7.5	4.3	3.3	1.0	3.2	5.8	3.3	2.5	0.8	2.5
	1987	8.0	4.7	3.5	1.2	3.4	5.7	3.3	2.5	0.8	2.4
	1988	8.2	4.8	3.5	1.3	3.4	5.6	3.3	2.4	0.9	2.3
	1989	8.1	4.9	3.6	1.3	3.2	5.5	3.3	2.4	0.9	2.2

* Rates per 1,000 married women aged 15-19.
† Rates per 1,000 married women aged 40-44.

Table 12.7 Conceptions outside marriage: numbers and rates by age of woman and outcome, 1979-1989

England and Wales
Residents

Age of woman at conception and year of conception		Numbers of conceptions (thousands)						Conception rates per 1,000 unmarried women in age-group					
		Total conceptions outside marriage	Conceptions leading to maternities				Conceptions terminated by abortion	**Total conceptions outside marriage**	Conceptions leading to maternities				Conceptions terminated by abortion
			Total	Outside marriage	Within marriage following marriage after conception				Total	Outside marriage	Within marriage following marriage after conception		
					All marriages	First marriage					All marriages	First marriage	
All ages*	1979	**203.5**	122.7	75.2	47.5	40.3	80.8	**54.0**	32.6	19.9	12.6	10.7	21.4
	1980	**208.6**	125.2	80.1	45.1	38.1	83.4	**52.9**	31.8	20.3	11.4	9.7	21.2
	1981	**214.3**	128.2	86.7	41.4	34.6	86.1	**52.0**	31.1	21.1	10.1	8.4	20.9
	1982	**226.7**	138.5	96.9	41.6	34.5	88.2	**53.0**	32.4	22.6	9.7	8.1	20.6
	1983	**236.4**	146.3	105.5	40.8	33.6	90.1	**53.3**	33.0	23.8	9.2	7.6	20.3
	1984	**263.4**	165.3	122.7	42.7	35.0	98.0	**57.5**	36.1	26.8	9.3	7.6	21.4
	1985	**283.5**	178.6	136.3	42.2	34.6	105.0	**60.0**	37.8	28.9	8.9	7.3	22.2
	1986	**304.6**	195.1	153.3	41.8	34.0	109.5	**62.4**	40.0	31.4	8.6	7.0	22.4
	1987	**337.1**	214.9	173.0	41.9	34.0	122.2	**67.7**	43.1	34.7	8.4	6.8	24.5
	1988	**351.5**	222.3	182.3	40.0	32.4	129.3	**69.6**	44.0	36.1	7.9	6.4	25.6
	1989	**365.6**	232.4	194.4	38.0	30.6	133.2	**71.7**	45.6	38.1	7.4	6.0	26.1
Under 16†	1979	**9.1**	4.0	3.4	0.6	0.6	5.0	**7.5**	3.3	2.8	0.5	0.5	4.2
	1980	**8.5**	3.9	3.4	0.5	0.5	4.6	**7.1**	3.3	2.8	0.4	0.4	3.9
	1981	**8.5**	3.6	3.2	0.4	0.4	4.9	**7.2**	3.1	2.7	0.4	0.4	4.1
	1982	**9.0**	3.8	3.5	0.4	0.3	5.1	**7.8**	3.3	3.0	0.3	0.3	4.4
	1983	**9.3**	4.0	3.7	0.3	0.3	5.3	**8.3**	3.6	3.3	0.3	0.3	4.7
	1984	**9.6**	4.2	4.0	0.3	0.3	5.4	**8.6**	3.8	3.5	0.2	0.2	4.8
	1985	**9.4**	4.1	3.9	0.2	0.2	5.2	**8.6**	3.8	3.6	0.2	0.2	4.8
	1986	**9.2**	4.2	4.0	0.2	0.2	5.0	**8.7**	4.0	3.8	0.2	0.2	4.7
	1987	**9.1**	4.2	4.0	0.2	0.2	4.9	**9.2**	4.2	4.0	0.2	0.2	5.0
	1988	**8.8**	4.1	4.0	0.1	0.1	4.7	**9.4**	4.4	4.2	0.1	0.1	5.0
	1989	**8.3**	4.0	3.9	0.1	0.1	4.4	**9.4**	4.5	4.4	0.1	0.1	4.9
16	1979	**15.3**	8.6	5.5	3.1	3.1	6.8	**38.9**	21.8	13.9	7.9	7.9	17.1
	1980	**14.6**	8.0	5.7	2.4	2.4	6.6	**36.1**	19.8	14.0	5.9	5.9	16.2
	1981	**14.9**	8.3	6.1	2.2	2.2	6.6	**36.5**	20.3	14.9	5.4	5.4	16.2
	1982	**14.5**	7.9	6.0	1.9	1.9	6.7	**36.5**	19.8	15.0	4.7	4.7	16.8
	1983	**14.8**	8.0	6.5	1.5	1.5	6.8	**37.7**	20.4	16.6	3.8	3.8	17.3
	1984	**15.5**	8.4	7.0	1.4	1.4	7.1	**40.8**	22.1	18.4	3.6	3.6	18.7
	1985	**15.7**	8.7	7.4	1.3	1.3	7.0	**41.3**	22.9	19.5	3.4	3.3	18.4
	1986	**15.0**	8.6	7.6	1.0	1.0	6.5	**41.0**	23.4	20.7	2.7	2.7	17.6
	1987	**16.2**	9.1	8.3	0.8	0.8	7.1	**43.3**	24.4	22.1	2.2	2.2	19.0
	1988	**15.5**	8.6	8.0	0.6	0.6	6.9	**44.3**	24.7	22.8	1.8	1.8	19.6
	1989	**14.9**	8.5	7.9	0.6	0.6	6.4	**45.2**	25.7	24.0	1.7	1.7	19.5
17	1979	**21.5**	13.5	7.3	6.2	6.2	8.0	**56.3**	35.3	19.2	16.1	16.1	21.0
	1980	**20.9**	12.9	7.7	5.2	5.2	8.0	**53.6**	33.2	19.8	13.3	13.3	20.5
	1981	**20.5**	12.5	7.8	4.7	4.6	8.1	**51.3**	31.1	19.5	11.6	11.6	20.1
	1982	**20.7**	12.9	8.8	4.1	4.0	7.8	**51.2**	31.9	21.9	10.0	10.0	19.3
	1983	**20.6**	12.5	9.1	3.5	3.5	8.0	**51.9**	31.6	22.9	8.8	8.8	20.3
	1984	**22.2**	13.7	10.5	3.2	3.2	8.5	**57.1**	35.3	27.0	8.3	8.3	21.8
	1985	**22.8**	14.2	11.5	2.7	2.7	8.6	**60.3**	37.6	30.3	7.2	7.2	22.7
	1986	**23.2**	14.6	12.2	2.4	2.4	8.6	**61.4**	38.7	32.3	6.4	6.4	22.7
	1987	**23.4**	14.6	12.6	2.1	2.1	8.8	**64.1**	40.0	34.4	5.6	5.6	24.1
	1988	**24.3**	14.8	13.0	1.8	1.8	9.5	**65.2**	39.7	34.9	4.8	4.8	25.6
	1989	**23.1**	14.2	12.7	1.5	1.5	8.9	**66.2**	40.6	36.4	4.2	4.2	25.6
18	1979	**22.7**	14.5	7.5	6.9	6.9	8.2	**63.8**	40.7	21.2	19.5	19.5	23.1
	1980	**22.8**	14.4	8.1	6.3	6.3	8.4	**62.3**	39.4	22.2	17.1	17.1	22.9
	1981	**22.4**	14.0	8.6	5.4	5.4	8.4	**59.7**	37.4	23.0	14.4	14.3	22.3
	1982	**23.3**	15.0	9.7	5.2	5.2	8.3	**60.0**	38.6	25.1	13.5	13.5	21.4
	1983	**23.6**	15.1	10.5	4.7	4.7	8.5	**59.8**	38.4	26.5	11.8	11.8	21.4
	1984	**25.4**	16.5	12.0	4.5	4.5	8.9	**65.7**	42.7	31.0	11.8	11.7	23.0
	1985	**26.7**	17.1	13.0	4.1	4.1	9.5	**70.0**	45.0	34.1	10.8	10.8	25.0
	1986	**27.5**	18.0	14.4	3.6	3.6	9.5	**74.1**	48.5	38.7	9.8	9.7	25.6
	1987	**29.2**	18.8	15.5	3.3	3.3	10.3	**79.0**	51.0	42.0	9.0	9.0	28.0
	1988	**28.4**	18.0	15.3	2.8	2.8	10.3	**79.5**	50.5	42.8	7.8	7.7	29.0
	1989	**29.0**	18.4	15.9	2.5	2.5	10.6	**79.5**	50.4	43.5	6.8	6.8	29.2
19	1979	**20.2**	12.7	6.8	5.9	5.9	7.5	**65.0**	40.9	21.8	19.1	18.9	24.2
	1980	**20.8**	13.0	7.3	5.7	5.7	7.7	**63.6**	39.9	22.3	17.6	17.4	23.7
	1981	**21.2**	13.4	8.3	5.1	5.1	7.8	**62.2**	39.3	24.4	14.9	14.8	22.8
	1982	**22.3**	14.2	9.3	4.9	4.9	8.1	**62.7**	39.8	26.1	13.7	13.6	22.8
	1983	**22.7**	14.7	10.0	4.6	4.6	8.0	**61.3**	39.6	27.1	12.5	12.5	21.7
	1984	**25.2**	16.3	11.7	4.7	4.6	8.9	**67.2**	43.6	31.1	12.5	12.4	23.7
	1985	**26.4**	17.2	12.8	4.3	4.3	9.3	**71.5**	46.4	34.7	11.7	11.6	25.1
	1986	**27.5**	18.1	14.0	4.1	4.0	9.4	**75.2**	49.4	38.3	11.1	11.0	25.7
	1987	**30.2**	19.4	15.7	3.8	3.7	10.7	**85.0**	54.8	44.2	10.6	10.5	30.2
	1988	**30.5**	19.3	16.0	3.3	3.3	11.2	**86.3**	54.6	45.2	9.4	9.3	31.7
	1989	**29.8**	18.9	16.0	2.9	2.9	10.9	**86.6**	55.0	46.6	8.4	8.3	31.6

* Rates per 1,000 unmarried women aged 15-44.
† Rates per 1,000 unmarried women aged 13-15.

Table 12.7 - *continued*

Age of woman at conception and year of conception		Numbers of conceptions (thousands)						Conception rates per 1,000 unmarried women in age-group					
		Total conceptions outside marriage	Conceptions leading to maternities				Conceptions terminated by abortion	Total conceptions outside marriage	Conceptions leading to maternities				Conceptions terminated by abortion
			Total	Outside marriage	Within marriage following marriage after conception				Total	Outside marriage	Within marriage following marriage after conception		
					All marriages	First marriage					All marriages	First marriage	
Under 20*	1979	88.8	53.3	30.5	22.7	22.7	35.5	48.1	28.8	16.5	12.3	12.3	19.2
	1980	87.6	52.3	32.2	20.1	20.0	35.3	46.2	27.6	17.0	10.6	10.6	18.6
	1981	87.4	51.8	34.0	17.7	17.7	35.7	45.5	26.9	17.7	9.2	9.2	18.6
	1982	89.8	53.8	37.3	16.4	16.4	36.0	46.3	27.7	19.3	8.5	8.4	18.6
	1983	91.0	54.4	39.8	14.6	14.6	36.6	47.0	28.1	20.6	7.5	7.5	18.9
	1984	97.9	59.2	45.1	14.1	14.1	38.7	51.2	31.0	23.6	7.4	7.4	20.3
	1985	101.0	61.4	48.7	12.7	12.6	39.6	53.8	32.7	25.9	6.8	6.7	21.1
	1986	102.5	63.6	52.3	11.3	11.2	38.9	55.2	34.2	28.1	6.1	6.1	21.0
	1987	108.0	66.1	56.0	10.1	10.1	41.9	59.6	36.5	30.9	5.6	5.6	23.1
	1988	107.4	64.8	56.2	8.6	8.6	42.6	61.0	36.8	31.9	4.9	4.9	24.2
	1989	105.1	63.9	56.4	7.5	7.5	41.2	62.0	37.7	33.3	4.4	4.4	24.3
20-24	1979	61.1	37.5	23.0	14.5	12.8	23.6	68.6	42.1	25.8	16.2	14.3	26.5
	1980	65.7	40.4	25.7	14.7	12.9	25.3	68.5	42.1	26.8	15.3	13.5	26.4
	1981	68.5	41.5	27.9	13.6	12.1	27.0	66.1	40.1	27.0	13.1	11.6	26.1
	1982	74.5	46.4	32.0	14.4	12.9	28.1	67.0	41.7	28.8	12.9	11.6	25.3
	1983	79.1	50.2	35.5	14.8	13.3	28.9	66.2	42.1	29.7	12.4	11.1	24.2
	1984	90.4	58.1	42.0	16.1	14.6	32.4	70.9	45.5	32.9	12.6	11.4	25.4
	1985	99.8	64.0	47.5	16.4	14.9	35.8	73.7	47.2	35.1	12.1	11.0	26.4
	1986	109.5	70.7	54.2	16.5	15.0	38.8	77.4	50.0	38.3	11.6	10.6	27.4
	1987	122.8	78.7	61.9	16.8	15.4	44.1	85.0	54.5	42.8	11.6	10.7	30.5
	1988	128.1	81.1	65.5	15.7	14.5	47.0	88.5	56.0	45.2	10.8	10.0	32.4
	1989	132.0	83.5	69.2	14.4	13.3	48.5	91.7	58.0	48.0	10.0	9.2	33.7
25-29	1979	28.9	18.1	12.0	6.1	3.4	10.8	76.8	48.0	31.9	16.1	8.9	28.8
	1980	30.0	18.6	12.3	6.3	3.6	11.4	75.6	47.0	31.0	16.0	9.0	28.6
	1981	31.6	19.8	14.0	5.8	3.3	11.8	74.5	46.6	32.9	13.7	7.9	27.9
	1982	34.6	22.1	15.8	6.4	3.7	12.4	76.2	48.8	34.7	14.1	8.1	27.4
	1983	36.7	24.1	17.3	6.7	4.0	12.6	75.3	49.5	35.6	13.9	8.2	25.8
	1984	42.6	28.3	20.9	7.5	4.6	14.3	80.7	53.7	39.5	14.1	8.6	27.0
	1985	48.0	31.7	23.7	8.0	5.1	16.3	82.8	54.7	41.0	13.8	8.8	28.1
	1986	54.3	36.5	28.0	8.5	5.5	17.9	84.5	56.7	43.5	13.2	8.6	27.8
	1987	63.1	42.3	33.2	9.1	6.1	20.8	89.9	60.3	47.3	13.0	8.7	29.7
	1988	69.3	46.0	36.5	9.5	6.6	23.3	90.4	60.0	47.5	12.4	8.6	30.4
	1989	76.7	51.2	41.5	9.7	6.9	25.4	91.9	61.4	49.7	11.7	8.3	30.5
30-34	1979	16.1	9.8	6.6	3.1	1.2	6.3	60.9	36.9	25.1	11.8	4.6	23.9
	1980	16.5	9.8	6.9	2.9	1.1	6.7	58.3	34.6	24.5	10.1	4.0	23.7
	1981	17.3	10.5	7.3	3.2	1.3	6.8	57.1	34.8	24.1	10.7	4.3	22.3
	1982	17.6	11.0	7.9	3.1	1.2	6.5	57.1	35.9	25.8	10.0	3.9	21.2
	1983	18.5	11.8	8.6	3.2	1.3	6.7	58.0	36.9	26.9	10.0	4.2	21.1
	1984	20.4	13.2	9.8	3.4	1.4	7.1	61.2	39.7	29.4	10.3	4.2	21.5
	1985	22.1	14.5	11.0	3.5	1.5	7.6	63.6	41.9	31.7	10.1	4.4	21.8
	1986	24.6	16.6	12.8	3.9	1.7	8.0	67.2	45.4	34.8	10.6	4.7	21.8
	1987	28.0	19.0	14.9	4.1	1.8	9.0	72.2	48.9	38.4	10.5	4.7	23.2
	1988	30.5	20.8	16.5	4.3	2.1	9.8	74.1	50.4	40.1	10.3	5.1	23.7
	1989	34.3	23.4	19.0	4.5	2.2	10.9	77.7	53.1	43.0	10.1	5.1	24.6
35-39	1979	6.6	3.4	2.4	1.0	0.3	3.2	33.6	17.2	12.2	4.9	1.3	16.5
	1980	6.7	3.4	2.4	1.0	0.4	3.4	32.2	16.0	11.2	4.8	1.9	16.1
	1981	7.5	3.8	2.9	0.9	0.2	3.6	32.6	16.8	12.7	4.1	1.0	15.8
	1982	8.3	4.4	3.2	1.2	0.3	4.0	32.5	17.0	12.5	4.5	1.2	15.5
	1983	9.1	5.0	3.7	1.3	0.4	4.1	32.4	17.8	13.1	4.7	1.4	14.6
	1984	9.9	5.6	4.3	1.4	0.4	4.3	33.4	18.9	14.3	4.6	1.3	14.5
	1985	10.4	6.0	4.6	1.4	0.4	4.4	33.0	19.1	14.7	4.4	1.3	13.9
	1986	11.3	6.7	5.2	1.5	0.5	4.6	34.1	20.2	15.6	4.5	1.4	13.9
	1987	12.3	7.5	6.0	1.5	0.5	4.8	36.7	22.4	17.9	4.5	1.5	14.3
	1988	13.0	8.0	6.4	1.6	0.5	4.9	37.9	23.5	18.8	4.7	1.5	14.4
	1989	14.0	8.7	7.1	1.6	0.6	5.3	39.9	24.8	20.1	4.7	1.8	15.2
40 and over†	1979	2.0	0.7	0.5	0.2	0.0	1.2	10.2	3.7	2.8	0.9	0.2	6.5
	1980	2.1	0.8	0.6	0.1	0.0	1.3	10.4	3.9	3.2	0.7	0.2	6.5
	1981	2.0	0.8	0.6	0.2	0.0	1.3	9.8	3.7	2.9	0.8	0.1	6.2
	1982	2.0	0.8	0.6	0.2	0.0	1.2	9.4	3.7	2.9	0.8	0.2	5.7
	1983	2.0	0.8	0.6	0.2	0.0	1.2	9.2	3.7	2.9	0.8	0.2	5.4
	1984	2.2	0.9	0.7	0.2	0.0	1.3	9.2	3.7	2.8	0.9	0.2	5.5
	1985	2.3	0.9	0.7	0.2	0.0	1.4	9.2	3.8	2.9	0.8	0.2	5.4
	1986	2.4	1.1	0.9	0.2	0.0	1.3	8.9	3.9	3.2	0.8	0.2	4.9
	1987	2.9	1.3	1.1	0.2	0.1	1.6	9.6	4.4	3.6	0.8	0.2	5.2
	1988	3.1	1.5	1.2	0.3	0.1	1.7	9.7	4.5	3.6	0.9	0.2	5.2
	1989	3.5	1.6	1.4	0.3	0.1	1.8	10.2	4.8	4.0	0.8	0.2	5.4

* Rates per 1,000 unmarried women aged 15-19.
† Rates per 1,000 unmarried women aged 40-44.

Table 12.8 All conceptions and conceptions outside marriage: proportions by area of usual residence, age of woman and outcome, 1989

England and Wales

Area of usual residence	Total number of conceptions (000s)	Percentage of all conceptions		Percentage of all conceptions		Total number of conceptions outside marriage (000s)	Percentage of conceptions outside marriage				Terminated by abortion
		Within marriage	Outside marriage	Leading to maternities	Terminated by abortion		Leading to maternities				
							Outside marriage			Within marriage following marriage after conception	
							Total	Sole*	Joint†		
1989	**a. All women**										
England and Wales	**864.7**	**57.7**	**42.3**	**80.2**	**19.8**	**365.6**	**53.2**	**14.9**	**38.3**	**10.4**	**36.4**
England	**818.9**	57.7	42.3	80.0	20.0	**346.3**	52.9	14.7	38.2	10.2	36.8
Wales	**45.8**	58.0	42.0	83.7	16.3	**19.3**	57.6	17.4	40.1	13.0	29.4
Standard regions											
Northern	**46.9**	55.9	44.1	85.3	14.7	**20.7**	63.2	19.0	44.2	11.1	25.7
Yorkshire and Humberside	**81.4**	56.9	43.1	83.2	16.8	**35.1**	58.3	16.4	41.8	11.4	30.3
East Midlands	**64.1**	60.1	39.9	83.5	16.5	**25.6**	57.7	16.1	41.6	11.2	31.1
East Anglia	**31.1**	64.3	35.7	83.7	16.3	**11.1**	53.4	13.4	40.0	12.9	33.7
South East	**323.6**	57.6	42.4	75.7	24.3	**137.3**	45.9	11.6	34.3	9.3	44.8
South West	**69.5**	62.6	37.4	84.1	15.9	**26.0**	53.9	14.0	39.9	12.4	33.8
West Midlands	**92.2**	57.6	42.4	80.1	19.9	**39.1**	54.3	15.7	38.5	10.0	35.7
North West	**110.0**	53.3	46.7	82.2	17.8	**51.4**	60.0	19.3	40.7	9.7	30.2
Metropolitan counties											
Greater London	**149.7**	50.8	49.2	69.2	30.8	**73.6**	42.6	11.5	31.2	7.3	50.0
Greater Manchester	**46.2**	51.9	48.1	82.3	17.7	**22.2**	61.4	19.0	42.5	9.3	29.3
Merseyside	**25.1**	48.9	51.1	81.2	18.8	**12.8**	61.8	22.8	39.0	8.2	30.0
South Yorkshire	**21.2**	54.8	45.2	82.3	17.7	**9.6**	57.8	16.8	41.0	11.8	30.4
Tyne and Wear	**17.6**	52.3	47.7	84.1	15.9	**8.4**	63.7	20.6	43.1	10.1	26.2
West Midlands	**50.2**	54.5	45.5	78.4	21.6	**22.9**	55.2	17.1	38.1	8.5	36.3
West Yorkshire	**35.6**	56.9	43.1	83.7	16.3	**15.3**	59.4	16.8	42.5	11.0	29.6
	b. Women aged under 20										
England and Wales	**117.5**	**10.6**	**89.4**	**64.4**	**35.6**	**105.1**	**53.7**	**18.9**	**34.8**	**7.1**	**39.2**
England	**110.4**	10.6	89.4	64.0	36.0	**98.7**	53.3	18.7	34.6	7.0	39.7
Wales	**7.1**	10.0	90.0	71.3	28.7	**6.4**	59.2	21.0	38.2	9.1	31.7
Standard regions											
Northern	**7.8**	7.7	92.3	73.5	26.5	**7.2**	64.0	23.5	40.5	7.6	28.4
Yorkshire and Humberside	**13.4**	11.3	88.7	70.0	30.0	**11.9**	58.9	20.1	38.7	7.7	33.4
East Midlands	**9.2**	10.7	89.3	67.4	32.6	**8.2**	56.5	20.0	36.4	7.4	36.1
East Anglia	**4.0**	13.0	87.0	63.8	36.2	**3.5**	49.8	15.1	34.7	9.4	40.9
South East	**35.3**	11.4	88.6	55.8	44.2	**31.3**	44.7	14.9	29.8	6.2	49.1
South West	**8.6**	9.6	90.4	62.7	37.3	**7.8**	50.8	16.9	33.8	8.3	40.9
West Midlands	**14.4**	12.3	87.7	64.7	35.3	**12.6**	52.8	18.7	34.1	7.5	39.7
North West	**17.8**	8.3	91.7	70.2	29.8	**16.3**	61.8	24.1	37.7	6.1	32.2
Metropolitan counties											
Greater London	**15.6**	12.9	87.1	53.9	46.1	**13.6**	43.6	15.1	28.5	4.7	51.6
Greater Manchester	**7.8**	9.3	90.7	72.2	27.8	**7.1**	64.2	24.2	40.0	5.5	30.3
Merseyside	**3.9**	4.7	95.3	69.3	30.7	**3.7**	63.4	27.4	36.0	4.7	32.0
South Yorkshire	**3.6**	9.8	90.2	68.6	31.4	**3.2**	58.4	20.4	38.0	7.3	34.4
Tyne and Wear	**3.0**	6.7	93.3	72.8	27.2	**2.8**	64.9	24.9	40.0	6.2	28.8
West Midlands	**8.2**	14.2	85.8	66.6	33.4	**7.1**	55.1	20.0	35.1	6.6	38.3
West Yorkshire	**6.0**	14.1	85.9	72.6	27.4	**5.2**	60.4	20.4	40.0	8.1	31.5

* Conceptions leading to births outside marriage registered by the mother alone.
† Conceptions leading to births outside marriage registered by both parents.

Table 12.9 All conceptions and teenage conceptions: numbers and rates
by area of usual residence and outcome, 1989   **England and Wales**

Area of usual residence	All conceptions				Conceptions at ages under 20				Conceptions at ages under 16			
	Number (000s)	Rates per 1,000 women aged 15-44			Number (000s)	Rates per 1,000 women aged 15-19			Number	Rates per 1,000 women aged 13-15		
		Total	Maternities	Abortions		Total	Maternities	Abortions		Total	Maternities	Abortions
England and Wales	864.7	**78.6**	63.0	15.6	117.5	**67.6**	43.5	24.0	8,382	**9.4**	4.5	4.9
England	818.9	**78.8**	63.0	15.7	110.4	**67.4**	43.1	24.3	7,922	**9.5**	4.5	5.0
Wales	45.8	**75.2**	63.0	12.3	7.1	**70.5**	50.2	20.2	460	**8.8**	4.8	4.0
Standard Regions												
Northern	46.9	**71.1**	60.6	10.5	7.8	**74.3**	54.6	19.7	625	**11.5**	6.2	5.2
Yorkshire and Humberside	81.4	**75.9**	63.1	12.8	13.4	**77.3**	54.1	23.2	1,031	**11.6**	6.0	5.6
East Midlands	64.1	**73.3**	61.3	12.1	9.2	**67.1**	45.2	21.9	742	**10.4**	5.0	5.5
East Anglia	31.1	**71.0**	59.5	11.6	4.0	**57.8**	36.9	20.9	328	**9.1**	3.4	5.6
South East	323.6	**83.8**	63.4	20.3	35.3	**59.5**	33.2	26.3	2,245	**7.5**	3.1	4.4
South West	69.5	**71.0**	59.7	11.3	8.6	**54.3**	34.1	20.3	661	**8.3**	3.6	4.7
West Midlands	92.2	**81.8**	65.6	16.3	14.4	**79.2**	51.2	27.9	1,029	**11.0**	5.0	5.9
North West	110.0	**79.7**	65.6	14.2	17.8	**80.3**	56.4	24.0	1,261	**11.0**	6.4	4.6
Metropolitan counties												
Greater London	149.7	**95.6**	66.2	29.5	15.6	**67.2**	36.2	31.0	866	**7.7**	3.4	4.3
Greater Manchester	46.2	**81.4**	67.0	14.4	7.8	**85.8**	61.9	23.9	561	**12.0**	7.2	4.8
Merseyside	25.1	**81.0**	65.8	15.2	3.9	**77.4**	53.6	23.8	253	**9.7**	5.8	3.9
South Yorkshire	21.2	**75.2**	61.8	13.3	3.6	**80.0**	54.8	25.2	289	**12.7**	5.9	6.9
Tyne and Wear	17.6	**72.6**	61.1	11.6	3.0	**77.7**	56.6	21.1	240	**12.2**	6.6	5.5
West Midlands	50.2	**90.1**	70.7	19.4	8.2	**89.6**	59.7	29.9	566	**12.0**	6.1	5.9
West Yorkshire	35.6	**78.8**	66.0	12.9	6.0	**83.0**	60.3	22.7	407	**10.8**	6.3	4.5
Regional health authorities												
Northern	46.9	**71.1**	60.6	10.5	7.8	**74.3**	54.6	19.7	625	**11.5**	6.2	5.2
Yorkshire	60.2	**76.1**	63.5	12.6	9.8	**76.3**	53.8	22.5	742	**11.3**	6.1	5.2
Trent	74.7	**73.3**	61.1	12.2	11.3	**70.4**	47.9	22.5	907	**11.0**	5.3	5.7
East Anglian	31.1	**71.0**	59.5	11.6	4.0	**57.9**	36.9	20.9	328	**9.1**	3.4	5.6
North West Thames	68.1	**85.2**	62.5	22.7	6.7	**55.1**	29.3	25.9	399	**6.6**	2.6	4.1
North East Thames	78.6	**92.2**	66.6	25.6	9.2	**71.5**	39.6	32.0	505	**7.9**	3.2	4.6
South East Thames	67.9	**86.1**	65.1	21.0	8.0	**63.7**	37.2	26.6	569	**9.2**	3.9	5.3
South West Thames	50.8	**79.3**	61.5	17.9	4.8	**49.5**	25.6	23.9	292	**5.9**	2.5	3.5
Wessex	45.8	**73.5**	60.8	12.8	5.8	**58.3**	34.7	23.6	470	**9.3**	3.8	5.5
Oxford	43.7	**75.0**	61.1	13.8	4.9	**53.8**	32.1	21.6	340	**7.3**	3.0	4.3
South Western	48.2	**70.4**	59.6	10.8	6.0	**54.3**	35.0	19.3	448	**8.0**	3.8	4.3
West Midlands	92.2	**81.8**	65.6	16.3	14.4	**79.2**	51.2	27.9	1,029	**11.0**	5.0	5.9
Mersey	40.4	**77.4**	63.3	14.1	6.1	**73.1**	49.6	23.5	409	**9.4**	5.3	4.0
North Western	70.2	**81.1**	66.9	14.2	11.8	**84.7**	60.4	24.3	859	**11.9**	7.0	4.9